BOX
FR of OGS

BOX of FROGS

Iain Hollis

Memoirs of a Canoeing Cyclist

Matador
9 Priory Business Park,
Wistow Road, Kibworth Beauchamp,
Leicestershire. LE8 0RX
Tel: 0116 279 2299
Email: books@troubador.co.uk
Web: www.troubador.co.uk/matador
Twitter: @matadorbooks

ISBN 978 1785898 648

British Library Cataloguing in Publication Data.
A catalogue record for this book is available from the British Library.

Printed and bound by CPI Group (UK) Ltd, Croydon, CR0 4YY
Typeset in 11pt Gill Sans by Troubador Publishing Ltd, Leicester, UK

Matador is an imprint of Troubador Publishing Ltd

For Hannah

Thank you for supporting C.E.S. UK charity

Best wishes

[signature]

'If you're going through hell, keep going.'

- Sir Winston Churchill

Contents

Chapter 1.

Cockleshell Cop

Parking in the city centre had always been a problem. Real estate comes at a premium and there was little concession for the emergency services. Budget cuts meant that the police had already downsized the main central station, from the once imposing fortress on Charles Street, to now sharing a multi-storey office block with a private company.

With the move to Mansfield House came an even smaller car park, with barely enough room to manoeuvre the emergency vehicle fleet let alone park your own car. In short, it wasn't permitted. Some of the senior officers had allocated parking spots. Perks of the job, I suppose. I mean, of course, they really needed them… NOT!

It was the shift workers who would have benefited most. Public transport isn't always available to those starting early or finishing late. It was one of the biggest gripes that local officers had, the fact that they were penalised for simply coming to work. Their colleagues in the outlying stations had free off-road parking or at least could park close by in the street, but for us lucky fellows it would be the NCP.

There was a small concession, a 'police discount'. Instead of £5.50 per day it was only £3.50, but in a typical month that could total in excess of £70.

I avoided these charges whenever possible and usually cycled to work. Cyclists were fortunate as there was a bike rack in the main car park. As a cyclist you could weave through the congestion and be almost certain of avoiding delays. Sometimes I would run. That was OK for getting there but running home had potential problems. I typically arrived expecting to do an eight-hour shift. Quite often this would be extended due to incidents. Even if I had the energy to run home after doing extra hours, the rest period between arriving at home and needing to return to work the next day could be so short that it was hardly worth it. That might mean sleeping in the office.

It was perhaps better to manage a combination. Have options. Ride to work and run home one day then run to work and ride home the next. That worked to a degree. An extension of the options was to catch a bus or share a lift whenever one was available. A further extension would be to use my kayak.

The battered old craft had been gathering dust in my garage. It was rarely used. Not because I didn't enjoy it, but instead because whenever I took it out or wherever I went, I would always have to use the same route back. In other words, 5 miles paddling one way, meant turning around to repeat 5 miles going back over the same scenery. I had already explored the local waterways. They no longer held any mystique but my new idea had some benefits.

An ankle injury meant I struggled to run as often as I used to. My marathon days were certainly over. Kayaking I could do sitting down. The water connection existed virtually from my front door to within about 600 metres of the police station. It was only 8 miles of paddling, and pretty much the same route I took when I ran or cycled. I gave it a try. It took me two hours. Not bad, but carrying the heavy 14ft fibreglass kayak across the busy city roads was hazardous. It was difficult to look both ways and the sheer length could cause collisions with obstacles, pedestrians or vehicles. On the positive side, it was a perfect fit behind the cycle rack.

Feeling very pleased with myself, I had a refreshing shower and then joined my colleagues in the office. They couldn't quite believe what I had done. I was ridiculed. They all laughed and told me I was mad. I couldn't see the big deal. I was buzzing from the endorphin release. I'd had a fantastic experience and this was something I intended to do regularly from now on. The laughter and jibes continued. Not just for the next few minutes, or all morning, or even the whole shift. They continued right up until the last voyage about two years later.

To make the transition from canal to station, I chopped up an old pushchair and, using bungees, fastened the wheels to one end. Throwing my oars and kit bag into the cockpit and then grabbing the rope toggle of the opposite end, I could pull the now almost weightless boat along like a trolley. I got some funny looks in the city and the occasional horn toot from 'White Van Man', but I didn't mind.

They say that 'madness is doing the same thing over and over, expecting different results'. I was perhaps mad to think they'd ever stop laughing but otherwise I was quite happy with my routine.

My colleagues were driving to work and fighting through congestion. They would often have to face similar congestion when leaving the city, either way, they were paying for fuel – at least £100 per month. Using the car park daily

– approximately £70 per month. Paying for gym membership – another £40 per month. What do they do when they get to the gym? Running machine, exercise bike and rowing machine. Need I say more?

I didn't paddle every day, and rarely there and back. A late start or an early finish were ideal occasions. There was once even a night-time excursion. With tomorrow being a scheduled day off, I marched out of the station gates about midnight. Pulling the boat behind me, I paraded past crowds queuing for the nightclub. There were a few double-takes and the bouncers were looking for the hidden TV cameras, thinking it was some kind of practical joke. Gradually the station accepted the sight but there was always someone seeing it for the first time who would stand and stare open-mouthed in disbelief.

I capsized only once. Heavy rain had caused the water levels on the River Wreake to rise and the current had increased significantly due to flood drain-off. I set out as usual with Tina Turner on my CD player that had been made water-resistant by a knotted sandwich bag. That low-hanging branch didn't normally cause me a problem but at 5am on this dark winter morning and with today's unusually high water level, it suddenly appeared in front of me. I couldn't duck forward to clear it or lean back low enough. I anchored my arms around the branch but the build-up of pressure from the water flow was now dragging my boat away from me. I had nowhere to go. Splosh!

The cold water took my breath away but I didn't panic as my life jacket immediately justified its existence. I kept hold of the kayak and started to swim over to the eastern riverbank. My CD player was still working – I couldn't believe it – but it lasted only a few seconds more before drowning poor Tina. Today I was the one 'Rolling on the River'. Having bailed out the kayak, my options were to either refloat and paddle for two hours while soaking wet, or drag the boat back home, warm up with a hot shower and grab an extra hour in bed before driving to work. The latter sounded most appealing.

On one occasion the canal waters by Abbey Park were frozen over. The rest of the route had been fine but this stagnant section was covered in a thin sheet and the kayak had to smash through like one of those ice-breaker ships.

Throughout the spring and summer I became familiar with the locations of nesting ducks and swans. The protective fathers ushered me away to the opposite bank. I think gradually they got used to me and it was a real delight to eventually see the various sets of parents leading out their fluffy offspring for a trip on the river.

After about six months, rumours of a 'canoeing cop' had spread. It was the *Leicester Mercury* that first seized the story. A colourful photo and an interesting write-up stirred a mini media frenzy. Next thing, I was being filmed on the canal for *Central News*, I was invited to BBC Radio Leicester for an on-air interview, and I was in the *People on Sunday* and the *Metro*. On one occasion I was at Crown Court to give evidence and there was my picture in a newspaper cutting pinned to back of the door in the CPS room.

I had told the reporters how much I loved doing it. I enjoyed the wildlife, the swans, ducks, fish, herons and kingfishers. I had even seen a turtle once, although I suspect that that was someone's discarded pet. The peaceful and calm canal waters enabled me to collect my thoughts and plan the day ahead. I avoided congestion, got free parking and outdoor exercise. It was all good. The reporters wanted another perspective; a few words from my supervisor, Sergeant Fred Keal.

"I think it is splendid," he said. "He's a very good officer who works on a lot of important jobs, but he is as mad as a box of frogs."

Photograph credit to the *Leicester Mercury, 2005*

Chapter 2.

GO IAIN

In *The Great Escape* movie, James Coburn plays a captive Australian airman. Having tunnelled out of the POW camp, dressed in civilian clothes and carrying a large suitcase, he strolls into a village, steals a bicycle and rides casually away towards freedom. That got me thinking… On a low budget with basic needs, how far could I get on a bicycle?

September 1996, early evening, Portsmouth. I was excited about the trip but at the same time tinged with sadness. This place was evocative. I had dated my first love for four teenage years but our military careers prised us apart. It was the Royal Marines for me while my partner had gone on to become an officer in the Royal Navy. Although we had split up some nine years before, we were still in contact and I knew that she was currently stationed nearby. For a brief moment I travelled back in time. There she was. A quarter Spanish with olive skin and beautiful dark eyes. I lamented my loss. Could I have done things differently? Will we ever be together again? Unlikely; my life was a mess.

Stood on the upper deck I looked port side across the harbour. Moored up for breaking was HMS *Fearless*. This also made me sad. I had been aboard her once during my basic training. This was one of the Royal Navy's aged amphibious assault ships, an LPD (landing pad and dock). The landing pad was for two troop-carrying Sea King helicopters and the dock, well, that was something special. The stern of the ship had gates that could be opened to enable partial flooding to allow the release or receipt of landing craft. Indeed this was the very ship that had rescued 007 and Agent XXX at the end of my favourite James Bond film, *The Spy Who Loved Me*.

I had twice served afloat on her twin sister, HMS *Intrepid*. First time through the Suez Canal bound for Oman in 1986 and second time coming home from Gibraltar in 1988. During the latter, Taff and I had drawn galley duty. The flat hull accentuated the effects of the Atlantic swell in the Bay of

Biscay. Preparing dinner for the ship's company followed by washing-up was hilarious. Splashes and spills everywhere as the ship rose, fell, rocked and rolled. We were drenched. The recollection made me smile.

My tooth hurt. It'd be fine… I hoped. Couldn't turn back now. The ferry was already heading out to sea and the Bay of Biscay loomed once more.

It was through a competition that I had won a 'mini cruise for two'. Three days with P&O from Portsmouth to Bilbao and back. Originally I intended to take my new love interest but she had declined the offer and we broke up soon after anyway. As an alternative, I invited my good friend Andy Shaw. Not for a mini cruise, but as a free one-way ticket to Spain. Our plan was to ride bicycles from Bilbao to Barcelona and then head north over the Pyrenees, through France and back to Blighty. 1,200 miles in fourteen days. The ride would be broken by two days of sightseeing in Barcelona. No drama.

Andy had been a sailor on HMS *Hermes* during the 1982 Falklands War, but he was now the landlord at my local pub, The Barley Mow. Unfortunately, my pal suffered an injury at work just days before the intended departure and was unable to participate. The heavy beer cellar trapdoor collapsed on his head damaging his neck and back. Clumsy matelot. I would have to go alone.

I drove from Leicester to Portsmouth, parked my car in a side street, took my bike from the boot and rode to the ferry terminal. With loaded panniers, an old Bergen (backpack), Pusser's slug (military sleeping bag) and roll mat (foam mattress), I embarked.

I met a fellow biker in the bar. He was doing a similar ride. We compared routes and timetables; however, at that point it became clear that we would not be compatible as adventurers. His bike was a 600cc Suzuki Bandit.

The voyage itself was uneventful. On-board prices were inflated so I remained in my cabin. I was broke at the time and effectively homeless. As a recently divorced, twenty-seven-year-old father of two, financially crippled by the CSA, I could not afford to buy or rent. Having departed the former matrimonial home I spent the early months 'house sitting' an old cottage in the sleepy village of Rothley. The property had been bought as an investment but the owners had run out of funds for the renovation. Rather than have the premises stand unoccupied and at risk of vandalism or squatters, I would be able to stay there rent free but have to pay for my electric. It was a good arrangement while it lasted but by now things were different. Sometimes I would sleep at the office, work's attic, friends' sofas, The Barley Mow or wherever I laid my hat.

I had surrendered the old mortgage endowment policies to release some funds. Robbed by early exit fees, I had just enough to buy a second-hand VW Golf and a decent hybrid bicycle, a Univega Activa.

With my bike, a camping stove, metal mug and a Gore-Tex bivvy bag, I was adequately equipped for the forthcoming expedition. My pauper's diet would be chicken and mushroom Pot Noodles (two a day). Discarding all of the plastic cups, I emptied the dehydrated meals into individual sandwich bags. I ate the first one in my cabin. My tooth still hurt. Why now?

September 1985. Commando Training Centre, Lympstone, Devon. Week one.

Royal Navy Dental Officer: "You have got film-star teeth. It may be difficult to maintain dental hygiene in the field but if you give them a thorough clean once a week they'll last you forever."

Later that same day, 296 Troop received foot drill practice. Military drill boots have hobnailed soles and horseshoe-type heels. This makes that impressive crunching sound as a formation marches in step. Left, right, left, right, crunch, crunch, crunch. In every new recruit class there is always someone who doesn't know his left turn from his right. I have no idea who got it wrong but when the drill instructor screamed at the class to, "Get down and give me fifty!" (press-ups), we moved like lightning. I threw my arms down and kicked my feet backwards to commence the punishing exercise. The recruit in front of me did the same but unfortunately he kicked me in the mouth.

There was no blood or pain, only shock at seeing chippings of tooth enamel on the heel inches away. Running my tongue over the front upper right incisor I could feel unfamiliar jagged edges. I stood up and brought this to the corporal's attention. He asked if it hurt. I said it did, and he sent me off to sick bay. He made me finish the press-ups first, obviously.

Royal Navy Dental Officer: "Have you been fighting?"

He said it was an 'awkward break'. The root was fine but the lower half of the tooth was broken off exposing the internal dentine to infection. A crown was affixed. This would break off six months later. A new crown was affixed. That lasted a bit longer but broke off as before. The third lasted beyond my five years of service and well into my new career as a police officer.

It was sometime in 1995 that the pain started. It got gradually worse over a week or so. An X-ray by my local dentist revealed an abscess had formed around the root of my problem tooth. The surgeon proposed drilling through the broken incisor, through the root and into the gum bone, thereby breaking into the reservoir of high-pressure pus. This would then be left to drain for several days and the infection would clear up through use of antibiotics. The procedure was going to hurt me more than him but it sounded like a good plan.

Let's just say that it was absolute torture. Then came the bad news. All that drilling hadn't worked. He had missed the well. We had not struck oil. He would have to do it all again on the perfectly healthy neighbouring tooth. I was shivering and shaking uncontrollably. This first attempt had done nothing to alleviate my pain, quite the opposite. He sat me back in the waiting room for about twenty minutes. My sorry state must have caused some anxiety for the other patients waiting for their appointments. The poor dentist himself looked apologetic and afraid that he was causing me so much suffering. It seemed that I had to give him reassurance. "It's all right, Doc, I trust you; let's just crack on."

Sometime later came success. There was instant pressure release and no more pain. My two hollow teeth were now like drinking straws. For the next few days I would be sucking pus and blood from the hollow in my gum bone. The next problem was a catch-22. The void created by the departed abscess was a breeding ground for infection. Antibiotics would kill that infection but stop new gum-bone growth and therefore prevent the hole from closing up. Root canal fillings would be made once the infection was cleared but that was simply sealing an entrance to the hole. I was advised that if any infection had remained inside, it would just be a matter of time before a reservoir of pus filled up again. More complicated surgery would be required if that was the case.

Self-diagnosis in my ferry cabin told me that a new abscess had indeed developed. I had no travel insurance and limited funds. I had some paracetamol and a Swiss Army knife. Only one thing for it… unpick my root canal fillings. The knife had many blades and functions but was no match for a dentist's drill. Alas, I could not remove the fillings or burst the abscess. The paracetamol was helping though. Perhaps I could soldier on?

After two nights at sea came the disembarkation. Adrenaline and a euphoric buzz probably blanked the tooth pain on that first day. Greeted by warm Spanish sunshine I started pedalling. Leaving the port area I spent most of the day climbing. That said, I clocked up approximately 110 miles. I rode until exhaustion, which was pretty much last light around 7.30pm. I slept in a maize plantation, right on the edge of the field. I figured I would have to move early next morning though in case I got chopped to pieces by a mechanical harvester.

The second day was flat. I had reached the plains. Long straight roads stretched out for miles in front and looking back gave similar views. Hardly a car on the road. A photo opportunity presented itself as I entered the village of GOIAIN. My first name has an unusual spelling yet here was a sign telling me what to do. I pressed on towards Zaragoza and saw much of the Spanish countryside.

By the third day I was fighting a losing battle. I had lost all interest in my scenic surroundings and my sole focus was on reaching the airport for a self-funded medical evacuation. The tooth pain was severe and I knew I was not going to be able to complete this epic ride. That night I was unable to lie down as it made the throbbing pressure in my head unbearable. I was reminded of *The Elephant Man*. I sat up with my back resting against a tree in a roadside lay-by. I don't think I got much sleep.

I reached the Mediterranean on the fourth day. I parked my bike, stripped off and ran into the waves. Cupping my hands together I scooped up some of the warm seawater and splashed it onto my face. I then rubbed my fingers down the sides of my nose towards my mouth in a face-cleaning motion. I screamed with pain. What had I done? It felt as though I was now walking with a spear stuck in my face and someone was strumming the staff from the opposite end. I found a car mirror and took in my facial appearance for the first time since leaving my ferry cabin days earlier. I was unrecognisable. My face was distorted and severely swollen on one side. I needed to get home.

Signs led me to Barcelona Airport and I managed to get a flight that day. At the check-in desk I struggled to speak. I tried to explain that I did not normally look like this but the words made little sense in English, never mind Spanish. Putting my bike on board was no hassle. Just had to deflate the tyres and loosen the handlebars.

I don't remember at which London airport I arrived but the bike ride into the centre took a couple of hours. I first needed to inflate my tyres. I had a hand pump but an air machine would be quicker. Welcome back to 'rip-off Britain'. In Spain, air and water were free at every service station. Not so here.

There was a demonstration taking place in Central London and I asked a good old British Bobby for directions but he sent me round in circles. I was very agitated. Eventually I boarded a train back to Portsmouth, found my car and blasted up the motorway hoping to get emergency treatment at my dental surgery or at the very least the Royal Infirmary. Back in Leicester I was too late. The out of hours' emergency message from my dentist directed me to A & E but they had no emergency dental treatment available until 8am. My local dentist would be open at 9am. So I would have to endure another night in agony and unable to lie down.

Morning could not come quickly enough. I managed to jump the queues but the swelling was too severe for them to operate immediately. My despair was short-lived however, as they quickly produced almost a pint glass full of liquid antibiotics. I downed this and was sent home for a few hours. The swelling reduced quite soon after, the pain subsided and I fell asleep.

The surgery that followed was almost enough to turn me into a complete coward who never wants to experience pain again. Having said that, the treatment was successful and they managed to save my teeth.

The proposed 1,200 mile bike ride across Spain and France was a disastrous failure. Yes, I had ridden 410 miles from Bilbao to Barcelona in just four days, but I had not enjoyed it. What should have been an almost free holiday proved very expensive at a time when I could least afford it. I incurred charges for the flight home, train back to Portsmouth and a hefty bill from the dentist.

I would have to do better next time. Much better.

Chapter 3.

False Start

Your first memory; what is it? How far back can you go? The inevitability of time suggests that childhood memories will pale into insignificance. Certainly the finer detail will fade but having a reference point can help preserve events by allocating the filing positions to either 'before' or 'after'.

That reference point came early in my life allowing the 'before' section to start when I was just three years old. At the time of writing this I am forty-seven, so it was a long time ago. I don't really want to go back there, to be honest, but to have insight as to what makes this author tick, it is necessary.

I fell over. Cold water went straight up my nose and I didn't enjoy the stinging sensation or the salty seawater that I had just swallowed in massive gulps. Someone helped me to my feet and I stood there, coughing and spluttering. As I rubbed my eyes and recovered my sight, I saw bikini-clad thighs wade past in front of me. That was head height at the time. I didn't get to be much taller in adulthood. The beach was flanked by a high brick wall and I got warm again, wrapped in a towel inside our windbreak. I also remember the white and red rotating poles outside the barber's shop and that ice cream was delicious.

It was the summer of 1972 and I was on the beach at St Ives in Cornwall. I returned with my own children in 2009. It was like déjà vu. The place hadn't changed much and those barbershop poles were still spinning. Apparently this is where we always went for our holidays. Grandfather Hollis owned a farm down there. His wife, Marcia, was not my natural grandmother. She was his new partner. Divorce seems to be a family trait as will become apparent. They had two children, Adrian and Anita, technically my uncle and aunt but they were described as 'cousins' because they weren't much older than me. They also had chickens that laid eggs. Of course they did. That's what chickens do and it was a farm after all. Apart from walking down the back garden path with Adrian, to collect some fresh eggs from the straw-lined hen house, I don't have any other recollection of that holiday.

Our family home was a brand-new three-bed semi-detached house; 181 Long Furrow, East Goscote. We moved in on my first birthday, 13th March 1970. Before that we had lived on Martin Street in the city but that house has been knocked down now. My father, Frederick Stanley Hollis, was a TV engineer who worked for the Co-op supermarket chain. It was through work that he had met my mother. I'm not sure of her first name. Many called her Lesley but it might have been Dorothy or Patricia. I called her 'Mum'. I know that her maiden name was 'Haynes', as in the famous vehicle maintenance manuals. My mum had been a manager in the Co-op groceries department. A brunette with dark brown eyes, I remember her as being very pretty but with a short temper and she would grit her teeth when she was angry, a habit I would inherit.

I had one brother, Tony. He was two years older than me. I know that I was born at Roundhill Hospital and I know that I went to playschool. That was probably at the nearby St Hilda's Church but I cannot be certain. For much of my early memory, East Goscote was a building site. The roads were muddy, dumper trucks regularly drove by and there was always a pile of builder's sand to play in.

I suppose we were a normal family. We had a dog, a ginger cocker spaniel called Amber. We also had a tortoise called Claw. He escaped and despite our searches of neighbouring gardens we never found him. We had a large aquarium but it wasn't the fish that interested me. I would be glued to the glass, watching bubbles rise from the helmet of an ornamental deep-sea diver.

I had a tricycle, toy soldiers, Action Man, Tonka toys, Dinky and Matchbox cars, cowboy and Indian outfits and a log-cabin play tent. Sometimes my mum would overturn the wooden dining table, throw a bed sheet over the table legs and tell me it was a pirate ship.

I had jigsaws. I remember one in particular. The scene was inside a bakery and lots of pixies were helping to make a delicious-looking cake. Most of my jigsaws were stored in the same box but each piece had a number written on the back. All the pieces from the first jigsaw were numbered '1'. The second were '2' and so on. I created my own pictures from Fuzzy Felt and I especially liked the animals.

I had a collection of Ladybird books and my favourites were *The Three Billy Goats Gruff* and *The Three Little Pigs*. I was horrified that the first two pigs were eaten by the wolf but the apples that featured on the last few pages made my mouth water. I also had a copy of *The Princess and the Pea*. I scribbled on most of the pages as I learnt to write my name. I remember being told off for that.

Disney's *Dumbo* was the first film I remember seeing and my parents warned me that my ears would grow if I sneezed too hard. I believed them.

Occasionally we would visit Great Uncle Ubert Hollis. He was a former army guardsman but by then a police officer and I used to wear his flat cap. Another cop used to visit our house. Uncle Phil would nip in for a cuppa while I sailed the seas in my imaginary ship. He wasn't my real uncle, just a family friend. I remember his blue shirts but it was the slip-on boots that fascinated me. They had an elasticated section on the inside ankle. It was arch-shaped and reminded me of a window in TV's *Playschool*.

I liked to watch *Star Trek*. Even today the original theme music takes me back. I liked *Play Away*, *Trumpton*, *Dixon of Dock Green* and *Z Cars*.

Dr Who was John Pertwee, although Tom Baker (the narrator of *Little Britain*) would assume the role around that time. Daleks and Sea Devils frightened me, but the scariest thing was that piercing theme tune played over the ending scene of a time tunnel. My perception of that footage was that it resembled the insides of my ear. The combination of high-pitched sound and inner-ear image penetrated my head. I hated it and would run to hide behind the sofa, burying my face in a cushion, eyes tightly closed, covering my ears, teeth clenched and screaming to drown out the noise until it had finished. How strange.

At Christmas time we visited the festive displays at Thorn Lighting. There would be illuminated Disney character statues around the perimeter gardens, decorated fir trees and dazzling light-bulb displays on the factory's exterior walls. These included Humpty Dumpty and marching soldiers in red coats and bearskins. It was an impressive sight and took place most years but gradually diminished over the decades.

I also remember running into the living room door with a coin in my hand. I woke up on the sofa with a cold flannel over my brow. I had knocked myself out and the coin had slotted itself into my forehead, leaving a permanent scar.

A 'Happy Meal' was a hard-boiled egg with buttered bread soldiers. Sometimes my mum would draw a smiley face on the eggshell before we bashed its head in with a teaspoon.

A special treat before bedtime was a mug of warm milk or Horlicks and some Malted Milk biscuits with their distinctive cow motif. I liked the way the frothy drink would create a false moustache on my young face and I would stand on the bottom stairs tiptoeing to admire my new mature look in the mirror.

One night we all took off our socks. Each of us practised writing and drawing holding a pen between our toes. First you had to pick up the pen using only your toes. I couldn't do that. Maybe mine were just too small at that age. I went behind a chair and cheated. Now holding the pen like the rest of my family, I joined in with the silly art display. I was a normal and happy little boy. If only things could have stayed that way.

With Mum, 1969

With Dad at Wicksteed Park, 1969

With Tony, my big brother, at Martin Street

Easter egg hunt in front garden of Gynsill Lane with Tony and Grandma
Dorothy, 1973

It was behind the scenes that decisions were made. Adult talk. Still only a four-year-old, I was the youngest and last to know. I don't remember how the news was broken but I do remember sobbing every night in my bed (the small box room at the front of the house). My mum had moved out taking Tony with her, leaving me alone with my short-tempered and no doubt stressed dad.

It wouldn't be long before I was reunited with my brother. We were now at my maternal grandparents, Grandma Dorothy and Grandad Raymond who we all called 'Nin'. Apparently that was the name I gave him when I was very young. It was one of my first words. He was a tall man with white hair and smoked a pipe. In later life the actor Stewart Granger's appearance would evoke memories of Nin.

My grandparents had a three-bedroom house, 26 Gynsill Lane in Glenfield. There was a massive back garden with climbable trees and the big drive at the front was the resting place of two Morris Minors. They had probably been intended as a restoration project by Nin but were great fun to play in. The bedroom had no carpets, just a few rugs over bare floorboards. I shared bunks with Tony. A decorative doll covered the spare toilet roll and the kettle whistled when boiled. Occupying pride of place in the wooden parquet-floored hall was a photograph of Grandma. She was in her army uniform from service during the Second World War. To me she looked like Queen Elizabeth II, who had performed similar duties during that conflict. Sometimes at night I would sit on the bedroom windowsill and look out across the fields. In the distance were all the street lights of Anstey.

Occasionally I would stay with Great Aunty June at her house near Aylestone Road. She was Grandma Dorothy's sister. Aunty June would take me fishing down the local section of the River Soar and using a small net we caught minnows and sticklebacks which we collected in jam jars with wire handles. She took me to church once. I didn't like it. I watched her as she knelt down to pray. It horrified me that Jesus had nails hammered through his hands and feet but I was already sceptical about the existence of gods.

I slept uneasy at Aunty June's. Beside the bedroom fireplace was an old stuffed crocodile, stood up high on its back legs with its mouth open and sharp teeth at the ready. It made me a little uncomfortable and I had to keep checking that it hadn't moved. I have seen similar monsters in Thailand but I don't believe that they can be brought legally to England any longer.

It was a stressful time for my mum too. Her temper got the better of her on many occasions though I know not if it was anything I had done. For some reason I was returned to my dad. Childcare issues or schooling perhaps. I continued with the nightly sobbing.

"I want my mummy!"

"Well she doesn't want you, tough, shut up, stop crying and go to sleep," was the typical response.

My mum's best friend was called 'Do' (pronounced dough). She was married to Bob but not for long. They lived just a few doors away on the opposite side of Long Furrow near the mound on the playing fields. Do was mad about Dalmatians. She had two but also collected ornamental ones and had way in excess of 101. Do was a teacher at Ellis Primary. She was also, informally, my childminder. Consequently I attended infant school a year earlier than I was supposed to.

East Goscote was a modern housing estate given a 'village' status. At that time the residents were probably all white. The schoolchildren at Ellis were almost exclusively Indian. It really didn't bother me but it was a strange new environment. I had never seen brown faces before. Each pupil was a year or two older than me. They took me under their wing and treated me as someone very special. I remember some of the Sikh boys having handkerchiefs tied upon the heads and many of the girls wore skirts while at the same time wearing trousers underneath. I remember tripping on the old stone staircase and cutting my chin. As I played in the classroom sandpit with a plaster on my face, everyone was sympathetic and kind. I enjoyed my time at Ellis and have fond memories.

After school I would go for walks with Do and her dogs. We often did the fields near The Gate Hangs Well pub. She had chocolate-button treats for the dogs but I liked them too. I would have my evening meal with Do before going home to Dad.

One day she told me that pudding contained a 'SURPRISE'. I was excited. One reason for my excitement was because at that age and with limited vocabulary, I didn't fully appreciate the difference between a 'surprise' (which is simply a shock – pleasant or unpleasant) and a 'prize' (an award or gift given at parties or competitions). In my mind I was looking forward to the latter. Dessert was Banana Angel Delight or Instant Whip. Before allowing it to set, she had added some chopped-up Mars bar and banana slices. It wasn't that thrilling as a 'PRIZE' but as a pudding I really enjoyed it.

Most weekends I would go back to Gynsill Lane to be with Mum, Tony, Grandma Dorothy and Nin. I suspect Nin worked at the Palitoy factory in Coalville because he often brought Action Man figures home with him. I had so many. Some with beards, eagle eyes, gripping hands. Some with pull-cord activated voices. Some with parachutes, Arctic gear, boats, tanks and helicopters. Action Man and Action Man accessories everywhere. Grandma Dorothy had some wonderful ideas. She decided that all these troops needed some female company, so we ended up with a couple of 'Cindy'-type dolls too. She even made small swords out of sticks so that they had alternative weapons.

The exact timeline is vague. I know that sometimes I had to go to work with Dad. These were probably just the occasional Saturday mornings as my parents shared weekend access… of me. I remember spinning in the office swivel chair, drawing on computer paper and jumping from the ramps in the loading bay. Dad drove a white MKI Ford Escort estate. It usually had a big TV in the back.

One day I met Dad's new girlfriend, Marilyn. She was a beautiful blond and friendly to me. She bought me a set of paints in a tin with a folding lid. The lid featured an African safari scene with lots of wild animals. *Nice lady, Dad, you've done well*, I thought, but once she moved in it was different. She changed into the stereotypical 'Evil Stepmother'.

I remember her taking me to Broomfield for my first official day at infant school. We entered a mobile classroom which was located just inside the gate where the library currently sits. The initial introductions were made and Marilyn turned to leave. I knew I was expected to stay but turned to walk out with her, hoping that no one would notice. I was called back by the teacher and told to join the others sat on the carpet. In future I would walk to school by myself, it was only about 400 metres away. Once I had been safely seen across the Long Furrow it was pavement the rest of the way.

I settled in at my new school but Marilyn had no interest or time for me and I became very sad at home. I was shouted at and told off constantly. I remember once being in the back double bedroom changing into my pyjamas. I caught my reflection in the window. I had been crying after becoming victim to some recent injustice. Seeing how sad I was, stood there in just a white cotton vest with tears streaming down my face, I thought that I was the poorest boy in the whole world. That makes me laugh now having seen others suffer much greater hardship but this was the mind of a five-year-old boy.

Weekly payday meant Friday-night shopping. Dad and Marilyn would go. If I was with them that weekend I would be dropped off at my other grandma's. My dad's mum, Grandma Iris Newby, was my favourite. Whereas Grandma Dorothy resembled the Queen, Grandma Iris was the double of the Queen Mum. She had married Ken, a war hero with many medals. He had glasses, smoked a pipe and drank bottles of beer, lots of them. He collected the beer-bottle tops and there was a big box full of them in the kitchen. It resembled a pirate's treasure chest, full of gold coins.

Their house was an old Victorian terrace called Hamilton Villa, at 95 Loughborough Road. It's still there. The front reception room was rarely used. There was a coffee table which was home to some jars of Humbug sweets, toffees, fudge, sugared dates and assorted nuts. The sweets were an obvious attraction but that room was cold. Better to be in the middle room next to the coal fire and kitchen. Warmer in there. The room was small. An extendable dining table was pushed against the wall. It was collapsed to enable dinner for two. The placemats had fox-hunter scenes of riders in red coats, jumping horses, and packs of hounds. On the wall was an ornamental galloping black horse. In the hallway were some Toby jugs on a shelf but also some ornamental heads nailed to the wall. Almost lifelike hand-painted faces, a turban-wearing Arab, a pirate and a pipe-smoking old sailor. I used to scrutinise them closely, expecting each character to come alive and speak. Weird.

I vaguely recall that there was a cellar but I was too scared to go down there. It was cold and dark. The monsters would obviously get me.

I would sit upon Ken's knee as he bounced me up and down giving me pretend horse rides. Grandma told him to stop. He was too old and I was too heavy for him. Ken ignored her and carried on while smoking his pipe. No such thing as passive smoking in those days. He was my friend and I loved him dearly. I wasn't his proper grandson but he was the best grandad anyone could ask for.

All too soon, Dad and Marilyn would return and collect me. Ken always gave me two shillings or a new ten pence for an ice cream. By today's standards it would be close to a pound. I would put the money in my coat pocket. My usual coat was an olive green parka with a grey furry hood, orange quilt lining and a draw string waist. The toggle ends resembled acorns and I used to chew them. It was similar to the Arctic jacket worn by my Action Man. Once I got back in the car Marilyn would say, "I'll have that." She stole my money every time. I hated her.

It wasn't long before we left Long Furrow. Marilyn was Dad's new lady and did not want to live in the former matrimonial home, so we moved to her folks', on Cranmer Street near the Hinckley Road-Narborough Road junction. We were only there a few months but that was long enough for me to change schools. King Richard III Primary. I was certainly there for my sixth birthday. I remember it. In school assembly you were called up to the stage on your birthday and given chocolate Smarties. One for each year. Not a pack, just six small sweets. I remember wishing that I was older.

I can't visualise Marilyn's mother or recall her name. Her partner, possibly Marilyn's father, was called Jack. He was German. I don't know if he fought or if so, on whose side, but the ends of some of his fingers were missing and others had no fingernails. He was not unkind to me but his hands freaked me out a little. I do remember that the terraced house had a small brick wall around the tiny front garden and that I spent most of my time alone in the front room, either drawing pictures or playing with Lego. These new relatives had no further influence on me. I never saw them again. From there we moved into our new house. Marilyn's house.

Beaumont Leys was a modern housing estate under construction. Like my early years on Long Furrow, Milton Crescent had muddy roads, dumper trucks, piles of builder's sand and even an outdoor water tap for the cement mixers. Houses were being built everywhere, but ours, number 44, was ready and we moved in.

We had another holiday in Cornwall. One benefit of the Escort estate was that when the seats were down, I could lay in the back with a pillow. I remember lying there and looking up at the high-low section of the M5 motorway. This is where the road cuts into the living rock of some cliffs. The southbound is the 'high' and the northbound is the 'low'. It is close to Bristol and I have travelled that way many times since. The prominent landmark is nowhere near Cornwall but I always associate the two.

On this trip we were driving down a country lane. It was raining heavily. We came across an overturned army truck. There were obvious casualties and I had to stay in the car. Marilyn didn't move either but my dad leapt into action. After his initial assessment he returned to the boot, took out his massive parasol-type fishing umbrella and ran back to the crash site. The raindrops collected on the windscreen and obscured the view. He was gone a long time and I fell asleep. He didn't say much about it.

I didn't stay on the farm with Dad and Marilyn. They did their own thing. I was dumped with some other family who had kids my age. I had a good time. I was spoilt. I remember eating some sweets that were presented in a small grey plastic helicopter. Could have been a Wessex or a Whirlwind. It was good weather and I think us children spent most of the nights in a tent in the garden.

I swapped schools again, Buswell Lodge, and immediately fell in love with my teacher. She used to let me sit next to her on her chair as she read stories to my peers, all sat cross-legged on the carpet in front of us. I was praised for my art work and general attitude towards school. I loved it. Monday to Friday it was where I needed to be. Home was Hell.

After school, I would have to go straight home. I could walk myself but had to do so in timely fashion. On arrival I would be sent to my room. The house had that new smell about it. My room was a good size. Probably seemed bigger than in reality because there was nothing in there. Just a bed. The walls were blank and painted summer blue and there were tiny scars in the plastering. There was a dark blue carpet. I sat on it with my back against the radiator. There I would sit until called down for my evening meal.

Every day was the same. Two slices of white bread with butter and strawberry jam, cut into four squares and served on a plate with a cup of sour milk. I knew very well what milk was supposed to taste like. We were given a small bottle every day at school before morning break. At home, we had a fridge and the milkman delivered a fresh pint daily, but mine was always spoiled. It had those curdled floaters on the surface and tasted acidic. I was being given sour milk on purpose. Marilyn didn't like me. I was hungry and thirsty so regardless of its condition I swallowed it.

On completion I would be sent back to my room. I didn't have to sit down against the radiator. I could look out of the window at the un-turfed gardens of the developing plots, some bordered by wire fencing. The only interesting feature was the large leafy tree. It would blow in the breeze and change shape. Sometimes it looked like the head of a helmet-wearing policeman. I wished he would take Marilyn away.

I would hear Dad come home. That was a small blessing and might give me some protection from the often subtle cruelty applied by Marilyn but at the same time he was not the cavalry. My prisoner status was unchanged.

My next activity would be the bedtime routine. I didn't have a wristwatch and couldn't tell the time but I knew when to make my move. Every weeknight there was a soap opera called *Crossroads*. When the closing theme tune blared out from the TV downstairs, I was prompted to act. I'd take off my clothes and put on my dressing gown, which was blue quilted on the outside with a red lining. I would make my way downstairs and walk through the lounge towards the kitchen diner. Dad would be sat on his tanned leather sofa reading the newspaper. There was no need for me to acknowledge him. I wasn't allowed to talk in that room unless spoken to.

Stood at the kitchen sink I would remove my robe to stand naked. The kitchen door would be deliberately left wide open giving a potential full view to the girls next door. Tracey, the older of the two, was my age and I quite fancied her if that was possible for someone so young. The open door was intended to humiliate me. It worked. I was hardly big enough to reach the taps let alone wash in the metal kitchen sink. I was barred from washing in the bathroom. I had once dirtied a towel because I hadn't cleaned my hands properly. Thereafter I would only be permitted to use the kitchen sink.

The next level of cruel abuse was the teeth cleaning. I would have to use soap. Why? Because there was no toothpaste. I was supposed to remind her that she needed to buy some in the shopping. Well, that's interesting. Were Marilyn and my dad cleaning *their* teeth with soap? Of course not.

"When will there be some toothpaste?" I'd ask. "When I go shopping," would be the response.

There never was any toothpaste and even today I can still taste the soap. I mentioned this to Grandma Iris. She told me that if there was no toothpaste, I could just use water. I liked the sound of that and raised it by way of protest at my next opportunity. Marilyn rejected the proposal claiming she was in charge, not Grandma. It wasn't as though I could just pretend to use soap. Marilyn would load the brush for me.

7pm, early summer. My bedroom curtains are drawn but it is still light. Other children are playing outside, yet I'm in bed and wide awake. My tongue is finding undissolved pieces of soap in the gaps of my teeth. How can I sleep? No books, not tired. All I can do is sing quietly to myself. Every song I know. 'Happy Birthday', 'Jingle Bells', 'When Santa got stuck up the Chimney', 'P.L.A.Y.' (*Play Away*) and Brotherhood of Man's 'Save Your Kisses For Me'.

I had no toys. They had all been confiscated soon after moving in. The reason was because I was playing at night instead of going to sleep. I wasn't tired. A friend from school heard of my hardship and gave me a small toy motorbike. The imagination of a little boy is such that this one toy could give great adventures. I smuggled the contraband item into my room and hid it in the pillowcase. On my very first ride across the undulating pillow landscape, I was caught.

My angry dad charged in, snatched away my one and only toy, before pulling down by pyjama bottoms to lash my backside with a bamboo cane. My screaming pleas were ignored. Attempts to protect by buttocks with the palms of my hands were in vain. I was too small and not strong enough. The blows found their target many times. I remember being shocked by the results. When the tears subsided and the stinging reduced, my fingers were able to examine deep furrows and bamboo imprints across my soft skin.

There was another punishment for not being able to sleep.

"Why are you still awake?" I'd be asked. "Not tired," I'd say.

That was the wrong answer. They'd make me tired. I was marched down to the foot of the staircase and made to stand to attention with my face about 6 inches from the wall. Try it sometime. See how long you can last. It's not long before the knees click, the legs ache and the weight shifts from one foot to the other. Eventually I would have to crawl back upstairs on my hands and knees because the legs could no longer support me.

Morning would come. Great! I'll be at school soon. But first, breakfast. Two Weetabix with sour milk. Then out of the front door for a few hours' respite. I looked forward to school and especially school dinners. Any seconds or extras, I would be first with a hand up. Desserts often included a jug of custard. Left standing, a film would develop on the surface. Dinner ladies would ask, "Who wants the skin?" There were never any takers but I'd always shout, "ME!"

By this point I was spending most weekends at my mum's. She had a new man with whom she had bought a house in Anstey. Paul was quite a bit younger than my mum. Proper blond, leather jacket and drove a Triumph Dolomite Sprint. He was OK with me. I remember us sitting down and doing some colouring with felt tip pens. They were quite a novelty in those days; far better than crayons.

The house was a three-storey end terrace, 45 Cropston Road, just up from the main village centre. There was loads of room, a big back garden with a climbable tree, but, most importantly, I would be away from Marilyn and back with my big brother. I would get there on a Friday night and stay until Sunday evening. It was absolute heaven.

Every Friday night we would watch *Hawaii Five-O*. Tony enjoyed a lie-in on Saturdays but I was always up early, raring to go. Sadly nobody else would be. I'd go in to Mum and Paul so as to wake them up. That wouldn't happen. Instead my mum would pull me in under the covers and hold me there for the kind of cuddle only a mother can give. It was warm, I was safe, I was loved, I was happy.

At this house I was allowed to use the bathroom. Looking in the mirror I saw that I had started to get freckles on my face. I didn't like them but no amount of scrubbing would remove them.

There were very few TV channels back then and no video or DVD. Saturday morning was the golden spot. A choice of *Swap Shop* or *Tiswas* interlaced with adventures of *The Three Musketeers*, *Tarzan*, *The Banana Splits* or *Arabian Knights*. Afternoon was ITV's *World of Sport* or BBC's *Grandstand*. I found horse racing and wrestling incredibly dull, so Saturday afternoon would be playing-out time. We would nip to the shops for a small bag of sweets.

I wanted to blow bubblegum balloons like Tony but first needed Santa to deliver my two front teeth. I especially liked sherbet dips and small white chocolate mice. I'd often save one as a pet friend for my return to Beaumont Leys but would normally eat it before arriving rather than risk confiscation.

Saturday night was essential TV. *The Six Million Dollar Man*. Afterwards, Tony and I would recreate the episode highlights. Being the oldest he would of course play the lead character, Steve Austin. There was no official sidekick so Tony invented my role. "You can be my bionic brother, Jim."

That was acceptable to me. He was my hero and I was just happy to be with him. I had to be Spock while Tony was of course Captain Kirk. He was Tarzan, I was Jai. He was Captain Scarlet, I was Captain Blue. He was the Lone Ranger, I was Tonto. He was Steve McGarrett and I was told to "Book him, Danno!"

Sundays were eventful. Tony went to the Boys Brigade. I wanted to go too. Firstly because he was going. Secondly because they wore a uniform which included a cap that looked similar to those worn by International Rescue in *Thunderbirds*. Alas, I was too young, so I was dumped at Sunday school. It was not particularly religious. Just somewhere safe for me to go while Mum prepared Sunday dinner. I would sit colouring in pictures of biblical characters. I had no idea who they were supposed to be, but I liked the one with the multi-coloured coat.

After the Sunday roast, we might clean Paul's car, visit his mum, Grandma Dorothy and Nin, or go to Bradgate Park for adventures, climbing on the rocks, rolling down the hill from 'Old John' and hiding in the old hollow oak trees.

Time just flew by and it would always be over too soon. 'Bohemian Rhapsody' was in the charts for many months. The radio counted down the singles chart every Sunday. We would enter the 'Top 10' by about 6pm. Just as the *Crossroads* theme music meant it was time for bed in Beaumont Leys, the last notes of this Queen song meant my happiness would soon be at an end and it was time to leave. Hearing that amazing and iconic tune today still evokes great sorrow.

Milton Crescent wasn't far from Cropston Road. A short drive along Anstey Lane linked the two addresses. I wouldn't need to be fed on Sunday night and I could escape the kitchen routine and soap-flavoured toothpaste by being ready for bed on arrival. Next Friday would be too far away but at least I had school to look forward to tomorrow.

Dad wasn't poor. He was important at work. The Taxman used to come to our house to sort the company's accounts. My dad kept fish in the garage. He had shelves stacked with fish tanks like a shop. He had Oscar fish. I remember that name because 'Oscar' was one of the main characters in the *Six Million Dollar Man*. No resemblance. He had angelfish, clownfish and even had some small sharks. He had angling equipment in a large wicker basket. Colourful fluorescent-tipped floats and trays full of maggots. He had a pet parrot in a large cage in the dining room. I remember how the beak resembled a Brazil nut. It wasn't smooth though; it was flaking as the bird grew in size and I wanted to pick at it. He had an expensive remote-controlled aeroplane that he would fly at a proper airfield. All this money, yet I was sent to school in shorts throughout the winter. I remember sitting in a sheltered corner of the playground with my knees pulled up to my chest trying to stay out of the wind and wishing break-time would soon be over. That was my only bad memory of Buswell Lodge.

I particularly enjoyed mixing the powdered paints and making green from yellow and blue. I can still smell the paint and remember cleaning the tray pallets. I also remember my rehearsed lines from the school's presentation to parents. At the appropriate time, I had to stand up in the crowd and announce, "MOST PEOPLE LIKED RICE PUDDING!" Shy and embarrassed I sat back down as quickly as I could.

Back at home, the Marilyn situation got worse. One morning she slapped me across the face. One of her fingers made contact with my eyeball and I yelped and screamed. I couldn't see. She panicked then. She was worried. She embraced me, comforted me and tried to mitigate that it was an accident. With her face close to mine I could see how her top lip was cracked and split in the centre. It looked painful. Perhaps she needed to stop smoking? She sent me to school with an enveloped note, presumably to explain my late arrival, and waved me off from the front door like a loving mother. I don't know what she wrote.

That day after school she was particularly nice to me. I was able to sit on the sofa and watch TV in the lounge until dinner. A small squad of toy soldiers appeared too. Marilyn was pregnant and she allowed me to put the soldiers on her swollen tummy. When the baby kicked, the soldiers tumbled and I tried to stand them all up again before the next tremor.

Alas, this new friendship was short-lived. My eye was fine. The next day I came in from school and sat on the sofa. "What do you think you're doing?" she asked, and I was sent back to my solitary confinement.

I remember on one occasion Marilyn screaming at my dad during a full-blown argument. I heard Dad remark, "Well, they say he's all right at school." Marilyn countered that she'd had enough of me and shouted, "Either he goes or I go!" The next day she was gone. Was it really that simple? Just me and my dad from now on? Cool.

"Do you see what you've done?" asked Dad. "I know; great, isn't it? She's gone," I said.

We went out together. He flew his aeroplane as I watched, munching away on a Mars bar. They were so big in those days. We were bros and I was happy again.

I don't recall much of the pregnancy but next came the new arrival. Amanda was my first little sister. That much I understood. I had no animosity towards her and was happy to be a big brother, but this tiny little bundle in a Moses basket was accompanied by Marilyn. She was back and so were her wicked routines.

The summer school holidays arrived and I was allowed to play out on the front. I regularly drank from the builders' tap, choosing to stay well clear of Marilyn's house. One day I decided to run away. I say run, I actually just walked. I knew the way. Today there are dual carriageways and busy main roads criss-crossing that area but back then it was just a narrow country lane. To avoid detection I walked inside the treeline that ran parallel to the road. It was perhaps regarded as too far for a seven-year-old to wander but I made it. Having turned up at my mum's I was promptly returned to Dad and the next thing I knew I was dropped off at Westcotes Children's Home.

The summer holidays were eight weeks long back then, and I spent most of that time at Westcotes, although I still had some weekends in Anstey. I loved it. Big back garden with a treehouse and rope swing. There was a TV room and that caused some bickering, particularly when the resident teenagers wanted to watch *Top of the Pops* while us younger ones pleaded for cartoons. Apparently, I slept there at night-time but I don't remember that. I must have been so exhausted from all the fun. Staff walked us to a nearby park that was bordered by green-painted metal railings. On the way, we all got some sweets from one of the corner shops. I had a bag of liquorice torpedoes. I had never heard of the word 'torpedo' before that. It seems strange that hearing it now makes me think of confectionery whereas most would consider a seaborne missile.

I remember two boys, a little bit younger than me. They were identical twins with that 'Milky Bar Kid' blond hair. Staff simply called them 'The Twins'. Their grandad used to visit them regularly. He brought them sweets. He brought us all sweets. We liked it when their grandad came and we would swarm around him, vying for attention, with staff holding us back so that 'The Twins' could have some quality time with their visitor.

I was totally unaware of the adult talk going on or that my future was being decided. Social Services had concluded that the only proposition that I could accept was for Mum and Dad's reunion. How they decided that I don't know. They were very wrong. I was happy to be with Mum and Paul, I was happy with Do, I was happy at Westcotes and at Buswell Lodge. The only place that I was unhappy was with Marilyn.

I was given a social worker; Ann Guy was her name. An old lady, a bit like the TV detective, Miss Marple. She drove a noisy yellow Citroen 2CV. She would take me for a spin and ask me loads of questions. Then one day she introduced me to Lynne and Ivor Wright. These were experienced foster carers. Veterans. They'd looked after more than thirty kids before me. They even brought one with them, a two-year-old half-Jamaican girl, Donnamae. They asked me if I'd like to live with them.

"Sure, why not, provided I can still see my mum and dad, oh and of course my big brother."

I wasn't desperate, I quite liked it at Westcotes, but I seemed to be getting a good deal and Donnamae would be my new sister. I took her for a walk around the garden and showed her off to the other kids. "My new sister." Within days I would visit the foster home and confirm that I wanted to go.

"When do you want to come?" they asked. "NOW!" I said.

I went back to Beaumont Leys and told my dad I was moving out. I wasn't going to miss the parrot and I wasn't allowed anywhere near baby Amanda. I hadn't fed her, held her or even seen her smile. One more night of strawberry jam sandwiches. Ha, I can cope with that.

The next morning, the white Escort estate was loaded with all my long-forgotten toys and my dad pulled up outside 6 Wentbridge Road, Rushey Mead. I remember that on the day, his eyes were watering and his nose running quite badly. I challenged this and he said he had a cold. I accepted that explanation for many years. Only in adulthood did I come to realise that he was actually holding back his tears.

I spent what was left of the summer holidays playing out on the front and making friends with the kids on my street. Gary from number 10 was my first friend. I was out in the road with my wind-up 'Evel Knievel' stunt motorbike toy. Annoyingly, that long-term storage had bent the front forks and consequently the bike no longer travelled in a straight line. We didn't exchange names on that first occasion. When he called for me the next day he simply asked, "Is the boy playing out?"

I soon had a whole squad of friends. We had adventures in the woods and paddled down the brook. We made catapults and fought each other by firing unripe plums. They really stung if you were hit in the back, much more dangerous than paintballing and we had no protection. Summer of 1976 is remembered for being one of the hottest on record. Hosepipe bans and droughts. Yes, that's how it was. Running around playing 'hide and seek' would quickly lead to a thirst, dry and dusty air making things worse. Disappointingly, the cold tap dispensed warm water during the day and sometimes going home was too much effort so we'd drink from the brook. How I am still alive I'll never know.

New surroundings. On the sofa at Wentbridge Road 1976, aged seven.

Chapter 4.

Damaged Goods

My new life was certainly an improvement. I had clothes, food, my own bedroom, toys, a new large and extended family, a new school, and lots of new friends, fresh milk, real toothpaste and access to a bathroom. Everything I needed. The thing is, some of this I didn't need and some of it I didn't want.

This may sound ungrateful or at least strange. Certainly for many it will be ambiguous. Given the trauma I had suffered for almost half of my life and most of my living memory, I ought to have been wholeheartedly embracing the opportunity to become a member of this welcoming family. But that is not what had been initially agreed at Westcotes (I would live with them but still see Dad, Mum and Tony).

I may have only been a seven-year-old but as far as I was concerned, I was now old enough and wise enough to choose my own destiny. In my mind, I was already a man. I didn't need a 'new' mum and dad. I had those people in my life already and felt no need or even desire to consider my foster parents as replacements. So when they suggested that I call them 'Mum and Dad'... I refused. Their names were Lynne and Ivor but that was too informal. We compromised. Instead I would address them as Aunty Lynne and Uncle Ivor. I was comfortable with that. I had called Do, Aunty Do. This was the same.

The other factor in my logic was that I did not see this as a long-term arrangement. My mum had already told me that I could live with her when I was eleven. By then I would be old enough to have my own key and let myself in after school. I would be eleven in a few years. In the meantime I would see my dad fortnightly for a few hours on a Tuesday night. We'd go for a drive and visit a pub. Sometimes it was the Malt Shovel to look at their resident otters. Sometimes it was the Gate Hangs Well. Marilyn did not attend; it was just the two of us. I would also have regular weekend stays at my mum's and play with my brother as before.

It angers and infuriates me now to see how I was manipulated. Seeing Dad or Mum and Tony was regarded as 'unsettling'. Naturally, I would be sad on return and slightly offhand in my attitude but consequently, those visits would become less frequent and eventually dry up almost completely. That upset me even more. I had expected to be fostered only short-term, as a temporary placement. I didn't need to settle and had no intention of doing so.

From the outset, Lynne and Ivor wanted to adopt me but I rejected that notion. They were offering a stable environment with unlimited love and support but I pushed them away. I may not have been an oil painting but I was certainly no blank canvas either. I had a history, I had memories and I had unwavering loyalty to my own family. Unaware that I was actually being groomed as 'Iain Wright', their eldest son, I fiercely resisted being forced into that mould.

Lynne and Ivor were good people but they weren't my people. They were doing their best for me but no matter how hard they tried I was never ever going to be anything other than a square peg in a round hole.

They were practicing Christians, indeed Ivor had even trained as a priest. I don't hold being religious against them, but that was their choice and I had ideas of my own. I wanted nothing to do with it. I told them that I didn't believe in gods and they were very disappointed. They questioned whether I would be celebrating Christmas or be wanting Easter eggs? They pointed out that Donnamae went to church and enjoyed it, but she was too young to know anything different. My lack of knowledge concerning Bible stories was also a shock to them.

We were taught a bit of religion at school. We had interesting lessons in RE (Religious Education). I was fascinated by the Golden Temple at Amritsar. I used to be able to draw it perfectly from memory. During assemblies we had to sing Christian songs while one of the teachers played the piano. I didn't like this singing, in the same way that I hated being told to change channel on Sunday so that my foster parents could watch and sing along to *Songs of Praise*.

I found religion quite absurd. What is my religion? Church of England? Why?

I suppose most people inherit a belief from their parents. They accept it without question because that is the way they were raised. It's tradition. My parents were absent. If I had gone to a school with just white kids, I may have been less dismissive of Christianity, but at Herrick Junior, most of the pupils were Hindu, Sikh or Muslim. One of my best friends was Baljinder. He was a Sikh and I spent many hours at his family home. I wasn't persuaded by Sikhism and I did not believe in any of the Indian gods, but at the same time I had to be prepared to look at the alternatives. I had already laughed off those of the Greeks, Romans, Egyptians and Red Indians but I saw no greater credibility in the Bible. Buddhism had some merit but at the end of the day, it should be my choice. I could believe in one or believe in none. I had already made my decision.

It seems very wrong that in a school where the majority were of Indian ancestry, and there were only a small number of white kids and even fewer churchgoers, we were all being made to sing those Christian songs. Some of us amused ourselves by altering the lyrics. "CUCUMBER, my lord, CUCUMBER."

Lynne and Ivor said that they were sending me to Sunday school, so I could learn more about their faith. No way. They couldn't make me go to church and they couldn't make me go to Sunday school. I think they realised that they would get nowhere with that idea. If I used that as an excuse for running away (which I threatened to do) they would have abused their position as foster parents. Religion became the first barrier to our relationship.

They did a lot for charity. Tremendous work for Mencap and helping people with Down's syndrome which included staging shows at De Montfort Hall and running 'It's a Knockout' events. I helped, I didn't mind; it was a worthwhile cause and when I was there, I usually had a good time, but it wasn't my hobby, it was theirs, and helping once didn't mean that I wanted to be a regular volunteer. The whole concept of volunteering involves choice rather than obligation. These social events were completely alien to me. Perhaps I just wasn't ready for the large crowds. I had spent so much time in isolation that my new freedom was something to relish. I wanted to be out playing with my street friends rather than being put on a leash and dragged around.

As time went on the terms of address would again surface.

"You ought to be calling us Mum and Dad. We have done more for you than your own parents and calling us Aunty Lynne and Uncle Ivor is confusing for Donnamae."

My new sister called them Mum and Dad, she didn't know any better. She'd been there since she was a baby. For me, the use of those titles implied permanence whereas my stay was only temporary. I wouldn't budge. It angered me that I was even being asked to do so. Had this proposal not been forced upon me, I may have been willing. Given sufficient time, I may have even requested it, but this way was wrong. I would never do it. Even today I resent the issue.

This seemingly innocuous conversation would have a lasting impact. Probably because it was repeated on several occasions.

"Why won't you call us Mum and Dad?"

"Because you are NOT my mum and dad."

"But we have done more for you than Fred and Lesley."

That resonated over and over.

"Right, I don't want you to do anything else for me," I said.

Given the choice of accepting that 'conditional assistance' or doing things for myself, I would choose independence every time. I didn't want their help any longer. This would now be an additional barrier to our relationship.

The issue of calling them Mum and Dad was non-negotiable. I would hear them arguing over this downstairs. I wasn't being awkward. Losing my real mum and dad was painful. They were the two special people who owned those titles. They weren't dead, I missed them and I wanted to still see them. I certainly wasn't ready to forget them. It hurt me to even say those words as it was a painful reminder of that loss. For me, the concept of addressing new people as Mum and Dad was, in effect, to sack and disown my original parents. I didn't need to do that as I would be reunited with them soon. Furthermore, I wasn't required to call Paul, Dad or Marilyn, Mum. This was just stupid and perverse.

The dictionary defines torture as 'the infliction of pain for the purpose of punishment or persuasion'. To me, this very discussion was absolute torture. I hadn't done anything wrong but I felt sick every time the subject was raised. They were only words but I just couldn't say them. I so wanted all this to stop.

Eventually, for the sake of keeping the peace, I conceded.

"OK, OK, I'll call you Mum and Dad from now on."

I would, but only in written form: birthday cards and Christmas cards, etc. Verbally, I did not call them anything. Neither Aunty Lynne nor Mum, Uncle Ivor or Dad. I'd just go into the room and speak directly.

"Anyone want a coffee?" "I'm going out now; bye!" "I'm going to bed; goodnight."

In order to successfully mask this new style, I subconsciously applied it to everyone. Nobody had a name. When meeting someone for the first time it is customary to introduce yourself. I never grasped that ritual. I had no need of it. I didn't communicate that way and names meant nothing to me. People might tell me their name but it would go in one ear and out of the other.

Every cloud has a silver lining and I think this helped me later in the police. With a mind empty of names, I was better able to remember faces. They were either friend or foe. Names of friends had no significance because I'd just call everyone 'mate'. But when it came to facial recognition of criminals and naming them, I was outstanding. So I was operationally effective, particularly for surveillance, but socially flawed. It would be many years later in a counselling session that I discovered this permanent scar. A scar that exists not because of Marilyn but because of my time in care.

The second lasting impact is my reluctance to seek or accept assistance. I enjoy helping others but I hate being in a situation where I need to ask for even the most basic favour. Such occasions fill me with dread and make me feel quite nauseous. I have many good friends falling over backwards and ready to assist me at any time and in any way but I just cannot bring myself to ask. Why?

"Because we've done more for you than…"

I don't ever want to hear that again. Being uncomfortable in that situation would be a second permanent scar from my time in care. That is not to say that I got where I am today unaided. I had lots of help. Some people recognise where help is definitely needed and act accordingly. They make no fuss and demand nothing in return. I am grateful to those people. The world needs more of them.

My social worker was required to make regular welfare checks. I would have to stay in and miss the opportunity of playing out with friends after school, just to have a ten-minute private chat in my bedroom. I didn't need this; things were bearable. My situation was not permanent; I'd be eleven eventually.

Ann Guy retired and I got a new chap. I didn't want to speak with him either. I think I told him so. One way of getting rid of the social worker was to be adopted. The subject was brought up. As foster carers, Lynne and Ivor were paid to look after me, but they weren't financially motivated. They wanted to adopt me as their own.

"We will legally become your mum and dad. Fred and Lesley will just be people you know."

They desperately wanted me to be their son but that was out of the question. Forget it. Not happening. This is only a temporary arrangement and why on earth would I wish to discard my real family?

Anyway, life rolled on. I went to see *Star Wars* on my eighth birthday, joined the Cub Scouts and got an arm full of badges. I did my cycling proficiency test, rode my skateboard, collected Panini football stickers and played marbles. Just like a normal boy. I also built dens in the woods. Just like a normal boy; only mine were more than dens. They were emergency housing should I decide not to go home. I wasn't settled. I was just sitting it out, waiting for my liberation.

I ran away a couple of times. The first occasion was after I had joined the 39th (later 54th) Cub Scout Group at Soar Valley College. 1977 was the Queen's silver jubilee year and we all wore a special commemorative badge on our uniforms. That summer, there was a sponsored walk around Bradgate Park. It was four or five laps around the perimeter to make a total distance of 20 miles. That was a very long way for an eight-year-old. This was a time before Nike trainers. In those days it was either Clarks leather upper shoes or lightweight black canvas plimsolls.

Having successfully completed the distance on a hot and dusty Sunday, I arrived back home late afternoon. I was then told to jump into the bath and get ready for bed. The logic was that the bath would promote recovery after my long march and rather than put on a fresh set of clothes, I could relax downstairs in my pyjamas until bedtime. That was a perfectly innocent, sensible and reasonable proposal, but the initial instructions provoked a surprisingly unnatural reaction.

I totally flipped. The suggestion horrified me to a point of uncontrollable panic. I must have had some kind of flashback to the Beaumont Leys bedtime routine. It was like pushing a burn victim towards the flames. I wouldn't submit to reasoning and was beyond persuasion. I stubbornly protested that I was not getting ready for bed so early and threw a major tantrum during which I said things like, "You can't tell me what do," and "You ain't my mum and dad."

With old wounds now open, I wasn't going to budge on this issue. I was very upset and decided that this foster home was no longer the place for me. When the coast was clear, I opened the bedroom window and climbed out onto the porch roof. My escape had been easy thus far but I soon realised that this spontaneous action was ill thought out and would require greater consideration and planning before execution, so I climbed back in. I was still angry though and wanted to teach my foster parents a lesson, so I hid under the bed and tested their response.

When they discovered an unoccupied bedroom and saw the curtains flapping at the wide-open window, there was panic. "HE'S GONE!" I remained undetected during their frantic cursory search but was soon discovered when they became more methodical. By the time they had finished berating me it was well past normal bedtime.

Later that year, I also did my first long bike ride. It was on a yellow 'High Riser', the cheaper version of the Raleigh Chopper. Same design with that big banana seat and the Sturmey-Archer gear lever on the upper crossbar. I rode to Anstey. I wasn't actually running away on this particular occasion, I was just paying a visit. The journey was about 5 or 6 miles and took me a while. Navigating wasn't that difficult; I knew the way.

The problem was that I fell off while descending the steep decline on Anstey Lane. In doing so, I injured my left shin. There was a deep open wound with blood everywhere. Seeing my insides for the first time was quite a shock. Adding to my fears was a passing funeral cortege. I thought they might be coming for me but they didn't stop. The gash would eventually need three stitches.

When I reached Cropston Road, I saw Tony and asked for help with my leg. He was being looked after by Grandma Dorothy and called her straight away. She cleaned and dressed the wound before telling me that she was going to ring my mum. I panicked. I was too far from home and would be grounded for sure. Best thing I could do was get back home quickly and pretend nothing had happened. I was out of Anstey before Grandma had even picked up the phone.

A couple of hours later I casually rode up the street to be greeted and instantly interrogated by Lynne. The word had got back and people had been out searching for me. I was in deep trouble.

"Where have you been?" she asked. "Just riding about locally. Oh and yes, I fell off my bike," I said.

I was scolded, grounded, bike confiscated, yet still had blood trickling down my leg.

There were issues at the health centre that played out partly in my favour. I was a 'ward of court', Social Services was responsible for me and my foster parents were unable to give consent for anaesthetic. Although sought, the appropriate authorisation could not readily be obtained and consequently I would have to be treated without the local injection. The stitches took my breath away but they would be my main punishment. Being grounded was inevitable. I couldn't play out anyway because of the wound and as for losing the bike… well, I wouldn't be rushing back to Anstey. I was unfairly bitter towards Grandma Dorothy. She had acted appropriately and in my best interests but through my immaturity I felt she had betrayed me.

Having made my view on adoption quite clear, I was then talked into taking the name, Wright. It was suggested that school parents' evening was awkward when the teachers asked for Mr and Mrs Hollis. I couldn't see the issue myself and today I realise that that was just utter bullshit. I did not mind being called Wright but I was not going to stop being Iain Hollis. My nickname at school was 'Lollies'.

I was told that I could be Iain David Hollis Wright. I liked the idea of a double-barrelled surname but that novelty wasn't on offer. I would become Iain Wright on the school register but I could introduce myself as Hollis Wright if I so wished. This was not a deed poll change, just a non-permanent and informal arrangement. If need be I could revert back at any time.

Being in a foster home was interesting to say the least. I was there long-term. So was Donnamae. But others would have shorter stays; a couple of days, weeks or months. Over the next few years I was big brother to many kids. Three little Indian boys: Abanesh, Brianesh and Nilesh. I walked them to school, shared a bed 'top and tail' and we laughed all night. A handful of a two-year-old half-Jamaican boy, Jason, stayed for a couple of weeks. A white lad, my age, Andrew, stayed for a few months.

There were many others but my favourite was F (not her real initial but I don't know how she would take being identified), a newborn Muslim girl, taken into care because she was considered at risk. Mum had mysteriously fallen down the stairs while heavily pregnant (pushed more like, as they wanted a son). She was now my baby sister. I fed her, changed her nappies, rocked her to sleep and received her first smiles. I was heartbroken when we gave her back. She was much bigger by then but not yet ready to eat apples. She was returned to us after allegedly choking on one. She hadn't even got teeth. "They're trying to kill her!" I said. She eventually went back to her parents and they were regularly supervised. Crazy world.

My eleventh birthday neared. I was excited. I'd be moving on soon. Hadn't discussed it properly with my foster parents or social worker but I had done so with friends. Their advice was that I should stay put. I had everything I needed and was with people who had done more for me than… "STOP!"

They say 'the grass is always greener on the other side' but I was under no illusion. I knew that my new life was much more privileged than Tony's, but they also say that 'blood is thicker than water' and I would have gladly accepted a lesser standard of living just to be returned to my own clan.

ELEVEN! Finally! I'd been waiting for this day for a third of my life. Alas, the move was not happening. Apparently it had been decided that I was settled now; a move would be too disruptive and against my best interests. Also, Donnamae and the other children would miss me. Rubbish! I was due to start a secondary school in September. That was six months away, so there was plenty of time to make the arrangements. This was just a foster home. Donnamae was not my real sister and she saw her natural mother regularly. Such disparity. The final word from my mum was that she could not cope with both Tony and me, so it would be better to stay where I was.

My disappointment was off the scale and this news absolutely destroyed me. Being abandoned by Mum meant I had also lost Tony and my reaction to her devastating decision demonstrated my true colours. Lynne and Ivor now knew that despite my seemingly passive exterior, deep down I had not settled over the last three and a half years and I didn't want to be with them. That was the third and final barrier. It was insurmountable.

My mum had reneged on our arrangement which led to feelings of betrayal, rejection and utter humiliation. This was made worse by the fact that soon afterwards, she and Paul produced a daughter, Andrea. My heart was ripped out and I was totally dejected.

Who am I supposed to be now? Who will I be in future? I am really messed up. Can't go back to Mum, Can't go back to Dad. I don't want to stay here. The only person who matters to me now is Tony, and we've grown apart. He has my mum but I'm on my own. I don't want to be, but where can I go? Nowhere! Who can help? No one!

I was alone. All hope was shattered. I was abject, broken and numb. Looking back, it may have been better if I'd returned to Westcotes at that point. My mental and emotional development was being damaged beyond repair. I was living with perpetual torment. The longer I was fostered, the more opportunity there would be for Lynne and Ivor to do things for me. That increased the pressure to express gratitude. I didn't want that obligation, I wasn't there by choice. Being dumped by my mum didn't change the way I felt about my custodians. I didn't belong there and shouldn't have been there. It was like being an innocent convict in an open prison.

Perhaps a better analogy is that of a wounded or abandoned animal. It doesn't matter how well the rescuers treat it. The longer that creature is removed from its natural environment, the harder it becomes to return it to the wild. Eventually it becomes suspended in limbo, belonging to neither place.

Many years later my younger children were watching *Tracy Beaker*, a TV show based on life in a children's home. In this particular episode, a brother and sister combination was split. He remained at the home while she was taken in by foster carers. The brother's attempts to contact his younger sister were blocked by the new parents on the basis that this was 'unsettling', and they were trying to persuade the girl to address them as Mum and Dad. My children were fixated by the unfolding drama but it obviously evoked memories of my early years. I lost control and fled to break down behind the kitchen door. As a grown man, it shamed me that I couldn't hold it together. It seems the pain will never go away. It is my Achilles' heel. I just have to avoid exposure to it.

I didn't want to be with Lynne and Ivor. I didn't want their religion, I didn't want their help and I certainly didn't want to call them Mum and Dad. I had desperately held on to a false hope of reunification but had been played for a fool. Being with people from a similar background would have made me feel normal. Staying where I was made me odd. I was now an outcast and a recluse. That's the way it would stay.

I left Herrick Junior. I lived in the catchment area for Soar Valley, where most of my friends were going, but Rushey Mead was a much better school so I would be going there. I made new friends at school but most did not live locally. I shut myself away in my room after school each day, similar to the Marilyn routine but without the cruelty. I had my dinner and went to bed. My foster parents would moan at me for being belligerent and anti-social but that did not alter my behaviour.

I had a TV in my room, a black and white portable. There were only three channels to watch but it was adequate. A record player and radio cassette provided alternative entertainment. *Steve Wright in the afternoon* (no relation) was actually on Radio 1 in those days. On Sundays I would record the chart countdown and make my own compilation tape recordings. The problem with cassette tapes was that with continued use they would get chewed up in the player but I became quite expert at repairs by cutting out the crimpled sections and reconnecting the ends with small pieces of Sellotape.

For my long walk to and from school, I would be alone. Everyone else in my neighbourhood went to Soar Valley. As a loner, I would be a potential target for bullies. To counter this I started to exercise. Holding the heavy portable TV by its carrying handle, I would do bicep curls. I did 200 sit-ups daily on my bed. I exercised with a 'Bullworker' and practised my punching on an old sports bag filled with footballs and jumpers. I was quite confident. My 'six-pack' was so hard that I could take punches for payment.

With the onset of puberty came an increased interest in girls. Lorna caught my eye. She was a very pretty green-eyed blond but she had several admirers. When the two O'Reilly brothers approached in the playground and told me to forget about Lorna, I stood my ground. I more than stood my ground. The big one pushed me in my chest while frowning aggressively. I frowned and pushed him back harder and rose my clenched fist, but he had already fallen over. He got back up and the pair retreated.

Later that day, I was told that 'Big Brother O'Reilly' was going to beat me up after school, over the earlier incident. Friends were rallying round trying to mediate. I wasn't concerned. I was strong from all my home training and I'd knocked him down earlier with just a push. *Bring it on*, I thought. The school bell rang and I headed out confidently to meet the challenge. Everyone told me I was going to lose. We'll see.

Shit! There were three O'Reilly brothers, not two. I had agreed to fight the big one rather than the middle one whom I had pushed earlier that day. I didn't really have a chance. Some years older than me, much taller and heavier. He even had a beer belly hanging over his trouser belt.

I had unwisely traded arrogant insults all afternoon and would not be able to talk my way out of this one now. We walked to an alley with a small audience in pursuit and the fight began. I went straight at him, pummelling his fat gut. My punches made no impact. In contrast, he hit me clean on the nose. The stinging sensation was a shock but I continued in vain. He struck my nose a couple of times more before deciding that I was no match. He then put me in a headlock and quite magnanimously told me to stop. This mismatched contest was over and Goliath had easily beaten David.

The crowd dispersed and I walked home, consoled by a few stragglers. Some of the earlier audience shouted and waved support for me from the upstairs of a double-decker as it drove past. It seems I had lost the fight but not my friends. I had also broken my nose, but within days I had won the girl. Asking her out was the easy part. What to do next was the problem. I had no big brother for guidance and few sources of advice. We didn't last long as she soon dumped me for an older boy.

Cindy showed an interest. She was a lovely girl with a great sense of humour. She lived near the city and would usually go home by the opposite route but now she was walking slowly with me. She could get a bus from the end of my road. We'd walk and talk and sit at the bus stop. She would ignore the first bus so we could talk longer. Did she fancy me? Was she waiting for me to ask her out, hold her hand or kiss her? I had no idea. I couldn't get it wrong. Her brother was a famous boxer (later World Champion). When it came to girls, I was useless. Cindy escorted me on several occasions but I never took the bait and she eventually gave up. Damn!

Chapter 5.

A New Hope

It is often said that 'orphans make good soldiers'. With parents out of the equation and fewer close ties, they perhaps adapt to life in the armed forces, quicker and easier, than those leaving behind the comforts and securities of an established or stable family environment. I wasn't an orphan but may as well have been. I looked to the military as a way of escape. I knew that I would be joining up at sixteen. No one could stop me. Well, actually lots of people could stop me but they would have been foolish to try. I was definitely going. Just hadn't chosen my branch or regiment. I had already informally interviewed a soldier of the Royal Anglians and the Army sounded good to me.

In April 1982, Argentina invaded the Falklands. The Parachute Regiment made an impressive and costly contribution towards liberating the islanders, but it was the Royal Marines who stole the show. I was soon influenced by the various documentaries which were broadcast following the British victory. At just thirteen, I had already made up my mind what I was going to do when I left school. It was the Commandos for me. The Paras were my second choice. People often ask which is better. Well, horses for courses, I suppose. They're different, but the Marines training was much longer, looked more challenging and sometimes they jumped out of aeroplanes just like the Airborne. It was an easy decision and one I have never regretted.

Out in Belgrave one evening, I saw a youth in army uniform. He wore a blue beret with a red patch but I recognised the cap badge as the Royal Marines. I followed him as he went into TS *Tiger*. He was a Royal Marine Cadet. I had no idea they existed. There were also young lads and girls walking around in naval uniforms. These were known as Sea Cadets and the girls were members of the GNTC or 'Girls Nautical Training Contingent'. In essence, Royal Navy and Wren Cadets. Wow, this is land-locked Leicester but Portsmouth is on my doorstep. I had heard of the Sea Cadets. I had seen a photograph of my brother, Tony, in his uniform. He had joined years before but I had no interest in the Navy. He hadn't either; his main enthusiasm came from the access to canoeing and kayaking.

My foster parents had been concerned about my 'loner' existence. I told them I had stumbled across the Marine Cadets and wanted to join. They resisted, suggesting this was simply a veiled attempt to reunite with my brother. So what if it was? I managed to persuade them it was in my best interests. They subsequently got approval from Social Services and I was signed up for training. Two-hour sessions, twice a week. Tuesdays 7pm-9pm and the same on Thursdays. There would be the occasional weekend away and a week-long summer camp. I joined Unit 211, X Company of Eastern Area Marine Cadets. Serial number 480. Tony had moved on so there would be no reunion but that didn't matter. I loved it.

After a three-month induction, I won the award for 'Best New Recruit'. At last, I had found where I belonged. The Royal Marines would now be my family. Fellow marines would replace my brother. The Queen and Prince Philip would be my mum and dad. I had come back to life. I had finally been saved.

I lived and breathed the Corps. Cadets taught many of the skills that I would need *when* I joined the regulars: discipline, drill, navigation, weapon-handling, fieldcraft, tactics, unarmed combat, regimental history and, of course, washing, ironing and polishing. So absorbed, I lost all interest in my academic studies.

In the penultimate year at school, I had to pick my subjects. My choices were influenced by their relevance to my intended career rather than any innate aptitude. I ditched biology for physics, history for geography, art for automobile engineering and PE for French. I only selected the latter in case I needed to meet 'La Resistance' in any future conflict.

I arrived at Mr O'Higgins' language class a little late. I had been on summer camp with the Cadets and that had culminated with a final twenty-four-hour exercise. I'd had little sleep. Consequently, I missed the first morning of term and arrived later that afternoon. When I knocked on his door, the class had already started. He suspended the lesson and walked out to the corridor before looking me up and down. My attire failed to impress. With very short hair, green bomber jacket, Union Jack T-shirt, jeans and high-leg Doc Marten boots, I looked like a skinhead.

"What do you want?" he asked.

"I'm Iain Wright, sir. 4 Bosworth R. I'm in your class."

"Surely not!" he said, before abandoning me in the corridor. Through the door window I watched him make a phone call. He promptly returned and invited me inside. Looking round the class, I had a choice. I could join the group of ten Indian girls, huddled behind the first row of vacant desks, or join Andrew, sat solo on the flank, still wearing full school uniform, despite it no longer being obligatory in our year. It seemed unfair to leave him sat by himself.

Mr O'Higgins wasn't English. He spoke fluent French and German, but when he lost his temper and shouted in my language, he sounded like a Nazi. He was friendly enough but scared most of the girls. My own silver-tongued pronunciation certainly impressed one of them. More on her later.

"Qu'est-ce que vous avez l'intentions affaire apres avoir finalement quitte l'ecole?"

"Monsieur, je voudrais entre les Royal Marines."

I may have looked like a skinhead but I was certainly no 'Paki-basher'. Quite the opposite, in fact. To Minesh and Bhavin, I was their regular escort/ bodyguard and they would no longer be bullied walking home after school, despite passing the walls displaying NF graffiti. Back then, I truly believed that meant Nottingham Forest.

In October 1983, volunteers were sought for the Trafalgar Day celebration parade to be held on Sunday in London. I went with my new best pal, Shane Booth. He was a year older than me but we were both equal in rank and service. Three Sea Cadets and two members of the GNTC would make up the Colour Party. Our job would be to raise flags, including Nelson's famous signal 'England expects that every man will do his duty', during the parade to be held in Trafalgar Square. Cadets were drawn from all over the country but it was our complement from TS *Tiger* that would have the showpiece.

We were driven down in a minibus on the Friday night and billeted at RAF Uxbridge. The RAF certainly lived well. Cream cakes and iced buns. All you could eat. Rehearsals were carried out all day Saturday. Our role wasn't difficult. We just had to stand to attention and wait for the piped signal to pull on the halyards. Our colleagues were all marching up and down being screamed at by a drill instructor.

In the downtime, Shane and I showed off to try and impress the girls. We were Marine Cadets, something a little more interesting than the Sea Cadets of which they were more familiar, or so we felt. I was no longer a shy guy;

the Marines had made me supremely confident. I fancied Karen and the early signs were encouraging.

Up early Sunday for the drive into London. We visited the offices of the First Sea Lord in Admiralty Arch, had a quick drink and toilet stop before taking up position on the square. The parade passed with military precision and we started the journey home. Unfortunately the minibus broke down. We were stranded for hours until the recovery wagon arrived. Karen and I took turns sleeping on each other's laps. It blossomed from there and we would be together for the next four years.

I volunteered for everything at Cadets and was determined to be as good if not better than the older guys. Cadets aged from thirteen to eighteen. There was no obligation to join the Royal Marines but many intended to do so and consequently there was a regular insight into the selection procedures. As a cadet became eligible it would be the main topic. What did they ask in the interview? How was the medical? Etc.... This gave me focus. I knew what to expect and the standards to achieve. I can't do fifty press-ups... Oh look, yes I can.

In the summer of 1984, the Yanks returned to Leicester. Veterans of the US 82 Airborne had been stationed locally during the build up to D-Day. Forty years on, they came back, and to mark the occasion various military cadet units paraded through Leicester's city centre. We were inspected by the famous General 'Jumpin Jim' Gavin, a veteran of D-Day, Market Garden and the Battle of the Bulge. It was a huge honour.

I had long been a fan of the Royal Marines Band and had many of their albums. When I came across a bugle, I discovered I could play it naturally. I became the official bugler of TS *Tiger*. I had to play the 'General Salute' for the opening parade and 'Sunset' for closure, every Tuesday and Thursday. I couldn't read music, I was self-taught and played by ear.

Shane and I competed with each other in a friendly way and were promoted together, first as lance corporals and then as corporals. He was as 'Corps pissed' (enthusiastic about all things Marine) as I was.

One of the Commando tests was a 9-mile speed march with kit. Shane and I would practise this on Saturday mornings. With rucksacks loaded with anything heavy, e.g. exercise weights, encyclopaedias and rocks, we would run from his house in Sileby all the way to TS *Tiger*. This caused a minor scare. On two occasions during routine activity, my knee gave way and I ended up on the floor. A specialist doctor concluded that it was the single-mindedness of my exercises that was the problem. My body was just not developed enough to cope with Commando tests at that young age and he said that I should do alternative training. He gave me a list of exercises and assured me that there was no permanent damage.

This goes some way to explaining my frame. I'm not particularly tall (5' 8"). The chosen activities of my puberty years seem to have influenced the way my body grew. I have permanently massive muscly thighs, ideal for load carrying uphill. A big chest from all those press-ups and long arms with 'Popeye' forearms from too many pull-ups (the Marines wanted eighteen. By the time of my medical, I could do forty-five). I was self-conscious about my height for a while but I look back at what this body has achieved and to be honest, I wouldn't change it now.

Inspection at TS *Tiger*, 1984. I am fifth from the right on the front row. Shane Booth is fourth from the right.

My own personal military kit inventory was expanding. Boots, uniform and field equipment filled my wardrobe. I had expressed interest in a German boot knife. This was an American-made dagger. The scabbard had a strong spring clip to enable the weapon to be fixed to a combat boot or a shoulder strap. This knife had only one purpose: to kill. I didn't need one yet but I intended that one should eventually complement my fighting order. Ivor cautiously handed over the gift, saying he felt I was a bit too young for the blade. I dismissed his concerns and told him it wasn't that sharp. In the privacy of my bedroom, I examined the weapon. It was shiny and perfectly symmetrical but could it slice down through a vertically held sheet of paper?

No. Slightly disappointed, I stabbed the paper instead. The metal went straight through the sheet of A4 and the layer of denim before becoming buried in my left thigh. Oh my god, I've only had it two minutes and I've already stabbed myself. I pulled out the blood-soaked dagger. It had gone in about an inch. I was slightly in shock but daren't call for assistance. I hobbled to the bathroom, rested my leg over the basin and cleaned the wound. I made a field dressing from a face flannel and tightly secured it with string. I then rinsed out the blood from my jeans and got dressed again. I had about fifteen minutes to get to school. Unable to hide the limp, I claimed to have overdone my exercises. My foster parents never found out about that incident but the scar is still visible today.

I was persuaded that my informal name change ought to be made legal by deed poll. My CV was developing and all my certificates were in the name of Wright, although I was officially still a Hollis. The confusion might have frustrated my Marines application so I agreed to the proposed change.

My TV debut happened in the Cadets. Seamanship skills were taught on an old-style sailing ship with masts, rigging and yardarms. I spent a week on the TS *Royalist* sailing from Norfolk up to Newcastle. Climbing the rigging in a rough North Sea can be quite daunting. I was a little concerned and at times I thought *I ought not to be doing this kind of thing, it's very dangerous*. The former Olympic swimmer, David Wilkie, joined us on board for a day's filming. He was presenting a programme about leisure activities called *Wheels, Wings and Water*. We put on a display by racing up the rigging. He climbed slowly and rather pathetically to the first-stage platform to admire the view from there. Being a little older now, I doubt I would have gone much further either, so well done, David.

A second TV appearance would happen on Noel Edmonds' *Late, Late Breakfast Show*. Noel Edmonds looked quite tall on screen but in real life he was actually smaller than me. He had what was called the 'Land Rover Challenge'. Load as many people as possible onto a Land Rover and drive it 20 metres. The Army had done so last week. This week was our turn. We spent a night at the Royal Marines Reserves barracks in London before heading off to the BBC studios on Saturday morning. We practised all day and smashed the record on live TV that evening. Sixty-nine of us. Those at the BBC lived well. Cream cakes and iced buns. All you could eat. Our record lasted a week until the Gurkhas broke it.

I was pretty fit by now as you can imagine. The PE teacher, Mr Bevan, asked me to represent the school in athletics. I wasn't that keen, as training and events might impact on my Cadet activities, but the next meet would be in school time. "OK, I'm in," I said.

My event was the 'under sixteen-year-old boys' 400-metre sprint. The Area Schools Final was in effect the heat stage of the City Schoolboys Final to be held next month. I turned up at Saffron Lane Stadium and waited for the event to be called. An usher guided me to a lane and I took my position. The gun was fired. I sprinted out of the blocks, relaxed down the back and then went flat out for the last 200. I crossed the line first but couldn't breathe. The air would not go in quickly enough. People were patting me on the back and I was immediately congratulated by a jubilant Mr Bevan. Then a man with a clipboard came over.

"Who are you?"

"Iain Wright."

"What school?"

"Rushey Mead."

"You're not on the list; you're disqualified."

Apparently I was supposed to register before the start of the race. Oh, bollocks. This was school athletics, not the Olympic Games. Mr Bevan protested on my behalf, initially in vain but he went higher. He could not overturn the disqualification but secured me a lane in the City Final as a 'guest'. That meant I could run but my result would not count. A pity because I won. Unofficially I am the 1984 City Schoolboy Champion. It probably helped with my Marines application but I would not be pursuing athletics.

My foster parents were generally supportive of my career choice although cautiously they wanted me to do well in my exams, wait until I was eighteen and try to go for 'officer'. The commission did not interest me. I just wanted my green beret. I had been robbed of so much in my early life. Once I had got that, it would be something that no one could ever take away from me.

I was still fifteen when I signed up at the Charles Street Careers Office. Had to wait to be sixteen before I could sit the entrance exam. Only a few weeks away now.

There were two loves in my life at that time, the Corps and my girlfriend Karen. Nothing else and nobody else mattered anymore. At home I was simply a lodger. I had weekly pocket money and earnt extra by babysitting, so I had sufficient funds for dating. I'd see Karen at Cadets and from home we'd talk on the phone when it was cheaper after 6pm. Calls in excess of an hour were too long and I was regularly reminded. We wrote love letters weekly, doused in my Old Spice and her Musk. I tried in vain to emulate her perfect handwriting. Most weekends we would meet by the fountain in the Town Hall Square. I'd usually get there first and often Karen would be late. I'd sit there waiting as the clock bells chimed at fifteen-minute intervals. We would grab a coffee, go to the cinema or go roller-skating at Granby Halls (the current stadium site of Leicester Tigers) and basically hang out like teenage lovers do. Sometimes I would walk the seven miles to her parents' house in Wigston so that we could bus ride into the city together. We managed all this without mobile phones which seems incredible today.

With my sixteenth birthday fast approaching, I was making plans for a special date with my lover. It transpires that a surprise party was being planned. Not a big one, just a table in a restaurant for the immediate family. There were six of us in our house at that time. Like me, Donnamae was still fostered but Mark and Claire had joined us some years back. Lynne and Ivor had adopted them as small babies but they were about five or six years old by now. Karen would be there too. She was in on the surprise. It backfired.

My foster parents had created reasons to keep me at home and free for the event, but it was the weekend, I was going out and no one could stop me. That attitude resulted in a heated argument during which they were forced to reveal their secret plans. They told me that I was 'so ungrateful'. I was furious. I didn't want to have a surprise party. I didn't want to go to a restaurant with the family. I wanted to have the special day with my girlfriend. I guess I pretty much offended everyone but I'd told them how I felt. I didn't want to be part of that family. The table was cancelled at short notice and I spent my sixteenth alone, sulking in my room. I was absolutely livid.

I sat and passed the entrance exam the following week. I had my medical while on exam leave. Regardless of my school results, I'd be out of there soon and I couldn't wait.

Chapter 6.

The Big Bang

I was awoken by Lynne quite early. Too early for a school day. She came over to my bed and hugged me. That was unusual; we didn't do that kind of thing. Then she started to cry. Ivor had died during the night. He had been admitted to hospital after suffering another heart attack but didn't survive. He was only forty. He wasn't a regular drinker but liked his cigars. He had been on tablets for many years because he was prone to stomach ulcers. I think he just worked too hard.

He was a managing director and accountant at two knitwear companies, he served at the church, he made and sold jewellery, sold watches, sold garments, organised charity events, ferried me back from Cadets twice a week, was constantly doing DIY projects and the rest of the time was a husband and father in our house.

I didn't see eye to eye with Ivor. Everyone loved him and wanted to be around him. He was a bit like Terry Wogan. Fun-loving and helpful, an all-round good bloke, but I felt smothered by him. He had even started to encroach on my Cadets escapism. Not content to simply pick me up at the end of the night, he had talked his way into the wardroom and would regularly have a couple of shandies with the instructors.

He could get people stuff, genuine stuff and at cheap prices, because he was respected and well-connected. So many at TS *Tiger* were wearing his watches, in particular the instructors and some of the senior cadets. He was so popular that he even got invited to one former cadet's graduation and Green Beret presentation. It was beneficial to me, I got to go too, seeing Lympstone long before joining, and his chats in the wardroom gave me precious time with Karen whose father was himself in there as a Sea Cadet officer.

There was even talk of him taking on an instructor position. He had no military experience but was very intelligent and could do anything. I resented that idea. If he had done so, I would have handed in my kit. He just wanted to be close to me. He wanted to be my dad. Although I'm sure that many people would've gladly taken my place, the truth is that I never ever wanted to be his son.

So now he was gone. I was the man in the house. I didn't want to be and felt terrible guilt. In a totally selfish attitude I cursed his timing. Nine years of tunnelling towards freedom and everything had caved in. The loss of Ivor was a massive blow to our household but my imminent departure would represent even greater imbalance and disruption from normality. I obviously couldn't join the Marines now and felt a moral obligation to stay put in a supportive role.

Then came the twist. Lynne had changed overnight. Yes, she was grief stricken. She loved Ivor for certain but now she was on her own. She became a stronger woman. Quite an amazing and inspirational woman, if I'm honest. She drew a lot of strength from her faith and had a huge network of support from the church. She wasn't going to stop me joining the Marines. That was out of the question. "You're going. Good Luck."

The house filled up with tearful friends and family. The kettle was overworked and eventually I decided I needed some fresh air. I walked to TS *Tiger* and sat on the canal bank. I would miss Ivor. He had done a lot for me over the years. Yes, I hated being smothered, but I didn't want him to die. I had a whole life flashback and was overwhelmed. I broke down and wept.

The funeral was at St Gabriel's where he had served. I had seen him once in his white robes swinging an incense burner. Now, though, the church was packed. Former cadets who had become professional Royal Marines, attended having secured special leave. They, other cadets, Karen and I were all in our best uniforms. It was an impressive sight and a fitting tribute to an extraordinary man.

Ivor passed away in May 1985. I had not yet sat my school exams. I completed them all and didn't do particularly well but got the important O-levels in English, Maths and Geography.

I spent the summer working at Templar Knitwear on Cobden Street, which was one of Ivor's companies. I pushed a trolley round delivering jumper parts from a store to the overlockers. I made up cardboard boxes and became slick with the masking-tape gun. I would stick Tesco-size labels onto clothing hangers and any other simple task as directed by the warehouse manager. £50 a week was good money. I'd soon be working much harder and getting paid less.

On 23rd September 1985, I boarded the train to start my life as a 'bootneck'. Lynne dropped me off at the station but didn't hang around. She would leave me alone so I could share a final moment with Karen. It would be thirteen weeks before I got leave. It should have been fifteen but the Christmas break interrupted the normal timetable. The clock was ticking and I would be off very soon.

What?! My mum is here. Why? Because she is my mother and wants to say bye to her son? Too late. You did that when I was eleven. She didn't stay long but it created an awkward atmosphere and I wish she hadn't come at all.

I got through the thirty weeks' basic training. Being a cadet had prepared me well. Of forty-six recruits that started, there were only twenty-two originals when we finished. That was a reasonable pass rate. It was often much lower. Those unable to continue were either discharged from service or 'back-trooped'. That is where you simply continue training from close to where you left off by joining a newer class. Foot or hand injuries were common causes. Over the initial months a close bond forms. No one wants to get back-trooped, firstly because you leave your mates and secondly because you prolong the pain and hardship. Best to get through first time. Easier that way.

Occasionally you'd hear blokes sobbing in the toilet cubicles. That was just pressure release. The training was hard. A typical day started around 5.30am and you'd be lucky to be in your bed before midnight. The British Military ethos is to 'train hard and fight easy'. The intense workloads and lack of sleep inevitably led to rubber-necking in lectures. For this reason recruits were known as 'nods'. It was quite a battle to stay awake when sat on a chair in a warm classroom. Occasionally you might be discreetly kicked or nudged by one of your colleagues who had noticed your heavy eyelids. Having passed my English and Maths O-levels gave me free periods while many of my classmates had to have lessons to bring them up to the equivalent standard. Those breaks were priceless.

Shane Booth from the Cadets joined two months after me. For a while we were in the same accommodation block. My class had the top two floors and his the lower two but we rarely had time for socialising. He would sail through basic training and go on to serve more than twenty-eight years, finally retiring as an RSM.

We had a week of survival training on Dartmoor in December, just before breaking up for Christmas. The extreme winter conditions and permanently wet feet meant that my toes froze. Many of them went white and numb. It was several weeks before feeling was restored. I would lose most of my toenails during the two weeks' leave but they grew back eventually.

Special 'troop trains' were laid on to transport the stampede of high-spirited young men being let loose for the festive period. The first of these would take us to Exeter and then a second would head north. The rowdy singing and drinking weren't something the public needed to witness. I jumped off at Bristol to grab my connection and board a fourth train for the final leg from Birmingham.

It seemed strange being back in Leicester. Dumping my Bergen on the floor, I looked at my old bed. A lie-in with a duvet was long overdue. Later that evening one of the neighbours visited to offer his condolences. Apparently I was dead. The TV and radio news had announced that a Royal Marine recruit, Ian Wright, had not made it home. He had been collected from Lympstone by a relative but died in a car crash during the journey. I assured the neighbour that I was still very much alive but how awful it must have been for the family of my namesake, for that Christmas and every Christmas that followed.

Returning to barracks in the New Year, I was greeted by shocked but relieved colleagues who had also heard of my demise. What were the chances of Iain Wright and Ian Wright going through basic training at the same time? A few weeks later his unclaimed laundry was mistakenly forwarded to me.

At the halfway stage (two weeks after the Christmas break) there was an open day. The recruits put on various displays of skills learnt during the first fifteen weeks. Friends and family were invited. Karen, Lynne and her brother Martin, came along.

I was fighting a fever and had been for about two days. I had no strength and was constantly shivering. There were only five of us in our six-man dormitory. One recruit had failed and left. I used the blankets from his open locker. I was still cold. One by one, the spare blankets from all of my roommates covered me. Thanks, guys. I survived the night, completed my tasks and was driven back to Leicester for my long weekend.

Still fighting the fever, a doctor was called. German measles. I posed a risk to pregnant ladies and would not be able to travel back by train for a number of days. That meant I would miss two days of the course. Would I be back-trooped? I hoped not. Fortunately my instructors said there was no need as I already had the relevant knowledge from my time in the Cadets. Phew.

Recruits needed to pass four physical challenges towards the end of basic training. These were known as the 'Commando tests'.

The first was the 'Endurance Course'. I found this one to be the most difficult. It involved walking four miles from camp to the start line. You had to walk but that was in your own time and not against the clock. A cooked breakfast was available every morning but that would be too heavy for this challenge. I would make do with either a pack of custard creams or some ration-pack porridge left over from an earlier field exercise.

We had already been divided into three-man syndicates during our practice runs. I was teamed up with Edwards and Porter. Syndicates would set off at minute intervals and navigate a series of tunnels and water obstacles for the first 2 miles. The syndicate had to stick together as a team for this phase which included the famous 'sheep dip'. Taking it in turns the first man would be fully submerged in a short and narrow tunnel. The second man would push him through and the third man would pull him out when he appeared at the other end. This sequence was repeated until all three had passed through. This was quite a daunting experience. Trying to hold your breath under icy cold water after running flat out is very difficult. Once that obstacle was cleared, it was a 4-mile dash back to barracks, every man for himself as quickly as possible. Having arrived soaking wet, covered in mud and gasping for breath, you finished on the rifle range where you had to successfully hit targets with your weapon.

I was the slowest member of our team, but our syndicate was the fastest in our class. So as to not get held up by other recruits, we would always be the first to depart. I would set the pace until reaching the sheep dip. No one would catch up with us. After the dunking, Edwards would disappear from view very quickly and I would just have to make sure I never lost sight of Porter. I couldn't keep up with either of them.

The 9-miler was perhaps the easiest for me. It was boring. I had practised this with Shane on those runs from Sileby. The class would run together as a formation against the clock and then fight a battle at the end. During the speed march, each man carried a rifle but volunteers were sought to swap these at the finish line and carry a heavier machine gun during the assault phase. I raised my hand. I could run better than most and I didn't consider this challenge particularly difficult.

The Tarzan Assault course was the shortest event. Its high obstacles, tunnels and climbs involved skilled techniques and sprints. If you weren't vomiting by the end, you had not worked hard enough. The high obstacles were where you could make ground. Some recruits would hesitate or pause, thereby losing valuable seconds. I had no fear over this event and quite enjoyed it. I'd done it enough times and would be attempting to beat the course record. Complacency crept in.

One obstacle was a horizontal rope. You were expected to crawl along this on your stomach and then drop over the side to dangle while maintaining a grip with both hands. To right yourself and continue crawling involved a technique known as a 'regain'. The first thing was to kick your legs up and hook your feet over the rope. Many struggled with this but not me. I could do it first time, every time.

Today, however, my feet missed; the clock was ticking. I kicked again and missed again. Oh no. This cannot be happening. No chance of the record now. My drill instructor was screaming at me but I couldn't hear what he was saying. On the third attempt my feet reached their target but what was the next move? I had a mental block. At this rate I would fail to complete in time. Fortunately, Corporal Tighe ceased shouting and now spoke softly. He told me to stop struggling and listen. Bit by bit he calmly and successfully talked me through the sequence of drills. "LEFT ARM OVER, RIGHT HAND BACK TO THE KNEE, TURN AND BEAT!" Oh yeah, I remember now. Back on the rope he reverted to the usual screaming manner of telling me to get a move on. I just made it in time.

The ultimate test was the famous 30-mile 'yomp' across Dartmoor. It was tough and made worse by extreme weather but the distance and eight-hour time limit were easily within my capabilities. For my good friend Andy Kirk, though, it would be much harder. He was limping before we started but he wanted to finish with the rest of us. We couldn't carry his kit for him and we couldn't let him slow us down. There was a safety Bergen which we each took turns in carrying. We could excuse him from that task and the navigation but nothing else. He whinged and moaned all the way. It was hard for everyone but especially hard for Andy. He successfully completed it with us and won his green beret. He then went straight to sick bay who told him his foot was broken. He graduated on crutches. What an amazing bloke.

Back row L-R: Bywater, Edwards, Wright and in front centre, Andy Kirk

The mood in camp was euphoric. Everyone had passed the 30-miler. Recruits were walking round the accommodation block in flip-flops and shorts, shaping their green berets, posing for photographs and becoming extremely vain looking in mirrors. This was the prize we had all sought for so long.

I was relieved. For several days I had been calculating just how many more miles my legs would have to endure before the Lympstone experience was over. I had made it but only just. Both legs were very painful now, my shins in particular were extremely sensitive to touch and it felt like they were ready to snap. It was a stress fracture that Kirk had suffered. Constant pounding was the cause. Surely I was close to a similar injury.

We only had our berets for a day, just enough time to shape them, label them with our names, and affix the cap badge. We then had to surrender them. They would be returned to us at the official presentation in front of our invited guests.

Most were excused from wearing boots after the 30-miler, just for a couple of days. Others were less fortunate. Those who had failed any of the tests would be given another opportunity. The 9-mile rerun was announced and a small group was ordered to parade. Being a superior runner, I was selected to join them as moral support and to help drag them around the course. In my mind, I wasn't physically capable of this and was very concerned about causing permanent damage to my legs. What would have been the point of all this training if I was left disabled at the end of it? I had done what I needed to do and qualified. It would be several months before my leg pain settled but now I was being asked to do an *impossible* extra 9 miles.

I reported to the commanding officer and expressed my concern. He slaughtered me with just a stare and then reiterated the 'Commando spirit', which was defined as 'courage, determination, leadership, *unselfishness* and cheerfulness under adversity'. He pointed out that everyone's legs were spent, but I was capable of this task. Maybe I was. Maybe I was just being selfish. No. I had volunteered to carry the machine gun on the last occasion but this time I knew I was struggling. I would have to dig very deep.

We embarked on the rerun and I pounded my legs once more. I soon got used to the pain and tried to ignore it. Head down and jogging at a constant pace known as the 'Commando shuffle', we pressed on. Sadly, the weaker runners fell behind again and couldn't keep up. I was in tears of pain and screamed at them. They had to work harder to stay on schedule. Alas, at 7 miles they were thrown in the back of the safety wagon. I was furious; they had failed again and those body-damaging extra miles had achieved nothing.

In fairness to my colleagues, I think the first rerun had been scheduled too soon, coming just days after the 30-miler. They all got through on the third attempt a week later. A whole squad of PTIs accompanied them, sparing the need for 'volunteer helpers' such as I had been before.

The 'passing out parade' on 23rd May 1986 was effectively our 'graduation day' but the Green Beret presentation went wrong. We were formed up in the theatre and the curtain opened revealing us to the seated audience of friends and family who responded with applause and camera flashes. One by one we were called forward to receive our prize. Marine WRIGHT IDH was stood next to Marine WRIGHT GK. They called my name. I marched up to Major Rowland, saluted and shook his hand. He presented my beret, we posed for a photograph and I marched away to the drill instructor. I removed my blue beret and cast it into a bin before placing the green one on my head and marching promptly back to my place within the ranks.

Well, that was what was supposed to happen. In reality, I was handed the beret belonging to WRIGHT GK. It was several sizes too small and didn't fit. I marched carefully away precariously balancing the tiny headdress. He in turn received mine, way too big, and it made him look like Frank Spencer. When the curtains closed we corrected the error.

I left Lympstone, physically drained with nothing left in the tank. I wasn't on crutches like Andy, but I could hardly walk. It had been worth it though. I had made it. I was a Royal Marine Commando. There was nothing I couldn't do now. The whole world was mine for the taking.

I was sent to Leicester Careers Office for a week as part of a recruitment drive. Reading between the lines, I think this may have actually been 'disguised' compassionate leave. The Corps knew that I had joined quite soon after a family bereavement and perhaps they had kindly considered that I might benefit from the extra time at home. It was almost exactly a year since Ivor had passed away. They told me it was to encourage new entrants but I was the only one to receive this kind of work.

So, I would return home as 'the local boy done good'. I visited some of my old teachers at Rushey Mead School, looking very smart in my Lovat's uniform and brand-new green beret. I also visited TS *Tiger* to further encourage the enthusiastic cadets. As for boosting our numbers, well, all those who walked into the careers office, I managed to dissuade. In my opinion they weren't up to it and I might have to work with them one day. That week ended quite quickly and then I was off to my unit.

Marine WRIGHT IDH with Karen (later Lieutenant Steele RN)

Chapter 7.

Life begins at 40

'Appear weak when you are strong, and strong when you are weak'
- Sun Tzu
The Art of War

3 Section, 6 Troop, Bravo Company, 40 Commando RM. Norton Manor Camp, Taunton. June 1986.

As a seventeen-year-old with no driving licence, I would rely on trains. Carriages have certainly changed over the years. Today we have airlock automatic doors that cannot be opened when the train is in motion and only open on the platform side. In the 1980s you could run to board a train that was already leaving the station. You simply had to yank the handle and jump on. Conversely, you could hop off before the train had actually stopped. You could leap onto the platform if in a hurry to make a connection, or jump out trackside to avoid paying the fare.

When on official business such as being posted to a new unit, a 'travel warrant' would be issued. This covered the out-of-pocket expense and existed in two forms, namely 'rail warrants', which were military forms that could be exchanged for tickets at a train station, or 'mileage allowance', which was simply a form submitted by the driver with details of the journey and total distance, then processed and paid out on the base.

The single serviceman had an annual allocation of four free travel warrants. That covered journeys home for the main leave periods at Christmas, Easter and summer, plus one other occasion. In reality one could use the warrants anytime. Married men were entitled to twelve such warrants. The thing is, most married men didn't need that many, if indeed any at all, because they tended to live close to base or in local married quarters. The system was open to abuse and this surplus was exploited.

If I had used all of my warrants, a return ticket would cost me about

£20 (almost half a week's pay). If I asked a married man to sell me one of his allocation, my journey would cost me just £5. I saw nothing wrong with this. There was a budget and its funds were paying for genuine travel. This was a reallocation rather than a misallocation of funds and I think a blind eye was turned to this particular practice.

It was slightly different for mileage allowance. It did not apply to me at that time but many must have been exaggerating their journey distances in order to claim a bigger reimbursement. Given that the allowance was paid per mile, why honestly claim for just 50 miles actually travelled when you could dishonestly claim for a pretend journey of 500 miles? The answer was because that is fraud. The company sergeant major warned us about this during every Friday parade.

"I don't want to see any mileage claims for visits to 'wee Granny McTavish in Cape Wrath'," he'd say.

I don't believe the lady actually existed. She was entirely fictitious; but Cape Wrath in the Highlands of Scotland was about as far from our base as you could get. New rules eventually clamped down on this.

Having arrived mid-June, it wouldn't be long before we broke up for three weeks' summer leave. Before the break we would be given a challenge and the winners could go home a day early. We were told to parade in civilian clothes, carrying nothing. No money, no bags, no food. Then every man was given a £5 note and told to board the coach. We then drove out of barracks and periodically the coach stopped. Two random names were called out. The pairs would alight and receive an envelope. The coach then drove away, leaving them stranded and the sequence continued. Jock and I were dropped on a slip road off the M5 motorway just outside Bristol.

The contents of our envelope was a note which read, 'Your mission. Go to the Royal Marines Reserve barracks in London and get a beer mat signed by Lieutenant Richards. You have twenty-four hrs. Don't break the law unless you have to and if you have to, don't get caught.'

I laughed. I wasn't going to bother. We were only 50 miles from our barracks whereas London and back was almost 300 miles. Returning to base seemed more realistic, but Jock was disappointed by my attitude and persuaded me to give it go. We jogged over fields towards the built-up area, eventually finding the train station. We travelled to London managing to evade the ticket inspector. Miraculously we did the same on a London bus. We jogged to the barracks only to be told that the relevant officer was in

South Africa. All that way for nothing. So as to prove we had at least made the target destination, we got the guard room to sign and stamp a piece of official headed paper and write words to the effect that the officer was unavailable.

We dodged the ticket inspector on the return train and by late afternoon we were back in Taunton. Neither of us had touched our money, the camp was only 5 miles away and we still had about sixteen hours left to complete the task. Content that we had made it this far and with the knowledge that if this was for real, we could easily run the last leg in time, I suggested we blow the money on a Chinese takeaway and get a taxi back.

There were some amazing stories. People had been sent all over the country. 'Get a stick of Blackpool rock', 'Get a postcard signed by wee Granny McTavish in Cape Wrath', etc.… People had been thumbing lifts and jumping trains. Some of the methods were never disclosed but it was rumoured that several vehicles had been 'borrowed'. The winners had managed to get to the Isle of Wight and back on a hovercraft.

On leave, I took up my old job. Not yet legally old enough to buy a beer, my wages were still just £45 per week, less than half that of the older guys, so I needed the extra money. I was also the youngest member of the group. The failure rate of sixteen-year-olds in basic training was so high that soon after my intake they had stopped being recruited. That would cause me problems.

For the forthcoming NATO exercise (Blue Fox-Bold Guard), one man from each troop (platoon) needed to carry the very heavy 84mm MAW (like a Bazooka). As the youngest member of 6 Troop, that would be my burden and remain so until someone younger than me was drafted in. That was the tradition but with a freeze in recruitment my replacement wasn't going to arrive anytime soon. In 1987 a book was published, *The making of a Royal Marines Commando*. Page 71 features the youngest member carrying the said weapon. Yep, yours truly in Norway in 1986. Up and down mountains with that and my kit was physically the hardest thing I have ever done in my life. It belittled all that I had achieved in basic training. I cannot overstate how difficult it was for me with my lightweight and athletic frame. I was forbidden from carrying it on my shoulders as that might have made me an attractive target to enemy snipers. Instead, it had to be slung round my neck and carried in front of me so that I resembled an ordinary rifleman.

Typically, our machine gunners were the biggest and strongest blokes, so I questioned the logic of dumping this lump of metal on me. The combined weight of my rifle and this medium anti-tank missile launcher was the equivalent of *two* machine guns. With a heavy Bergen pulling me backwards and my weapons acting as a counterbalance, I felt like a toy 'Buckaroo' whose back was about to break. The crushing load meant fully inflating my lungs was impossible and I had to march along taking rapid, short and shallow breaths through constantly clenched teeth. I sounded a bit like the Sugar Puffs' honey monster. There was no avenue for protest. It had to be carried, if not by me then by someone else, and whinging breached military etiquette. In any event the response to complaints was usually unsympathetic. "That's life in a blue suit," meaning 'Welcome to the Navy, hardship goes with the territory'. I felt massive self-pity over this perceived injustice. I was being paid the least yet physically working the hardest but apparently this was 'all good character-building stuff' and at just 11st 7lb, I needed bulking up.

The Norwegian Army and some USMC played our enemy during the exercise. When we had finally scrambled up the mountain to overrun their defensive position, I was ready to collapse through exhaustion but unit pride and esprit de corps took over. I wasn't going to give the Yanks the satisfaction of seeing a fatigued Royal Marine. A fresh wave of strength and determination lifted me. With a spring in my step, I bounced by the Americans, breathing in casually through my nose and with a relaxed look on my face that suggested the load was as light as a feather. I can laugh about it now but back then it was a very testing time and the rest of my life would turn out to be much easier by comparison.

MV *Bolero*. Norway 1986

We had sailed to Norway on a civilian ferry, the MV *Bolero* of the Fred Olsen Line. There were four of us in a luxury cabin with a sea view. We had bunks, duvets and our own en suite, including a toilet, shower and basin. We didn't even have to tidy our room as the Norwegian crew did it for us. We dined in the restaurants and the food was fantastic. Older marines told us not to get used to this. It would be much harder on a 'Pusser's grey' (Royal Navy vessel). Occasionally, announcements would be made from the information desk. The embarked forces burst into laughter as a Norwegian female accent read out the messages.

"Attention please, will all MUF divers report to Mike Hunt, I repeat, will all MUF divers report to Mike Hunt."

There were similar outbursts when the same voice asked, "Major P Ness to contact Private R Soul."

If we ever had to go to war, this would be the way to do it.

After a few 'Elephant Beers', ashore in Aalborg, Denmark, where a lovely local girl wrote with black marker pen, 'Jeg elsker dig' (I love you) on the leg of my jeans, we finally disembarked in Germany.

Given their status as aggressive shock troops, the Royal Marines and Paras were not permitted to be garrisoned in Germany. Politically that would be seen as provocation and cause an escalation in Cold War tensions. Instead we would spend our week there, living in trenches. It normally took several hours to build a fortified two-man firing trench with a roofed sleeping area but this time we were assisted. One of the lads had 'borrowed' a JCB. The deep chasm was scooped out in minutes. It took us both ages to fill it back in sufficient to enable a view over the top in order to fire our weapons. It hardly mattered anyway. No one attacked our position. It was rumoured that the enemy had gone on strike over harsh conditions.

When it was all over, we were taken by bus through the towns and city to an airport. The bus was unusual in that it consisted of two single-deck carriages joined together end to end like a train. Still covered in mud and wearing dirty clothes we boarded a Virgin flight back to England. We were even served drinks by flight attendants. I'd never been on an aeroplane before. Thank you so much, Sir Richard Branson.

Special rules applied to 40 Commando. The unit consisted of approximately 700 men and was the equivalent size of an army battalion. The old Nissen huts where we slept were sub-standard and consequently we didn't have to pay accommodation charges. Also, the main body had to be away from barracks for at least six months in every year so as not to overburden or disrupt the local town. That didn't always mean overseas. We spent time near Bridgewater practising surf drills with our boats or yomping over Scotland and the Brecon Beacons.

One of the scariest things for me was roping down from a Sea King helicopter as it hovered 100ft over a field. The side door was slid open and a thick rope suspended from an overhanging girder. In turn we would stand in the doorway, lean out and grab the rope with both hands, then wrap our legs around it and drop to the ground with rifle and kit. If you slipped or didn't hold on, you'd almost certainly be killed. There was no safety harness. I'm a lot older now and there is just no way I would do that again, but back then I was fearless and invincible. One man dropped his rifle from high up and it javelined down, with the muzzle burying itself deep in the ground.

It was the party trick of our troop sergeant to walk alone into a bar after a hard day's work and order a single pint of bitter. When the barmaid asked if there'd be anything else. He would say, "Yes, and twenty-eight pints of lager!" The next line from the barmaid would inevitably be, "Are you serious?" At which point he would shout, "Hi hooohhhhh!"

On hearing this we would all march in on our knees like dwarves, singing, "Hi ho, hi ho, it's home from work we go. With a bucket and spade and a hand grenade, hi ho, hi ho, hi ho, hi ho."

Our high spirits and exhibitionism would usually be well-received. Not always. 'Singing in the rain' was a song to which the squad would perform a striptease. Living life to the maximum was encouraged. We never knew what was around the corner, but if a conflict arose, we could expect to deploy at short notice. It was therefore important to grab a whole lifetime's worth of wine, women and song in as short a period as possible.

I worked with a wide variety of people. Many of my peers were school leavers like myself but in our company was a former bank manager and a stock broker. There were those who spoke with plums in their mouths too. Some had given up well-paid jobs in favour of joining the Commandos but we had some complete nutters too.

Taff Evans was a giant of a man who carried one of our machine guns. He was a constant moaner but quite funny with his accent. He liked to drink too. His party piece after downing a pint was to smash the empty glass over his forehead. Consequently he had scars in that area. If he returned to the dormitory when others like me were already tucked up asleep, he would rattle our wardrobes or shake our beds, seeking more booze. One night after a fruitless search, he drank aftershave. He saw that his bottle of Paco Rabanne contained alcohol. Crazy Welshman could have killed himself. The ABV would have been about 80%. He was ill for several days after that.

We actually had lessons on drinking. The main lecture room was an old theatre with a stage. It doubled up as a cinema. We had many presentations in there. There was the short film called *Army Medicine in Vietnam*, which gave horrific footage of battlefield casualties and the before and after effects of treatment. The assault engineers would give demonstrations on rigging explosives and the medics gave us first aid or drug and alcohol lectures. Apparently you can get high smoking the dried insides of banana skin and by inhaling the fumes of boot polish. The drinking lecture was presented as a series of stops on a bus journey. Each stop represented a side effect. Everyone was invited to get off the bus at the early stops which were the less harmful stages. These included feeling social, chatty, increased confidence, euphoria, talking at a higher volume. Subsequent stops included poor co-ordination, speech impairment and disorientation. Among the last three stops were 'greyouts' and 'blackouts'. A greyout is where you drink so much that you forget what you were doing until someone reminds you. I was a regular at that stop. A blackout is where you have no recollection at all, despite others filling in the gaps. The final stop was 'death'; consequently, any alcohol induced memory loss represented a dangerous level of consumption.

Sadly we lost people quite regularly through all sorts of incidents or accidents. Statistically a big workforce will have casualties. When a marine died, his belongings would be auctioned to raise money for his next of kin. His personal valuables would be excluded but everything else, be it military issue or privately owned, would go to the highest bidder. The kit sale would take place in the theatre. There was a warped sense of humour at these events and most people would be in fits of laughter, particularly as the more personal items were announced.

On one occasion the 'prized lot' was two pornographic magazines. *Razzle* and *Escort* had a retail price of about 80p each. The bidding commenced. It went higher and higher. People were expected to give generously as this was about fundraising but £50 for the pair seemed a bit extreme. A voice yelled, "£50 for one!" Then a different corner shouted, "£50 for the other!" The auctioneer banged the gavel. "SOLD!"

Within a few weeks I'd be away again. This time we sailed on HMS *Intrepid* through the Mediterranean. Those older marines were right. The 'Pusser's grey' was a much harsher routine. Woken each morning to the blare of the ship's piper, we also had to contend with cleaning stations, galley duties, man overboard lookouts and mess deck inspections. Water was rationed, so it would be ship's routine in the shower. This meant you spent a few seconds getting wet and then stepped aside to lather up with soap while someone else got wet. Then you would swap places in order to rinse off. Each action of the tap would involve the operator shouting, "Turning on" or "Turning off". We'd been taught this in basic training and it was a tried and tested system.

We obviously shared the ship with sailors of the Royal Navy. Our hosts told us that the title of 'embarked forces' was too formal and from here on we would be known as 'troops in transit' or 'tits' for short.

We disembarked at Gibraltar for the 'Rock Run'. Bottom to top as quickly as possible. It was a sailor who actually won. I walked when I could. It was very steep and far too hot.

Two cans of beer a day were permitted on board but in 'Gib' I would have much more. In one bar my corporal 'Lofty' sold me to the gay landlord. I left rather quickly.

I nipped across into Spain just to get my passport stamped. Got it stamped again on return. (La Linea and Gib).

Back at sea we kept fit on the flight deck and fired our weapons at floating targets. The rumour mill started when we were all issued with anti-flash masks which reduce facial burns in the event of an explosion. We had been told we were going to Oman for a joint exercise but the Yanks had just bombed Colonel Gaddafi's palace, killing one of his sons. We were within striking distance, hence the masks. The wise old sweats announced, "We're going to war, lads. Libya."

We weren't going to war. We finally landed at RAF Akrotiri in Cyprus. Spent a few nights in a big tent. The RAF lived well. Cream cakes and iced buns. All you could eat. Got our feet hardened up in boots with an acclimatisation navigation march over the island. A new experience for me was to see rain wetting people 20 metres to my left while I watched on quite dry. Slowly the torrent came closer until it engulfed and drenched me.

Then on to Egypt and a wander around the museum, the Sphynx and camel riding by the Pyramids. I'm seventeen and I'm getting paid or this.

Down through Suez and into Djibouti. We stayed at a French Foreign Legion barracks. Some ventured out for a look but I had spent most of my money already so I stayed put. Next day we went for an early morning run. It had to be early because of the heat. Gossip among the ranks was how one of the men had come across a one-eyed prostitute the night before. With AIDS being a relatively new development, the marine was taking no chances. Instead of vaginal intercourse he had made love to her armpit before removing the eye patch and ejaculating into her empty socket. The formation groaned in unison at this story's unusual climax. No pun intended.

In Oman some of the group hit the beach D-Day style. My section was dropped by helicopter onto the high cliffs and we set off into the starry night. The invasion was filmed for political purposes at a time of rising tensions in the Middle East. It was broadcast in England on the *News at Ten*. Next day the intense desert sun completely dried my bottom lip. Prince Charles was out here too. He was with the Paras and they were dropping like flies. Not through fitness but lack of acclimatisation. It had taken us five weeks to get here by ship. They had flown from a cooler climate to jump into the fiery furnace after just a few hours.

For my group, several days of marching culminated in a final mock battle. No idea who won. I just ran when they told me to. We made camp that night. The exercise was not over so the sentries were posted. I didn't need a sleeping bag. It wasn't that cold but so as to avoid snake, scorpion or insect bites I zipped up in my Gore-Tex bivvy bag. I awoke to find myself floating. The dry ditch that we had occupied was now a fast-flowing river. It hadn't rained here for more than ten years. The ground was baked solid and the flash flood swamped us. No one had been prepared for this. Kit was lost. Insurance claims made; I'm sure most were genuine.

In truth, the average marine took his privately-owned kit into the field. With the exception of a NATO helmet, gas mask and weapons, everything else was likely to have been acquired by the individual. You were presented with a green beret after successfully completing the Commando tests but everyone had at least two: one for parades and another for daily wear. Additional berets were privately purchased, along with unit T-shirts, Norwegian Army shirts, Helly Hansen fleeces, Arctic windproofs, SAS or Para smocks/jackets, Berghaus Bergens, day sacks, Yeti gaiters, Peak or Bluet stoves; the list was endless but all this replaced the inferior quality items that had been standard issue. It was better to have kit that was reliable and more efficient. Webbing, boots, knives, flasks, camouflage cream, compasses, map cases, torches – it all added up and would cost a small fortune. Exercise Saif Sareea (Arabic for Swift Sword) was brought to a swift conclusion.

Oman, November 1986

The voyage home was familiar with spells in Egypt, Cyprus and Gibraltar. As we headed north up the Suez Canal we came broadside with a Soviet warship. It was a squeeze in the narrow channel. We were permitted on the upper decks to look but ordered not to do anything to antagonise the enemy. That included removal of the quintessential Ron Hill Union Jack shorts and no photographs could be taken.

Their ship looked as sophisticated as ours. Many of her crew stopped to stare at us as we did them. It was a surreal moment. No shouting or jeering. No smiles or waving. Just sombre faces on both decks. They looked like us. We had already been warned that in World War III our life expectancy was forty-eight hours. These were the people who were going to start it. Why? They probably looked at us and had identical thoughts.

Home for two weeks over Christmas and then it was 1987.

Just eight months out of basic training and I'd already visited twelve countries. My group would soon be heading out to the Island of Borneo for some jungle training in Brunei. I wouldn't be going. I was gutted. The trip included acclimatisation in Hong Kong, a must-see before we gave it back to China. A skeleton garrison would have to remain to guard our barracks. This was something the married men usually volunteered for as it meant less time away but everyone wanted the Hong Kong experience.

Dave wasn't going either. He had been my No 2 on the 84mm during the last two trips. We were both pretty miserable at being left behind but couldn't grumble really. Seventeen and had already visited so many places. Folks our age back home wouldn't have done anything like that.

After morning parade one day we were both told to 'stand fast'. We were then invited into the troop commander's office. We were puzzled. Had we done something wrong? "Relax, gents; stand at ease."

"One of you is going on a parachute course." (Gold dust – not to be turned down.)

"One of you is going on Exercise Curry Trail." (Jungle training via Hong Kong – not to be turned down.)

We both wanted Hong Kong and said so. Our deployments would therefore be decided by the flip of a coin. When I eventually came back from the jungle I was greeted by a rather envious Dave who made a point of standing side on so that I could see the new Para wings badge on his shirt. I laughed.

They issued us with jungle boots and lightweight camouflage uniforms in February. Then we were sent on night navigational exercises in the snow-covered peaks of the Quantocks. Our jungle boots were American. They had a metal plate in the sole to protect from the punji sticks that were used against them in Vietnam. This plate was freezing everyone's feet but we had to break the boots in or so they said.

We flew out at the end of February from RAF Brize Norton. The RAF live well. Cream cakes and iced buns. All you can eat. Our DC10 touched down in Bahrain but we were not allowed off the aircraft. We were all in uniform. Perhaps they thought we'd seize the airport. After a refuel we landed in Sri Lanka. A welcome chance to stretch our legs and drink some cold water. Next stop… HONG KONG.

Kowloon Tong Ping Fong. That was the name of our barracks. Say

'Kowloon Tong Ping Fong' to any taxi driver and you would be brought back to the camp. "Don't forget it," said the guide. That was twenty-nine years ago. The camp's medical officer gave us some pertinent advice about sexually transmitted diseases and then we were let loose. I had never seen a more relaxed attitude in the Marines. Yes, we had to be back by morning. There would be a long route march as part of our acclimatisation but we'd be out tomorrow night too. We were guests, not a garrison, so there were no guard or galley duties and very few working parties.

The night markets were very cheap. Everyone was buying fake Lacoste polo shirts. I got two pairs of Pepe jeans. My Dad had sent me £200 birthday money. I wouldn't be eighteen until Brunei but I would celebrate early out here. The China Fleet Club included a respectable shopping arcade selling genuine items. From there I bought my Seiko Kinetic Professional Divers' watch. £180 was a lot of money but it was the timepiece I wanted and would last me thirteen years. Others bought fake Rolex watches off the market. Some lasted a while, but not as long as mine. The taxis were red and you had to pay in Hong Kong dollars but most journeys worked out at about 50p. Such an exciting place.

The Bottoms Up Club featured in James Bond's *The Man with the Golden Gun*. I nipped in for a beer just to say I'd done it. The topless barmaid wasn't as beautiful as the advertisement outside had suggested. I left soon after. A pub crawl was inevitable. Many bars had souvenir T-shirts. Most of us bought one from Ned Kelly's. By the end of the night I was with Sue. That stereotypical Hong Kong name. Sue was actually English and she got me back to barracks safely.

After the long march up and down the hills, most hangovers were worn off. Then it was a quick clean of kit, some of us booked a day trip to China for tomorrow, then we hit the town again. Tonight I was celebrating my eighteenth. *Too much beer yesterday; I'll pace myself tonight,* I thought. I teamed up with Jock again and we both fancied a massage after our earlier yomp.

We entered the establishment not knowing what to expect. We were greeted with an offer of drinks which included tea and coffee. I said, "I'd love a coffee." When it arrived it was a whole pint glass brimming with ice and with a couple of straws. Hadn't seen that before. We were handed a large plastic bin reminiscent of those we used to have at the swimming pool. "Put your clothes in here, then naked into the sauna." I had never had a sauna before. Who could last the longest? That was marine mentality and once a gauntlet is thrown, the competition would start. It wasn't long before we realised the futility of this challenge. A compromise. "We'll both do thirty press-ups and then leave." "Agreed."

Wrapped in the towel, I went over to a row of couches. Above these were bamboo scaffold bars. I laid on my back and waited. My lady was huge and not at all attractive. They'd be no happy endings from this one. She had good hands though and knew what she was doing. Hot towels on my face opening up pores, then some menthol lotion to cool. I had caught the sun on the route march but this lady must have wiped off my tan. When I thought the massage was over she took off her flip-flops, climbed on the couch, grabbed the scaffold bars and started walking up and down my body. Being massaged by her heavy feet, my bones were cracking. I thought I would die but came out feeling awesome.

"Right, it's my birthday. Beer!" I don't remember the rest. I woke up in a disco. Billy Lloyd carried me back to Kowloon Tong Ping Fong.

I was well and truly hung over for the China trip. A coach, a train and then another coach. Visited some terracotta soldiers and a school where the little kids sang to us beautifully. Then to a temple of sorts followed by a banquet Chinese meal and a lesson on using chopsticks. If you could use them, you could keep them as a souvenir. I still have mine.

Party time over, we arrived at our new base, Tutong Camp, Brunei. It was seriously too hot to do anything and the pace was adjusted accordingly. We would be sharing these barracks with Gurkhas. It was explained to us that some of their ways might seem peculiar.

Royal Marines were all taught personal hygiene to the same standard. That way there could be no excuses for uncleanliness. This wasn't petty. It derived from marines being seaborne troops. In a cramped ship environment, one person's poor hygiene could wipe out the whole fighting force through disease, infections and the like. It was so important that it was the first thing taught on day one of basic training. The class was made to gather around while the naked drill instructor demonstrated the use of soap and water. They even taught us to shave.

Gurkhas are embarrassed by male nudity and shower with their pants on. This was a direct violation of our practice.

Friends from the same village often hold hands; this is quite normal and not to be mistaken as a sign of homosexuality (forbidden by military law at that time).

When a Gurkha leaves the camp his minimum dress code will be shoes, shirt and trousers.

Royal Marines certainly know how to endear themselves.

"We'll soon stop these blouse-wearing poofters being embarrassed by male nudity."

That night many of the lads, completely starkers, cans of beer in hand, danced the 'conga' through the Gurkhas' accommodation block. Kukris were drawn, but no blood spilled. It didn't happen again.

After this initial lack of respect our attitudes soon changed. We challenged them to a game of basketball. We pitched all of our 6-footers against their average 5' 4". Our lot were decimated. The Gurkhas were so fast and wow, could they jump high?

Jungle school wasn't a building. We were dropped off by truck and marched down a long dirt track until we came to a clearing. Here, rows of felled logs provided classroom seating. We sat down and the outdoor lectures commenced. In front of us was an old gunnery sergeant of the USMC. His catchphrase in that lazy American drawl was, "Pay attention to detail." Half an hour in, he was boring the hell out of me. I couldn't be doing with his voice but then behind him the ground moved. Loud bangs and several bursts of machine gun fire. Blokes were diving for cover and falling off the logs. Two Gurkhas who had been lying about 5 metres away covered in leaves, stood up in their ghillie suits, let off a few more rounds and ran away before disappearing into the jungle.

We applauded. Slowly at first as people tried to understand how it was that they'd survived this close range massacre. Then realising it was just a demonstration with blank rounds, the clapping, smiles and sighs of relief multiplied. We had just been put in our place.

The jungle is the hardest environment. If you're cold in the Arctic, you move about to get warm. Hot in the desert, you can find or make shade. In the jungle you stay hot. All of the time. Day and night. So hot under the trees that at times it is hard to breathe. Then there are the plants that make it difficult to move. One appropriately named 'Wait a while'. It was a sticky creeper that snagged on you like barbed wire, stopping you in your tracks and prompting someone to say, "Wait a while!"

Navigation is difficult because all you can see are trees. We relied on a compass-bearing and someone counting how many paces we'd made in order to judge distance travelled. And things are trying to eat you. That is before you even consider fighting an enemy.

We trained hard. We were only there for three months and had to maximise the opportunities. We had time off from Saturday lunch until Monday morning. There'd be a beach barbecue most Saturday evenings but not a woman in sight or indeed any local for that matter.

By mid-tour we were given a long weekend. Four days off. Some went to the Philippines for some very cheap sex. Many went to Australia. From the photos I saw, it seems they had the best time. The English accent won them many favours. Some were offered jobs and others offered brides. I wanted to go to Australia but I'd only just turned eighteen. I was due a pay increase now but the money I had been on as a seventeen-year-old was small change. I had gone over budget in Hong Kong and given that we were due to return there before flying to England, I would need all I could save.

It was OK. For those peasants amongst us staying local, there was an opportunity to go waterskiing. I put my name down but it was popular and first come first served. There were two days available and I was listed for the second day. I stayed on camp looking forward to tomorrow but the mood dropped suddenly and we were mustered on the parade ground as the sergeant major broke the news.

Craig had been in an accident waterskiing. The boat had ran him over and the propeller had taken off his leg. He had lost a lot of blood in the water and was fighting for his life. He was being well looked after by the Sultan of Brunei's staff but all future waterskiing was cancelled. I felt sick. I knew Craig quite well. He had once asked me to help him with his running. There was a very sombre mood in camp. Most of the lads had an early night.

Five of us decided we had to do something to get away from camp, so we all chipped in and hired a Suzuki jeep for a road trip. We crossed the border for a day in Sarawak and had a few beers at the Fook Hin Cafe.

The second half of the tour we honed our skills to culminate with a sixteen-day final exercise. I had replaced the standard issue survival knife and golok (machete) with a Gurkha-style 'kukri'. Many of us did and we didn't regret it. I took mine everywhere after that and still have it at home.

We lost Pete to heat exhaustion. He was close to death and his body swallowed two whole drips during his medevac by Land Rover. One unlucky chap broke his leg when he put his foot through roots in the dried-up mangrove swamp. His leg went down and stopped while his body carried on forward aggravated by the heavy load he carried. He screamed so loud. We had to clear a landing site to get him airlifted by helicopter.

We camped early each night in the jungle. It is almost impossible to move silently and tactically in the dark. That was one consolation, plenty of rest. The night-time jungle is an orchestra of wild noises. Exotic birds, monkeys and insects. Out of tune was Rocky Stone. Something had crawled into his ear and sent him mad. He started running round the jungle bumping into and knocking over anyone who tried to assist him. He left too. We'd lost three men already and not fired a shot yet.

Being the dry season, water had to be flown in. The helicopter would hover and winch down Jerry cans-full. Some of the group carried large canvas bags. The water would be quickly transferred to the canvas bags enabling the helicopter to depart with the empty Jerry cans without loitering and giving away our position or indeed attracting enemy ground fire. From the canvas bags we would fill our bottles. The problem was that chemicals used to waterproof the canvas bags affected the taste of the water. It burned the back of your throat as you drank it. The more you drank, the more it burned. The more it burned, the more you needed to drink. This was going to be sixteen days of hell.

To make matters worse, all our rations were Arctic issue. We had them because of budget cuts. They needed eating before the use-by dates. They consisted of boiled sweets and chocolate bars which were melting and attracting ants and insects, and dried food such as noodles that needed water hydration. In the Arctic you have plenty of water because you can melt snow. These rations were totally inadequate. Orange powder masked the water's burning sensation but increased the thirst.

We couldn't cook for two reasons. Firstly from a tactical perspective and secondly because it was the dry season and the whole jungle might go up in smoke. We had on several occasions been called upon to fight natural outbreaks on the grasslands outside our barracks. We attacked those flames with fire beaters as the scores of snakes fled across the road. Fire was a real concern.

The only thing people could eat was tins of spam. Those that didn't like spam went hungry or munched on dried noodles, which would make them thirsty. I ate the spam. There were also fruit ants. Plenty of them about. Pick them up, squeeze their heads to kill them, then bite off the sack of sweet juice. Spam and ants it was.

When the sixteen days were up and we got back to camp, the queues formed at the ice-cold water dispenser. Clean cold water is so underrated. It is absolutely priceless.

Front left with another can of spam. Endex after sixteen days.

Some of us went to bathe in the South China Sea. Our clothes were rotting. So were my feet and my shoulders from the rucksack straps. The waves took away my dirty shirt. Had to explain that one to the quartermaster. Fortunately he didn't bill me for it. I thought he would.

There was an opportunity to see Craig before we left and I went along. He was out and about in the hospital's spectacular garden. Sat there eating an orange, he was quite chilled. The leg had gone below the knee but there were deep laceration scabs and scars across his lower thigh. Not nice. He was annoyed about missing the return trip to Hong Kong but happy he would beat us back to England.

Next time I saw him was a few months later at our base. He was back in uniform with a prosthetic leg. "What you up to these days?" I asked. "I am the company runner!" he said and jogged away.

In Hong Kong I found another English girl called Sue. We spent the day at the Sea World where we watched a few dolphins and killer whales perform. On the last night, all the lads got together in the bar of the China Fleet Club for a final beer or two or three and the party tricks started. Guys were racing each other at drinking pints while balancing upside down standing on their heads.

The most impressive act, you had to see to believe. A marine came round with a pint glass requesting a dollar from everyone who wanted to see a man lick his own penis. The glass overflowed and then another marine jumped onto the pool table, dropped his trousers, grabbed his manhood, bent over and flicked his tongue sufficient to raise cheers of amazement and approval. He didn't have a massive piece. He was just incredibly bendy and flexible. He jumped back down and collected his fee. He must have had the equivalent of £100 for a five-second stunt. I said, "I wish I could do that." Someone said, "Give him a tenner and he'll let you."

As soon as we landed in England, we all left for two weeks' leave. Completely by accident I returned to barracks a day late. As the youngest I was susceptible to wind-ups and it seemed everyone was telling me that I was AWOL (absent without leave). I didn't believe them. When I was told to 'stand fast' after the next morning's parade I realised I was in trouble. I had no excuse. Somehow I had confused the dates and turned up quite nonchalantly twenty-four hours late. My punishment was to work next weekend as 'advanced party'. I would help transport the baggage convoy for our next deployment.

The unit was off to the Altcar ranges near Southport for the APWT or Annual Personal Weapons Test. One week's live firing and marksmanship practice. On the last day, instead of returning by coach with the rest of us, one of the older marines got special permission to ride his bike back to our barracks in Taunton, 230 miles away. I was really impressed.

Next we started preparing a display for the 'Captain General'. That is a ceremonial title given to HRH Prince Philip. We may have been 'Her Majesty's Royal Marines', but Philip was our royal representative. He knew his stuff too. Prince Edward had been an officer candidate during my basic training but he didn't complete the course. I was more than happy with the appointment of Prince Philip anyway. He had done his bit in the Second World War and it was a huge honour to have him on board.

To mark our VIP's birthday there would be an amphibious cliff assault at Jennycliff Bay in Plymouth. We moved down to Stonehouse Barracks for a week and practised our boat drills and rope ascents. Evenings were spent ashore having beers and letting off steam on Union Street. The taxi drivers knew more of our timetable and what we were going to do than we did. It was supposed to be 'hush hush'.

D-Day arrived and I was in an LCU initially. That is one of those big landing craft. The forward ramp drops down and the troops charge out to storm up the beach. On this occasion, however, some of us would be off-loaded while out at sea into smaller high-speed craft known as 'Rigid Raiders'. They were something many of us enjoyed. They were so fast and lightweight with a powerful engine. They just skimmed across the surface and could even be propelled out of the water and directly onto the beach, allowing passengers to disembark with dry feet. But for this drop we'd get wet. The boats would deliberately fall short in order to loop back and bring in a second wave of troops.

Before that though we would have a surprise. A Sea King helicopter hovered above and the winch started lowering the Captain General into our LCU. He was dressed up in combat uniform and wearing his commando beret. Wow, that's Prince Philip. He was much taller than me and I remember thinking how old he looked. I had only ever seen green berets on the heads of young men but the sprightly prince was sixty-six. We gathered round to hear him tell us how great we all were and he wished us good luck. Jolly nice of him to drop in (literally). Sharing a landing craft with Prince Philip really made my day.

Anyway, we stormed the beach, scaled the cliffs and had a massive battle at the top. We were victorious and received rapturous applause from the public that had gathered to watch this invasion.

Cross-decking from a Mexifloat to an LCU in Norway 1986. Left of picture are two Rigid Raiders.

Then came the issue of the SA80. A new personal weapon. They had passed their trial period and would now be wholesale distributed. We had weapon handling practice until we could do everything with our eyes shut. I didn't like this new rifle, it had too many brittle or fiddly attachments. I only got to use it once. We did a practice night attack on a dockyard. I was supposed to be firing on automatic but could only manage a single shot followed by a jam. I cleared and fired another single shot followed by a further jam. I much preferred my SLR.

My summer leave and Karen's overlapped so I headed to Holland for a few days. I had been 'pen pals' with a Dutch lad since I was eleven or twelve. We had met on a camping holiday and wrote about once a year. Joost was now a student, living in a tiny flat in Amsterdam. True to stereotypical form he was a cannabis user. He had a jam jar full and would regularly roll a fat joint. My lungs were pristine. I didn't smoke cigarettes and wasn't about to start with the weed. In any event, I could lose my job and the local beer was quite adequate. I saw some of the sights while he did his studies and day job as a cleaner. Then we hitchhiked to his parents for the weekend in Voorburg.

Fun and games over, the unit started preparing for a tour of Northern Ireland. The threat from the IRA was a real one and they had started bombing the mainland. Two years from now, eleven soft target Royal Marine musicians would be murdered in a cowardly bomb attack at Deal and staff at Leicester Careers Office would have a lucky escape when a device attached to their minibus fell off and detonated on the road behind rather blasting them sky high.

At this point that is where I am headed next. However the deployment is in January and it is now September. If you don't have a career plan in the Marines you will be given one. All posts need filling. If no one volunteers, someone will be selected (pinged). As an expendable general duty marine (rifleman) you are first in the pecking order. It could be names in a hat or just a plain and simple order. Sought-after jobs such as vehicle mechanic or HGV driver had no shortage of applicants. These would be useful qualifications after leaving the service, but few had joined the Commandos to be an administrative clerk, a cook, a heavy weapons specialist or signaller (radioman).

I had been a general duty marine for more than a year. I had been on three tours and seen nineteen countries. Many of my peers had visited only Norway. I would be pinged soon if I wasn't careful. For the unit to deploy on operations, all of the technical posts needed to be sorted. General duty marines were less of a priority as they could be sourced directly from the newly qualified ranks leaving Lympstone.

I contemplated the roles. I didn't want any of them but had to choose. Clerk – too boring. Cook – ridiculous hours. Mortars – Nah. Signaller?

I had tended to shy away from the radio. In an exercise during basic training I had struggled to translate the coded messages. I could master it with application and signaller would open many avenues. My friend Martin had started as a signaller and had then become a telecommunications technician. He was one of the most highly skilled marines in the Corps and had qualifications that could serve him well in Civvy Street.

As a signaller I could be seconded to Special Forces and do all sorts of interesting stuff.

As a signaller I will have greater insight into what is happening when I'm in Northern Ireland and I won't get pinged for crap jobs.

Daily parade was held and we fell out to read the noticeboard. Nick Wade graduated after me and we'd shared that trench for a week in Germany. His name was on the draft list. S3 Course. He had been pinged for signaller training. He was distraught. He had carried the radio on the last exercise and his competence made him the obvious candidate. Would I be destined for Heavy Weapons, the galley or the filing cabinets?

No time to lose. I'd take his place. I cleared it with Nick. He was delighted and gave me an appreciative hug. I spoke with the sergeant major. I volunteered on the understanding that I would be returning to Bravo Company for Ireland. He said he couldn't guarantee I'd get Bravo Company but I'd definitely be coming home to 40 Commando because they were well under strength. My course would end at the beginning of December giving me plenty of time to rejoin and deploy with my outfit.

We headed into Taunton for my leaving do. After a first course of many ales, the tradition is for a 'death wet'. A pint of spirits made up of all the optics on the top row. Generous portions of rum, whisky, gin and vodka. If you keep it down, there's a good chance you'll die, hence the name. The warped theory is that you make a determined effort to drink it all. Usually to the chorus of, "Down in one, down in one, down in one!" If you struggle it is not a problem as you are expected to vomit anyhow. That is inevitable. To avoid shame you must finish the drink before you vomit.

I managed it. I was surprised, but then the saliva glands worked overtime. They were getting ready to neutralise the impending flood of acid and bile. The audience was waiting for my reaction and cheered when it came. I ran to the Gents' and 'jettisoned fuel' into the toilet. The cheers continued and there were a few congratulatory slaps on my back. Better out than in. At which point some of my artwork was scooped up from the toilet into an empty pint glass and taken back to be shared out among my supporters. You crazy bastards. That is brotherhood.

Chapter 8.

SOS

Almost two years after first moving into Lympstone, I was back. This time I already had a green beret and on the shoulders of my jumper were the title flashes that read 'Royal Marines Commando'. The way I would be treated now was completely different. No more 'military bullshit' and no one screaming at me or making me run everywhere. It was a great place to be.

I couldn't drive and still relied on trains in those days. I had turned up early and after finding a room I would have the weekend off. Then Bruce Godschalk arrived. He was a South African by birth but was now a serving Royal Marine. He was on the signals course too. Bruce had a car. We drove to Exeter so that he could get some last minute items, then went for a couple of beers which ended up being a full session. We ditched his car and caught the train. Instead of getting off at the barracks we continued to the end of the line and got out in Exmouth to find the nightclub.

Loitering around the DJ were three black men wearing thick winter coats and looking very cold. I didn't know it yet but one of them was Burt and he would be on my course too. I can't remember much of the rest of that night.

Most of the other course candidates arrived sporadically on the Sunday and eleven of us would commence course S3/2/87 on Monday morning.

Burt Rohan Riley wasn't a Royal Marine. He was a member of the Barbados Defence Force and would be training with us. His two friends at the nightclub were his fellow countrymen and they were on other courses here too. Our class make-up was like the line to a joke; there were Englishmen, Irishmen, Scotsmen, Welshmen, two South Africans (Bruce Godschalk and Bruce Swanepoel) and Burt from Barbados.

Over the next three months we would get to know our Clansman radios very well, master those ciphered messages, learn Morse code and be taught to touch-type. Nobody wanted to be there. No one had officially applied or volunteered. I had jumped before being pushed and it wasn't my ambition, but it could have been worse. With no real emphasis on the physical aspects, we were able to party hard most evenings and sober up during typing practice. It was a bit like being back at school. We spoke behind the teacher's back and messed around in class. We even had detentions. But we were all in it together and looking back it was quite a good laugh.

When the course ended the results were released and the draft orders announced. To my dismay, I was not returning to 40 Commando. I was going to 3 BAS. I had never heard of that unit. I protested but was told that I had finished 'top of the course' and 3 BAS was my prize.

I was disappointed that I was not returning to my original unit but I would make good friends at 3 BAS and, for coming top, my name would be gold painted on a large wooden plaque roll of honour in the Signals Training Wing.

As I left the building for the last time, I bumped into Nick Wade, the guy whose course I had just successfully completed. I quizzed his presence. He was about to embark on the next signals course. He had been pinged again. My earlier rescue had amounted to nothing more than a temporary stay of execution.

MOD Crown Copyright 1988, HMS *Heron*

Chapter 9.

Points Make Prizes

3 BAS did indeed turn out to be a prize but getting to RNAS Yeovilton by train was a pain and involved several station changes. A Royal Navy minibus shuttle service operated from the final stop, if I wanted to wait, otherwise it would be a long and expensive taxi journey to the barracks. Fortunately the minibus was ready and waiting as my train stopped.

My impending arrival had been expected and I dropped my kit off in temporary accommodation. I would parade at the company lines of 3 Commando Brigade Air Squadron tomorrow and then be introduced to the Signals Section.

They were a welcoming bunch but I was gutted. They were mostly older married men and I was still only eighteen. One of them looked quite young with a wispy moustache but when he took off his beret, he was bald like an old man too. Of all the aged dozen, he seemed the happiest to see me. This was Taff Phillips and he was only three years older than me. I was invited to be his roommate along with 'Harry the Bastard'. I was Harry's replacement and he would be leaving us after Norway, so for the time being there'd be three of us in the room.

Out of the whole section, only Taff and I were unmarried, and with the exception of our room, everyone else lived off the base. The Royal Navy Air Station (HMS *Heron*) was huge. It was said to handle more air traffic than any airport in Britain. It was certainly noisy with an almost constant thunder of jet engines and the whirl of choppers. All sorts of military were represented here. Obviously there were sailors and some Wrens, but there were RAF, Army Air Corps, army technicians, USMC and other foreign flying representatives of NATO.

The role of my new unit was aerial reconnaissance and anti-tank patrols using Gazelle and Lynx helicopters. I drew my Arctic clothing from the stores and would head out to Norway for my first winter after Christmas leave.

Deploying in early January meant that my two weeks of Christmas leave would commence one week before Karen's leave from the Wrens. We had hardly seen each other these past two years. She was so consumed during her basic training earlier that year that I didn't receive a single letter during my three months away on Curry Trail. Traditionally in the service, people with the surname Wright are nicknamed 'Shiner'. The absence of mail during my time at 40 Commando earnt me the nickname 'Shiner from Leicester with no letter'. I wasn't aware that I had an accent but when people addressed me by my nickname they exaggerated and mimicked my dialect, calling me 'Shina from Les-tah wiv no letta'.

I had made it to Karen's graduation at HMS *Raleigh* and we had spent some weekends in Weymouth near her new base, but the strained relationship ended in a row at Leicester Clock Tower. It was inevitable and for the best but it took a long time to get over her.

I flew out of Yeovilton on a Hercules. Landing at night-time in winter Norway, the Arctic air immediately froze at the back of my throat. That year I would learn to ski. Cross-country for the military role and recreationally on the downhill slopes. Our final exercise took place on the Yerkin Range where those snow-covered opening scenes from *Star Wars: The Empire Strikes Back*, were filmed.

One good thing about Norway was the LOA (local overseas' allowance) to compensate troops for the increased cost of living. Norway was more expensive than Britain and consequently a marine would receive just over £10 extra every day. Given that a winter deployment lasted almost three months the total LOA would be worth approximately £1,000. That was a welcome boost to me earning just £480 a month. It would certainly clear the Christmas credit card balance.

Many NATO countries took part in these annual winter tours which culminated with a joint final exercise. The war games were based on a Soviet-led Warsaw Pact invasion of Europe via the northern route (Russia into Northern Norway). Our ultimate aim was to deter and if necessary repel that advance.

We weren't yet exchanging fire – it was a Cold War stand-off – but we were still taking causalities. Every winter claimed someone's life. Treacherous driving conditions and avalanches took some. One poor chap slipped into the icy water while transferring from one boat to another. Heavily laden with kit he just sank in the freezing waters. In the local bars, a beer was about £3 but on camp a single shot of spirits cost just 10 pence, meaning some would die of alcohol poisoning. Occasionally someone would kill themselves through depression. Three months away from family can seem a long time. There was no internet or mobile phones. Keeping in touch meant scribbling letters or expensive telephone calls. I personally knew of one chap who came out of his tent and walked straight into a radio antenna. This pierced his eyeball and blinded him. But I had survived my first winter and would be heading home soon.

"Oh no, you're not. You're staying. One of the helicopters is going further north for another two weeks. You and Taff, as the only unmarried men, have been nominated to stay behind."

Cool. More LOA and, as it turned out, a view of the spectacular green Northern Lights.

As soon as we got back to England we were pinged again. We had missed Easter but still had home leave to look forward to. We had to take it immediately because two weeks later we would be heading off for six weeks in the Mediterranean. It was us two again because none of the married blokes wanted to leave their wives so soon after returning from three months away. Accompanying us would be one of our corporals, Nige Batley. Exercise Dragon Hammer in 1988 was probably the best six weeks of my life.

Martin 'Spud' Hart had been a senior marine cadet when I joined TS *Tiger*. He went on to become a Royal Marine Commando, a signaller and then a telecommunications technician. His entire family had taken me under their wing after Ivor died and from that day to the present, I was treated as one of their own. Joan and Jerry would always introduce me as 'one of our adopted sons'. Naturally, I should have been uncomfortable with that label but they didn't box me in and I felt quite honoured and privileged to be described that way. The endurance of our friendship means that my children regard them as grandparents. How fortunate I was to have met them.

Martin would get married on Saturday in Reading and I wouldn't miss it for the world. However, I was to deploy on Sunday morning and there were no trains to get me back to barracks in time. The taxi all the way to Yeovil cost a fortune but at least I was able to stay until the end of the wedding celebration.

We boarded a coach and drove all day to Arbroath, Scotland. Spent a night in the barracks of 45 Commando before embarking on an RFA (Royal Fleet Auxiliary) LSL (Landing Ship Logistics). We then sailed for several days, down the North Sea, through the English Channel and into Plymouth Docks where our ship received a single Gazelle helicopter from 3 BAS. I marvelled at the military genius. Why had it been necessary for me to rush back from leave, drive to Scotland and sail south for five days when I could have simply embarked at Plymouth?

From there we sailed to Gibraltar. There was another 'Rock Run' but I was even slower this time. Heading ashore later, we walked past a US warship moored behind ours. We were shocked to hear their ship's Tannoy broadcast.

"Duty Negro, close up to cleaning stations!" We couldn't quite believe what we had just heard. Were Americans really that backward? Apparently so. They still had segregation on board and armed US Marines guarded the various mess decks or sleeping quarters.

In one of the bars we met some American submariners and played drinking games. They were a good bunch. Later that night I was sat on the steps of the fish & chip shop. I was joined by Paddy Coulter. We had been on the same signals course but I hadn't seen him since. He was on another ship taking part in the exercise. I gave him some of my roast chicken and we reminisced. Such a small world.

With a few days' leave, Nige, Taff, Steve and I hired a small Vauxhall Nova and headed to Torremolinos and then Marbella. We met two girls on the beach. They were from London. One of them was a single mum, and her young lad had come over to play with us. That was the initial introduction but it was clear that I was in with the other girl. Guess what? Another Sue. We got on well and didn't want the party to end, so nominating the skint Steve as 'babysitter', five of us went out on the town. The next day we returned to our ship and sailed on to Sardinia. I'd catch up with Sue when I got back to England.

The main NATO exercise would only last three days. The USMC, Dutch Marines and French Foreign Legion were participating as well as the Royal Marines from 45 Commando. Our job was to man the radio. Four hours on, eight hours off, between the three of us. It wasn't that difficult. Periodically, I would have to change frequency but no one called my call sign. People wishing to use our helicopter were supposed to request it through us (a bit like ringing for a taxi), but I think our pilot must have simply made his own arrangements. Bored out of my mind I took up smoking. Cigarettes were very cheap on board and I opted for Benson & Hedges. I didn't like them and gave up before finishing a full pack. I also wrote to Annie Harris who played 'Jane' in the Australian soap opera, *Neighbours*. I asked if she'd consider dating a good-looking marine. She didn't reply and went on to marry a millionaire. Oh well, her loss.

We headed to Genoa, Italy for a resupply. We'd be there for five days and were free to come and go as we pleased. Taff and I headed for Rome. The train was crammed and standing room only for much of the journey. Taff managed to climb onto one of the overhead baggage racks and go to sleep. I was not so fortunate. In Rome we took in the sights: the Vatican, Colosseum and Trevi Fountain. When we got back to the ship we still had loads of leave left so we went the other way. This time to France: Nice, Cannes and then on to Monte Carlo. Preparations for the F1 Grand Prix were in motion. We bought souvenir caps and T-shirts but the race was still a couple of days away so we'd timed that wrong. Cannes was packing up after the film festival so we had just missed that too.

Taff and me in Rome, May 1988

Returning to the ship a second time, we still had loads of leave left. Taking an army helicopter mechanic who wished to tag along, we boarded another train to Pisa. It was late when we arrived so we tried door handles eventually finding one that was insecure. Gaining access to a large hallway at the bottom of a communal staircase to a multi-apartment complex, we bedded down for the night, with some ripped-up cardboard boxes serving as mattresses. We were awoken and evicted by a broom-wielding, female Italian cleaner quite early the next morning and ran off to climb the 'Leaning Tower'.

Once back in Genoa, almost skint, we chose to stay local. With high spirits later that night, I tried to invite myself aboard a private yacht in the harbour. With one foot on the boat and the other quayside, the craft started drifting causing me to do the splits. I fell, splashing into the water. That sobered me up quite quickly. My pals were in stitches, so I pushed them in. The four of us were soaked now. Back on board it seemed too early for bed, so we started jumping from the upper deck and then swimming back round to the gangplank. The night sentry found it quite amusing. We all jumped in several times.

Next morning, the ship's sergeant major (most of the crew were Royal Corps of Transport) entered our mess deck looking for the so-called 'Diving Display Team'. He wasn't angry with us but stressed we would all now need tetanus jabs in our buttocks. Our own captain had seen the funny side too but had to discipline us somehow. We would perform the 'guard of honour' for the forthcoming cocktail party. We had to stand looking smart as the distinguished guests arrived. Once they were all aboard we were free to go again but we behaved ourselves that night.

Naughty boys performing the guard of honour. Bottom right are three Dutch Marines.

We returned to Gibraltar and transferred to HMS *Intrepid*. This time we would disembark at Plymouth. Once back at Yeovilton, I stood in the queue for my evening meal. I was joined by Nick Wade. It was a shock but a nice surprise. What was he doing here? Apparently, he had finished top of his signals course. His name was now gold painted, next to mine, on the roll of honour plaque in the Signals Training Wing and his PRIZE… He was to join the Signals Section of 3 BAS.

I spent many weekends with the Sue that I had met in Spain. She shared a house near Waterloo Station. We did various bars around the capital, in particular those floating on the Thames such as the Tattersall Castle and I became familiar with 'the tube'. I have forgotten the name of Sue's single-mum friend but she started dating a guardsman and occasionally we went out as a foursome. Typical of the guards, this man was much taller than me but at least he wore the same desert boots. Unfortunately he deployed to Northern Ireland that year and was blown up in the first week. He lost an eye and badly injured an arm, the poor man. Sue was a bit older than me and her body clock accelerated the agenda. We disagreed one weekend and our brief romance was over.

The APWT arrived once more. 3 BAS headed for the ranges near Southport. I received a letter one morning. I didn't recognise the handwriting but it was from Holland. Lying on my bunk I opened the envelope. Flakes of dried cannabis leaf fell out onto my pillow. I think Joost was trying to be funny but I had to quickly sweep up and discard of the drug before anyone noticed. He was inviting me over for the summer. His flatmate was a rather large New Zealander. She was keen but a bit too tall for me and I decided to give it a miss.

I learnt to drive during summer leave instead. Took a two-week intense course and fortunately passed first time. Unwisely, I rushed to buy my first car. I picked up an overpriced banger of a Vauxhall Cavalier. It was a 1.6 litre but cheap insurance because it was so old. The radiator blew on the maiden voyage. After buying a brand new replacement and a water pump, the ignition failed. With a dozen dads giving me advice and remedies, we managed to get it going again. I had to first replace all the spark plugs and HT leads. On the first high-speed return to Leicester, the head gasket blew.

I traded the Cavalier the next day and got a generous part exchange but I had still lost a lot of money. I would lose even more money on the never-ending hire purchase agreement but at least this next car would be reliable. The replacement from a showroom on Abbey Lane was a nearly new Austin Metro. Tornado red. B296 KNR. An easy registration to remember. B for Bravo Company, 296 was my class in basic training and KNR was an abbreviation for 'Kooners', the local convenience store in Rushey Mead. It was very economical as a 1 litre and quite fast when it was just carrying me. Next priority was the stereo and speakers. Obviously.

In high spirits one day, Nick dived on the bonnet as I was reversing. I cringed. "Get off; you'll damage it and it's not paid for!" He ran over the top laughing. I stopped and inspected it. The bonnet was OK but there were three prominent dents in the roof where his heavy boots had trod. What was he thinking? The stunt was costly. After several quotes, it was decided I'd need a new roof. £456 was almost one month's pay. To his credit, Nick picked up the bill but it would take another winter in Norway to repair the dent in his wallet.

L-R: Spike, Shina, Taff and Nick. Going ashore (off camp).

With an uncertain future I considered my options. Life wasn't difficult; I knew my job inside out but we weren't being tested. I had recently been trained as a flight deck firefighter and as a first aider. I completed the skidpan driving course at Silverstone and the helicopter underwater escape drills in the brand new dunker but these were just basic rather than professional qualifications. A typical day involved a few light tasks each morning such as vehicle maintenance or painting things green. We would play volleyball most afternoons. I was bored. A fireman fights fires. Marines fight wars. That is not to say I wanted a war to start just to stop me being bored. Absolutely not; but the reality was, we were simply a 'break glass in the event of emergency' option. We were largely ignored and dormant otherwise. Promotion was slow, defence spending was shrinking, so training was limited, pay was rubbish and equipment was such poor standard that people bought their own. Some guys were happy with this stagnant, money for nothing existence but I wanted bigger challenges and better pay.

They would throw money our way if the trouble started but it didn't look like there was going to be any. The Cold War was coming to an end. I think it had something to do with Rocky Balboa fighting that Russian. It all happened quickly after that. I looked at jobs in the Corps. Very few marines had travelled as extensively as me and I did not wish to spend my entire career as a signaller. I would only be here for another year or two before being moved and at some point I would be drafted for sea service. There was just one avenue capable of keeping me in the Marines. I would volunteer to join the Special Forces.

I was invited along to participate in one of their exercises. The job was to liberate passengers being held hostage on a ferry in the English Channel. The Special Boat Service were given the task and I would help with communications. It was a very interesting weekend but one sworn to secrecy. I was quite keen to pursue this line of work but most of those I spoke to said they were leaving. They didn't get extra pay, most of the time they were in freezing cold conditions and nearly all were handing in their notice.

It wasn't just marines that were leaving. The British Army was withdrawing from Germany and soldiers were quitting in vast numbers. As the Cold War closed, the budgets shrank further. There seemed very little point in staying, so like many others I would seek a PVR (Premature Voluntary Release).

At the end of October 1988, I handed in my written request. I first had to see a captain who attempted to dissuade me. I told him I was considering joining the police. He told me I didn't stand a chance. There would be too many applicants and not enough jobs. I'd take my chances, thank you.

Then an appointment was made to see the commanding officer. There were 120 men in 3 BAS. Eleven of us were queuing outside the major's office that morning. We were all asking to leave. The major couldn't argue. He was leaving too. 10% of our strength. As a trained helicopter pilot he would seek work outside like the rest of us.

My request was endorsed but I would still have to serve out eighteen months' notice. If a dream job presented itself in the meantime, I could withdraw my application to leave. If another war came along, they could overrule my discharge and retain me. Indeed they could even call me back after release if necessary.

For the Arctic deployment of 1989 we would sail by LSL across the very cold North Sea. This year we were in Fagerness. Our barracks were quite luxurious – a holiday park near a big lake. We stayed in four- or six-berth log cabins. These had kitchen facilities but the toilet and shower blocks were a short dash through the knee-high snow.

Going ashore for a beer in the local nightclub was very expensive and consequently most of the lads initially topped up with the cheaper booze on camp. There was also a scramble for any small containers that could act as improvised hip flasks. With the Sarsons vinegar now in short supply, I had to make do with a Timotei bottle. I thoroughly rinsed and even washed the insides with coffee to remove the soapy taste before filling with Captain Morgan Rum. A last minute decision to go clubbing saw me rush back to the accommodation, grab my bottle and share a taxi into town. After concealing my liquor from the doormen, I topped up my overpriced beer. To my utter dismay, I had grabbed the wrong bottle. That frothy head on my lager was from shampoo. Every cloud has a silver lining and as a consequence of being less drunk than usual; I pulled. I managed to join an elite group that night; 'The Winter Wives Club'. I had a Norwegian girlfriend for the last few weeks. Britt was her name. I thought about maintaining a long distance relationship but it wasn't love and self-funded trips to Norway were way outside my budget.

The men were never encouraged to volunteer, but sometimes they were tricked. It was usually the inexperienced who would be caught out. With the company stood on parade an NCO might ask, "Who here has a driving licence?" Thinking they would be letting themselves in for a nice easy job behind the wheel of a warm and dry Land Rover, the hands would shoot up. "Well volunteered. You, you and you report to the galley." They would spend the whole day in the kitchens helping prepare food, cleaning the mess hall and washing pots.

I didn't fall for that one. Not because I knew better. I simply didn't have a driving licence the first time I heard it. They got me with, "Anyone here got O-Level Geography?" I raised my hand. I would spend the day joining up individual Ordinance Survey maps to make one massive chart for the main HQ.

When the sergeant major asked for volunteers to work on Saturday morning and that it would be in our interests, there was obviously a great deal of scepticism. I volunteered and could not believe what I was being told. "You lot will be in the next *Indiana Jones* movie."

A coach collected about twenty of us and we were taken to a stately home in Bicester. We were there measured up for our Nazi uniforms and given some German goose-stepping practice. It only took a couple of hours and they fed us too. The filming would take place on Wednesday evening. When the day came, we all got dressed up, took loads of photos and then went before the spotlights. They had us marching round in a semi-circle. There were three separate squads of about thirty men. When the leading squad was out of camera shot, the members had to sprint back to the start, reform and continue marching. On film, this would create the effect of an endless procession of soldiers. We soon got tired. We weren't getting anything wrong, it was other technical issues. After a few hours we were all fed up and when they finally gave us a break, everyone just collapsed on the road.

Sean Connery walked by with Harrison Ford. I was quite excited and shouted, "YO, SEAN!" and gave him a thumbs up. He smiled raising a palm and we all responded with loud cheers. That was a small boost to our morale but we were nowhere near as enthusiastic for the next session. They would have to get the sequence right soon. Our uniforms were getting tatty from lying about on the road and some of the props were getting damaged. In particular the golden eagles that were mounted on long staffs supporting swastika banners were mysteriously breaking off and disappearing. They were only moulded plastic but military personnel are renowned for trophy hunting and everyone wanted a souvenir. We were addressed over the Tannoy and told to take more care as these props were very valuable and needed for other films. That fell on deaf ears. A while later, the broadcaster effectively suggested that we were deliberately damaging and stealing the props and told us that we would be searched before leaving the site. Well, marines like a challenge.

I received £200 for my brief appearance in *Indiana Jones and the Last Crusade* (the book burning scene in Berlin). I gave half of that to Great Ormond Street Hospital. Some of us had done a sponsored run from HMS *Heron* to London but I had raised very little and this money was easy come easy go. I would have been happy to do the film for free. From time to time I visited various friends in the accommodation block. In some rooms there were golden eagles sat of TV sets, German helmets on coat hooks or swastika banners hanging from the walls.

The last twelve months were a drag. Taff was drafted elsewhere so I had the room to myself from then on. A few small field exercises took place and some of us spent a couple of weeks playing enemy for members of 42 Commando who were training for a Northern Ireland deployment.

I spent much of my time preparing for the police selection. I had been advised to boost my current affairs and political knowledge. *The Telegraph* was essential reading and Radio 4 was my new entertainment. Leicestershire Constabulary was recruiting but would only hold vacancies for six months, meaning I could not apply until I was closer to discharge.

The competition was fierce. After initial clearance from the vetting procedure, I had to sit the entrance exam. There were five test papers (four on English and one on Maths). There was a medical and then an assessment day during which the remaining twelve candidates were put through our paces. The day started with some fitness tests in the gymnasium followed by a sprint around the 'Oval' at Abbey Park. By commando standard, that aspect was a breeze.

We then had to act out various role-plays in problematic scenarios. One of these involved getting everyone across an acid river using three barrels, two wooden planks and a length of rope. Under the watchful eyes of our assessors, everyone was trying to impress by appointing themselves as leader. While they were all squabbling with each other, I focussed on solving the problem and was the first to present a solution. It was a ferry, propelled by the manual rotation of upright barrels. The crossing required two crew and could carry only one passenger on each trip. It was time-consuming but worked. We didn't even need the rope. As soon as I set foot on the opposite bank, I was silenced by one of the staff and my fellow applicants were challenged to continue without me. They abandoned my system in favour of an alternative but all died in the river. From my perspective, that was a positive start.

We then had to deliver a prepared ten-minute presentation. With the imminent privatisation of the industry, I chose 'water' as my subject. How to get the precious liquid in a survival situation. I knew that the solar still would captivate my audience. We then had to talk ad-lib for five minutes on a random topic thrown at us by one of the staff.

Most of the afternoon was taken up by interviews. With only one panel to focus on each individual, the other eleven candidates were given concurrent activity. We all had to write our biographies (a test that would give an indication of our evidential statement writing abilities).

When it was my turn for questioning, they absolutely tore me to pieces. It wasn't an interview, it was a verbal confrontation which pushed and provoked me. I was caught completely off guard but responded quite calmly. I came out of the room, white as a sheet, knowing that I had failed. I was gutted.

When the day drew to an end, they thanked everyone for coming and told us that we would be called out of the classroom, one by one, to receive our verdicts. I knew that they would call out the unsuccessful applicants first and I hoped to be the last to leave. First to be called was Geoff. I was shocked. He had been a really good bloke. If the police didn't want him, what chance had I got? I contemplated my next move. If I joined the USMC, I could get American citizenship. Uncle Sam beckoned.

Then they called me. My heart sank and my face filled with the embarrassment of my rejection, but out in the corridor they told me they were giving me 'the benefit of the doubt'. Geoff had made it, I had made it, but the rest had failed. Phew.

I queried their aggressive interview tactics and the panel apologised but said it was all designed to see how I coped. Most of the others hadn't been exposed to this type of onslaught. Their fates were already decided and they hadn't even reached that final assessment. It had certainly been a tough, mentally draining test and we all laughed about it.

After a final interview on 17th November 1989, I was formally offered the position. I would join after another winter in Norway. As a constable, my starting salary was equivalent to a Royal Marines sergeant. With allowances and overtime payments I would be receiving almost a 100% pay rise. Confident that I would have guaranteed work for the next thirty years, I planned to settle in Leicester.

In later life that would annoy me. From our regular foursome at 3 BAS, Taff had joined the Marines, left and became a firefighter in Weymouth. Spike from Manchester became a paramedic in Yeovil. Nick would initially stay the service, get promoted and earn a chest-full of medals before transferring to the Royal Navy as an officer. He now commutes from France. I was from Leicester and had come back. I'm still here.

I returned to Leicester most weekends, became a regular at The Golf

Range bar and started to make new friends. I met up with some old ones too. Kim was a girl I knew from school. She was dating Eddie and I knew him, originally from the Marine Cadets. He had gone on to join the regulars and had been in the same class as Shane Booth. Unfortunately, Eddie had fallen from the Tarzan course and damaged his ankle. After many months of rehabilitation he was medically discharged. He was now in the Paras but regularly home on leave. Kim's older brother, Sean, was previously in the TA and so I now had local friends with things in common.

After Karen, I had refused to commit to a serious relationship. Finding a woman wasn't difficult but the constant spectre of a short notice deployment meant planning a future was problematic. With my new career now pencilled in, I was ready to settle down with a partner. Through Sean, I met Karen number 2. She had many positive attributes and we soon hit it off. She had three jobs, working Monday to Friday in a factory, several nights as a barmaid and weekends as a taxi controller. She could hold her own in an argument, had a good sense of humour and liked me. I was quite impressed.

I hadn't managed to shake off the name 'Shina from Les-tah wiv no letta' because it resumed when I was reunited with Nick. Karen would soon change that. In Norway, mail didn't arrive every day. It was perhaps once or twice a week. The troops would gather round, hoping for their names to be called by the holder of the mail sack who read out the details on letters and parcels. In previous years they'd shout:

"Shina!"

I'd run up, excited about receiving unexpected mail. Before I could open what I had been handed, the announcer would say:

"Give that to Taff!"

Everyone would laugh. Except me.

This year was different. Not only was Karen sending me letters, she was sending magazines, food parcels and had even got regulars from the pub to drop me the occasional line.

The announcer was shouting:

"Shina, Shina again, Shina again."

In the end he just dumped everything on the pool table and told me to help myself.

I thought Karen was great. As soon as I had left the Marines, we moved in together, sharing a rented house with yet another woman called Sue.

Chapter 10.

PC 1597

My Marines service ended on 24th April 1990. Just six days later I was sworn in as a constable with Leicestershire Police. A couple of admin days at the brand-new FHQ in Narborough were followed by about four weeks at Blackbird Road Depot. After various classroom exercises they sent us out into the community for a series of attachments.

I spent day secondments with a victims of crime charity, a mental health organisation and a funeral directors. I hadn't ever seen an actual dead body before but that visit prepared me well for the eighteen deaths I encountered during my career. The most horrific was a teenage suicide. He had slashed his own wrists and throat in a hotel room but I am not prepared to describe that macabre scene further. For the next few months, his self-inflicted wounds reappeared on my own forearms causing me to grimace and clench my eyes shut until I could conjure up a less harrowing image. Most were just elderly people who had collapsed or died naturally but there were a couple of hangings, a horrendous chainsaw decapitation, a park-bench vagrant who despite being dead vomited when I moved him and a heartbreaking cot death.

Another was reported by neighbours on the St Matthews Estate. My nose soon found the source of the mysterious foul smell. I entered the flat to find a rotting corpse lying on a mattress. All the windows were shut and the flies were buzzing around. His skin had turned black. The ears and nose and lips had been eaten away by maggots. Was this a natural death or a crime scene? It was standard practice to roll the deceased to look for a knife in the back. As I moved him his body separated. Some of it stuck to the mattress and the rest remained in my hands. I needed to retch and ran outside holding my breath.

I could cope with the visual aspect, but my lungs rejected the putrid air.

It clung to me. When my sergeant arrived, I fumigated myself with one of his cigarettes. I couldn't stop itching and it felt like bad air was crawling all over me. We completed our tasks at the scene and then moved on to the next job.

That evening I attended Gordon Banks' testimonial football match at Filbert Street. I got to see Gary Lineker play in a Leicester shirt. He didn't manage a goal but what a day.

After Blackbird Road it was ten weeks at Ryton Police College which culminated with England's semi-final defeat to Germany during Italia 90. I was devastated and disconsolate. That was the Thursday night. I was collected by Barry, Dawn (from the pub) and Karen the next day. We were off to Cornwall for a long weekend via the 'high-low section' once more.

My car had recently been written off. Parked outside Karen's parents' house, it had been crashed into by an underage and therefore uninsured driver. I'd later salvage what I could from the MK2 Escort and buy a same model replacement old banger.

I hadn't enjoyed my time at Ryton. Some of the new teaching methods were bizarre and I was learning very little. We had to sit around in a circle and discuss feelings and perceptions. It wasn't dynamic enough for me and I was frustrated by the lack of legal input and clarity.

Being ex-military, I was tasked with training the class to march and perform drill. At the end of the course there were various competitions between the six classes. My lot took the trophy for this category.

Arriving at Charles Street Police Station was much better. I soon realised that I could do this job. I was a natural. My life experience so far enabled me to build a rapport and communicate well with criminals. It was exciting working in the city and for the most part, I enjoyed my career. Job politics and senior officers were my only negative episodes.

One of the worst early incidents occurred when I was off-duty. It was mid-morning on a summer's day. I had an old kayak on my roof rack and was making my way to the river for some 'me time'. I came across a car that had struck a tree. The bonnet was crumpled and there was steam hissing from the engine. The doors were open and the windscreen was smashed.

I pulled over to make a further inspection. As I got out of my car a teenage girl approached me, walking with her arms outstretched like an 'Egyptian mummy'. "Help me," she whimpered.

Her face was covered in blood and she couldn't see. I put my arm around her and sat her down against a wall. The blood was pouring from her head but I had no first-aid kit. My T-shirt was clean; that would have to do. With the improvised dressing, I applied pressure to her wounds and reassured her. A neighbour came out and I tasked him with calling for an ambulance.

The girl asked about her injuries. I told her she was fine and that I'd seen much worse. I lied. Her face was split open; a deep diagonal laceration from her forehead, across the bridge of her nose and through her eye. Her eyeball resembled a hard-boiled egg that had been sliced open. An image I have never been able to erase.

She had taken unauthorised absence from school with some of her friends. The unqualified driver had borrowed his parents' car and lost control. My casualty had been the front-seat passenger and had not been wearing a seatbelt when they'd crashed. Her head had gone through the windscreen and she was lucky to be alive. Her young friends had ran off in panic, leaving her behind.

The ambulance arrived quite quickly, as did some of my colleagues. My day on the river was cancelled as I had to make a witness statement about this crime scene. I was never an enthusiastic 'traffic cop', but it is this kind of experience that justifies a penalty ticket for those who choose to break the law by not wearing a seatbelt.

By the time Karen and I realised we didn't particularly like each other, it was too late. We were trapped with a mortgage to our small two-bedroom house at 45 Huntsmans Way, Rushey Mead, and Karen was pregnant. I'm not sure why we stayed together. Maybe I didn't want her to bring up my daughter on her own. Maybe I didn't want my daughter to be an only child. We agreed to work at our relationship and carried on.

When the contractions came, I drove Karen to the General Hospital. With each jolt or kick she would curse, "Oh ya cow bags!" I laughed and asked, "What are cow bags?" She said it was better than swearing. She was unable to maintain that composure, however. When the head finally appeared I was stood at her side. She suddenly lashed out and gripped my groin while screaming, "Ya fucking bastaaard!!!"

Kids are often named after older family members. My daughter was no exception. She would be named after Hannah Snell who was the only ever female Royal Marine (there are many now in the Band Service). Hannah arrived in January 1992. No trouble really. If she cried I'd dump her in the bouncy chair in front of the tumble dryer. She'd soon nod off.

I married her mother that September. The wedding was a real soap opera and the guest list proved very problematic. The bride's father worked for BT. Our reception venue, the BT Social Club, could host 120 guests. 80 of these would be people I felt obliged to invite. On paper, I alone had four mothers, two fathers, three brothers and six sisters.

There was my foster mother, my real mother and my dad's new wife Janice (my new stepmother). There was Paul and my dad. There were Karen's mum and dad. So when the photographer asked for both sets of parents… Talk about awkward. No one could decide where to stand.

Most weddings involve two families. Ours involved four and the choice of guests would offend at least one corner. Why is she a bridesmaid instead of her? That sort of thing. It was simply a farce. If there was ever to be a next time, I'd get married on a beach with a couple of witnesses and just let everyone know afterwards.

We had the night in the Holiday Inn and then came home. We couldn't afford a proper honeymoon but later had a weekend in a B&B at Mablethorpe.

Back at work, officers in need of urgent assistance used the code word 'TEN NINE'. On hearing this, fellow officers would drop whatever they were doing and stampede towards their beleaguered colleague. It wasn't heard very often, but when it was uttered you could expect the sirens and blue lights.

I met Hagrid at the family courts on Lee Circle. His children were being taken from him, to be placed in care. During his angry protestations, he had threatened the prosecutor, and consequently the judge sentenced him to six months' imprisonment, to take effect on completion of the day's hearing. I alone was sent to be the escorting officer. On conclusion of the session, I called for transportation but during our wait, Hagrid fled. He was halfway down the stairs before I noticed. I leapt over the railings and dived onto his shoulders. Together we tumbled down the staircase but he was first to his feet and ran out of the front doors. With superior speed and fitness, I had caught him within seconds, but what was I supposed to do next? The long-haired and bearded 7-footer looked down at me as I tried to pin him against the side of a lorry.

"Tell them I got away," he growled. I shook my head. "I can't do that," I said.

I had a truncheon but my hands were already being used. I had loose link chain handcuffs but stood no chance of applying them. I had a radio but couldn't yet press the button.

I looked up at him and waited for the blow that would surely render me unconscious thereby breaking this stalemate. He simply pushed me aside instead and started running again. They say that 'the bigger they are, the harder they fall'. I rugby-tackled his ankles and he went down. A police judo arm lock was my overly optimistic intended next move but he had grabbed my testicles by that point.

"TEN NINE, TEN NINE, TEN NINE... LEE CIRCLE!" I shouted in a rather high-pitched voice.

I was soon assisted by two workmen and together we were able to restrain my prisoner until the reinforcements arrived. My street neighbour, Val, had been on Lee Circle with her two small sons. They had all witnessed the drama unfold. Chris and Gareth later recounted to the other kids on our street that I was a policeman and they'd seen me arrest a *giant*.

My first near-death experience happened that year. One dark November evening on foot patrol around the St Matthews Estate, I came across a young lad sat in the driver's seat of a Cortina. The door lock was damaged and there was a screwdriver in the ignition. He explained that it had been stolen previously but had not yet been repaired. I didn't believe him and went to remove the screwdriver. There was a struggle during which he managed to start the engine and put it in gear. The car started to pick up speed with me still leaning in through the open window wrestling the driver. I couldn't get out and I couldn't get in. As the engine strained, calling for the gear change, the car shot across the T-junction and mounted the pavement before crashing through a brick wall.

The impact catapulted me into the car. I bounced off the inside windscreen and landed upside down in the pitch-black front passenger footwell. I remember thinking, this is the point where my life flashes before me, and that is exactly what happened. My last thought was of my baby daughter. Now it was just dark, quiet and still. Was I dead?

No, his hand was holding me down while he tried to kick open his now jammed door to flee. A voice in my head shouted, *Get him!* and I sprang back into life. A quick sprint along Manitoba Road and I had him on the ground. He was shouting to people for assistance. "Get him off me!" I'd lost my radio and couldn't call for back-up but fortunately someone had heard the crash and dialled 999. Within minutes blue lights came screeching round the corner.

The car was indeed an outstanding stolen vehicle but it was now a write-off. The teenager was charged with 'aggravated vehicle taking' but got a slapped wrist. I had torn my jumper, ripped my trousers, grazed my knee and broken some ribs. I didn't know it yet but I had also broken two discs in my neck.

I woke up next morning in my bedroom, looking up at the ceiling. I was stuck. I wasn't paralysed but any attempt to move my head would cause a severe piercing pain. An emergency doctor was called.

It was explained that the shock-absorbing discs between each vertebrae are like chocolate Rolos. They have a hard outer shell and a soft gel centre. The cracked discs had been seeping that gel since last night's impact and were by now squashed flat. Consequently the neighbouring vertebrae had altered position and were pressing on nerves.

Until now, I had gone two and a half years without a single day of sick leave but that record was over. This injury would need ten years of treatment before becoming tolerable. It required a neck brace, painkillers, neck-stretching physiotherapy and many breathtakingly painful injections to my spine. It would cause me sleeping problems for the rest of my life. Orthopaedic pillows did not help. I have to alter position frequently. It made watching TV painful and turning to check over my shoulder when driving very troublesome. One hard knock or even a bad night's sleep could put me out of action for days. Real life is not like the movies. If you get hurt, you stay hurt. Surgery to remove the damaged discs and fuse together the vertebrae would have meant a medical discharge. It looked like my career was already over but fortunately I was eventually saved by a physiotherapist.

Callum was planned but the pregnancy was problematic. In the early weeks Karen had a heavy discharge of blood and we were told we'd lost him. A subsequent scan revealed he was still very much alive but the placenta was only partially attached. Karen would not be allowed any heavy work and had to take things easy. That was difficult with our small baby Hannah. After several more weeks of our combined best efforts, there was more bleeding. We were booked in for a termination and were both upset but then a faint heartbeat was detected. He was still in there, but the placenta had torn away from the wall of the womb and was hardly hanging on at all. We still had three months to go. To ensure he got nourishment Karen drank two pints of full-fat milk daily. We hung on by our fingernails expecting a premature birth. Against all odds, we went full term and eventually he needed to be induced.

He emerged, let out a faint squeal and then went silent. The General Hospital staff were running around frantic. They threw Callum around like a doll and then laid him upside down before ramming a tube into his throat. He urinated all over them as they worked. He had swallowed too much amniotic fluid. A nurse told me this was perfectly normal but Karen and I knew it wasn't. We feared the worst. They wrapped up the little bundle and placed him in a clear glass crib with a heat lamp overhead. After a few minutes it looked to me like he was being sunburnt so I removed him. The little champ had survived.

Unfortunately that rapid first aid irritated his throat and he was very awkward to feed. He would cry because he was hungry but couldn't swallow. I would get up to do my share of the night feeds but whereas that was only a twenty-minute job with Hannah, it could take two to three hours with Callum. I had work to go to and couldn't accommodate this protracted routine. I never once managed and would lose patience. His mother was much better at this. They bonded. We didn't.

In December 1994 we bought a three-bed semi-detached in East Goscote. I was back. We lost a bit of money on the sale but saved a lot more on the purchase, so that was OK. We loved the house and the big back garden with a couple of sheds. We'd had four cats in the quiet cul-de-sac of Huntsmans Way. Sadly we'd lose two of those to the busy roads at our new house. There was plenty of grass for our rabbits and I got a dog. Victoria Chantelle was a very naughty Collie cross.

I sat in the back garden the following summer, watching the sun go down. I looked at my life, what I had achieved, where I was and what I had got. I liked my job and my house. I had a son, a daughter, a car, a camcorder, pets and even a kayak. There was a can of beer in my hand and a loyal dog at my side. I was still unhappy. I didn't love my wife. There was no one else, but we were about done. We'd lasted six years. She didn't love me either so it was not devastating news when we discussed our separation.

Access to my kids wasn't a problem but the maintenance would cripple me. The CSA formula would only take account of my accommodation charges if I could produce a rent book or mortgage statement. Still paying the five-year loan to cover what we'd lost on the first house sale meant I was penniless and nomadic. I couldn't afford to rent or buy so they hit me with the full amount.

I left the house on 4th July 1995. Independence Day.

Chapter 11.

Front Line

'Attitude Reflects Leadership'

- Remember the Titans

Life was a bit harder now but I would slowly get back on top. My workplace was the inner city St Matthews Estate and my base was a small satellite station in one of the council buildings. It was an extremely busy beat for a police officer. It was only 1 square mile but home to about 2,000 residents living in high-rise towers blocks or two-tier maisonettes. Approximately one-third of the local population would move each year from what was regarded as a stepping stone or temporary accommodation. Most didn't want to live there. My daily contact was usually with the weak, vulnerable or poorly educated. There were supposed to be five of us allocated to this problem area but cutbacks had shrunk our number to just two and we worked alternate shifts, rarely seeing each other face to face, like ships in the night.

When I was on duty, the control room would dispatch me to jobs via the radio or telephone. When I was off duty, they would send jobs for my attention to our fax. Woe betide I ever took a day off. Returning to the office, I would regularly be greeted by endless, unravelled fax scroll, spilling out across the floor in scenes reminiscent of a raid by the Andrex puppy. I could bat off some minor jobs through local knowledge, and a police mountain bike enabled me to rush between incidents, but I could never clear the backlog. The incessant juggling of priorities was exhausting and mentally draining. I had served there for almost five years but by now, living on my own, this constant pressure from a more than doubled workload and isolation from the real world was driving me crazy so I requested a transfer to Asfordby Street.

My move met with some resistance from the locals but it had little to do with my popularity. It was the fact that we were already massively understaffed, and allowing yet another officer to depart demonstrated a lack of serious police commitment to that community. As chair of the St Matthews Tenants Association, Jean Williams MBE was the loudest voice from the residents. She graciously consented to my move on welfare grounds (I was going through a divorce) but as a trade-off St Matthews suddenly became a policing priority and was promptly boosted back up to full strength with a new neighbourhood team. Well done, Jean; you managed to achieve what no one else could.

Asfordby Street Police Station was just up the road. It was an old fire station on a terraced street in the Highfields area. It was perhaps one of the toughest places to work in Leicester. People often celebrate my home city for being 'multicultural' but certainly back then it was not as Utopian as they suggested. There was some integration success in the suburbs but the inner city was actually carved up into zones. Birds of a feather, I suppose. Belgrave was for the Indians (mostly Hindu or Sikh), the Poles had settled in the West End, St Matthews would soon become home to the Somalians, and white people lived in Braunstone or Northfields. Caribbean folk had originally dominated the St Peters Estate in Highfields but their numbers were dwindling as Asian Muslims had become the main population. There was always some tension in Highfields and it was certainly not harmonious. This area was renowned for drugs, guns, robbery and prostitution, making it a very challenging yet exciting place to work.

It was around this time that the police service had been formally slated for being 'institutionally racist'. That was utter nonsense. Every officer knew on joining that; racism, sexism, dishonesty or use of excessive force would lead to almost certain dismissal. I was offended by that defamatory remark. It didn't reflect my attitude or any of my colleagues. We had joined to do some good and catch the bad guys. It didn't matter what colour or religion they were. I was not a racist. I couldn't be. At school I had been the ethnic minority. In an average class of thirty pupils, only two or three would be white and most of my school friends were a different colour to me. I had been given an award for a charity run that raised funds for the famine victims of Ethiopia in the mid-1980s. I had served as an equal with black military personnel and the Gurkhas. I was perhaps almost colour-blind through sustained exposure and it seemed unnatural to me that the attitudes of some still lagged behind. Certainly with my experience as a local boy brought up in care I felt some immunity from such a besmirchment. That gave me a freedom to operate less hindered by fear of negative perceptions.

Some officers had to tiptoe or shy away from potentially racially-sensitive situations. They didn't feel they had the support of management and were unable to do their job properly. They would express a desire to move to other stations, away from potential accusations. I agree that there was some ignorance. Officers recruited from outside the region might not appreciate the difference between a Sikh, Hindu or Muslim but with a default setting of trying to treat everyone the same, how relevant should that be? In response to the unfair labelling, senior officers and politicians were desperately trying to improve race relations, but in a bid to be seen as 'not racist', they actually went the other way. It's true, minority groups were under-represented but that was not because of the recruitment policy. It was partly a cultural thing, where potential candidates feared being disowned or rejected by their various ethnic or ancestral kin. I had a lot of respect for those black or Asian officers who had joined before me. They were committed professionals with a thick skin and strength of character. They were certainly competent as they had joined a predominantly white workforce and being so few in number exposed them to perhaps unfair scrutiny.

Ian Harding was the epitome. He was always first to volunteer for the dangerous jobs or to help those needing assistance. He rescued me so many times that I came to look upon him as a kind of guardian angel or invincible big brother. He was more than just a role model for black people. I and many others aspired to be as good as him. That alone demonstrated a forward momentum towards racial equality. Leicestershire Police were in fact leading the way.

However, the knee-jerk reaction was to switch from merit to mass and thereby create a genetically modified police force. There was a proactive campaign to encourage more applicants from minority backgrounds. In principle that was a good idea but in practice, it brought an obsession of allocating available posts to an even wider diversity. These were desperate times and the organisation wanted visible results, fast. Consequently they would take almost anyone meeting that description. Inevitably, the standards dropped but then there were concerns about discrimination against white recruits, so they dropped the standard for them too.

Things got quite messy. Some sergeants even lost the ability to deploy shift members without risking accusation of being insensitive to an individual's personal circumstances. This problem hadn't existed before but led to the more versatile officers being unfairly burdened. There was a lot of resentment but it wasn't just prompted by colour or race. They also felt the need to unveil people with disabilities or illness. We had officers who struggled to read or write and others who were unable to work night shifts, prompting the question: why had I been subjected to four English exams and a medical? This was the police force, for goodness sake. Cops work nights and do a lot of paperwork. Everybody knows that. Some (not all) of our new staff weren't fit for purpose but this pursuit of fashionable quotas meant that they would be retained at all costs. Some received extended training and others were hidden away to perform simple office functions. It was embarrassing, frustrating and demoralising. To use a football analogy, I was working hard to try and win every game but the management's tactics and some of its signings made me question whether or not I was at the right club.

Getting the best people was a lesser priority now, the main emphasis was on transforming workforce demographics. Quite how that could be achieved fairly I don't know but taking on more white officers wasn't a solution. This motive certainly contradicted the principle of equal opportunities. I accept there was imbalance and a need for change but evolution was already taking care of that at a natural pace. Accelerating that change through targeted recruitment was divisive and undermined the hard work of those minority officers who had joined before. There is obviously a significant difference in quality between a candidate who chooses to apply and goes through the system unaided against a pass or fail assessment, in contrast to a candidate who is invited to apply and goes through with a full range of support and guaranteed success. It will come as no surprise that some of these new officers were rapidly promoted outside their level of competence. They weren't proper cops, they were celebrities, and carrying them as passengers meant extra work for the rest of us.

Another unwelcome side effect of this less rigorous selection was the psyche of recruits. My generation and those that came before me were typically 'full-career professionals', looking to serve and at the same time develop new skills. We were long-term investments. Consequently, shifts had a wealth of experience and there was an abundance of best practice advice. Many of the new batch were 'uncommitted short-stint amateurs' with no real interest beyond adding a line to bolster their CV. To leave the service meant giving just two weeks' notice. Many left when the novelty wore off, others when the bubble-wrap was removed, exposing them to the harsh realities of policing. That surge in departures meant a frequent renewal of inexperienced officers, perpetuating a downward spiral of the blind leading the blind. The ensuing reduction in average career length created a skills shortage on operational shifts as well as a greater financial burden from training costs.

With my strong sense of fair play, I found this era quite worrying, but any dissent was regarded as bigoted. I guess we just needed to ride out this short-term chameleon propaganda and hope for the long-term greater good, but when I consider how difficult it had been for me to join only a few years earlier, this new trend of coaxing and nurturing desirable, yet often inadequate, candidates insulted my own achievement and short-changed the public.

It saddens me to speak of the service in this way but cops of all ranks are effectively gagged. Some may disagree, those from alternative vantage points might offer a different perspective, but this was certainly a commonly held view on the factory floor. I don't make this point to criticise any individual officers, they weren't to blame; after all, they simply took the jobs they were offered. I make the point in order to defend my profession from the original slur and highlight the detrimental impact of political interference.

By 2003, the government recognised that there were problems with retention, so they offered financial incentives to encourage people to stay. These included divisive and largely unattainable bonuses. It was too little too late. The damage was already done and the mess was entirely their making.

Then they said that we were disproportionately stopping black people. The statisticians labelled anyone who wasn't white as a being black, so even if you dealt with one white, one black, one Asian, one Oriental and one mixed race, you had demonstrated a propensity towards stopping non-whites. Furthermore, there was no allowance for those minorities that were actually stopped by minority officers. It was quite ridiculous, particularly as there were so few white people to even see in my policing area. In general terms, the Hindus and Muslims disliked each other intensely and there was similar bitterness between Africans and those from the Caribbean. Stuck in the middle, trying to act as referees, were the police. When fighting erupted between the various factions; the victims, witnesses, suspects and offenders were all of an ethnic minority. What was I supposed to do? Deliberately seek out white people to balance the figures? This was quite simply a by-product of mass immigration but it's always easier to cry police prejudice.

It didn't stop there though. Instead of focussing on police work we were sent out as data collectors. At one point we had to record every single encounter with a member of the public. The time, the date, the reason, the action taken, their details, including how they described their ethnic appearance. What this meant was that instead of casually reminding someone to wear their seatbelt or put on their headlights because it was dark, I now had to formally stop them and complete a survey form. Cops are supposed to interact with the public but this burden of paperwork at each contact was enough to make you want to avoid everyone.

Successive governments had promised to reduce bureaucracy but would always overload us with even more unnecessary tasks. One example was having to fill out daily questionnaires of how our time had been spent. On an eight-hour shift, that might mean the last half hour was wasted on another data form. The results might satisfy some office-dwelling academic but did nothing to improve our operational effectiveness.

Management became less interested in us being a law enforcement agency and started to run the service like a business. They even rolled out customer satisfaction surveys. They were more concerned about perceptions. It was better to be able to say that we had answered 999 calls swiftly, response times were on target and complaints were down, rather than perform any dynamic action or problem-solving that might provoke negative press. I hated this apathetic and misguided culture.

Illegally parked cars outside the mosque for Friday prayers were exempt from parking fines and officers were ordered not to arrest black people during the Caribbean Carnival. In my experience, the relevant communities were not requesting preferential treatment but as an organisation we were cowering under political pressure. This riled me. Why should one section of a population be given lawless days? What happened to 'unbiased policing' and acting 'without fear or favour' in a 'firm but fair' manner?

These were bad and hypocritical policies. The public usually accepted police intervention when they understood why it had happened. There was a mosque opposite our station and it was often the case that we would rush out of the offices in response to an emergency call only to find our police cars were boxed in. I wasn't particularly bothered about the weed smoke blown directly into my face at the carnival but drug-taking was not permitted at the music festivals in Donnington or indeed at any other occasion and the same conditions should have applied here. They didn't, and in my mind this disparity was not only unjust but also unnecessary. In essence, the 'softly softly approach' jeopardised our authority and created harder working conditions. A rule for one and a different rule for another was not a level playing field.

Crime statistics were one of the biggest deceptions. The service was under constant scrutiny and facing ever increasing demands for accountability. Everybody knew that drug addictions were the root cause of most burglaries, street robberies or theft from vehicles but certainly at senior management level there was a reluctance to allocate resources for drug enforcement.

The crime figures actually come from two sources: there are those offences reported by victims, and the offences discovered by police officers (e.g. drugs, guns, knives). The easiest way to reduce recorded crime is to take cops off the street. If there were no police patrols today, the only crime recorded would be that reported by the public. This is just one of the tricks that enables the government to boast of falling crime levels despite savage cuts to police numbers. The offences are out there but no one is dealing with them. Falling crime might sound good on a party election broadcast but hiding the truth under the carpet will eventually hurt us all.

It was the same sorry story about prisons. The cops had filled them to bursting point but the government's response to overcrowding was to stop locking people up and let others out early. That is such a kick in the teeth to those trying to clear up the neighbourhood and make people feel safe. I had one guy who admitted taking more than ninety vehicles. He was given a supervision order. I had spent many hours doing surveillance to catch this chap. What was the point?

I could probably write a whole book about what was wrong with the service but in the interests of variety and brevity I will share just a few more examples. I should re-emphasise that this was the mid-1990s and quite how much of this description applies to the modern-day police is for others to decide.

As a public service that made no profit, our budget was always under strain. When I first joined, shifts would overlap, enabling a period for briefings and or the handing over of incidents. If, for example, a complicated job was reported at 3.30pm and I was due to finish at 4pm, the control room would preferably dispatch someone rostered to finish their tour later in the day, thereby avoiding overtime payments. Shift patterns regularly evolved to try and satisfy greater demand with increasingly fewer resources. The shift overlap eventually disappeared altogether, meaning that officers would regularly be dispatched to incidents just seconds before they were due to go home. Staff initially responded to this with goodwill. Many of us arrived at work half an hour before we were due to clock on and that meant that in some cases we could act as an early relief, but inevitably this lack of cover saw a rise in overtime claims.

The government's response to the increased running costs was to suggest that we were performing 'Spanish practices' (hardly a politically correct term). They said that we were deliberately becoming involved with incidents at the end of our shifts in order to claim overtime and consequently we would no longer be paid for the first thirty minutes of any such occurrence. This caused absolute outrage and diminished the previous goodwill gestures by us early arrivals. We weren't the ones claiming for duck houses or second homes. We just expected to be paid for the hours we worked.

On one occasion I requested replacement uniform trousers from the stores department at HQ. They sent me the wrong size so I telephoned to arrange a return and correction of my order. The moron on the other end of the line insisted that instead of sending them back for an exchange, it would be 'easier' for me to attend HQ with the garments and allow the seamstress to make the necessary alterations. WTF?!

Perhaps the most infuriating incident was the chief constable's carol service. In a time of early austerity, we were told to save money by sending internal memos on scraps of paper rather than official printed forms and to use Sellotape or reusable treasury tags instead of staples. I arrived at work one day in December. The payslips had been delivered, and stapled to each one was a folded sheet of A4 paper. On this was a printed invitation to the carol service. With approximately 2,000 cops and an equal number of civilian staff, that meant 4,000 sheets of printed A4 and 4,000 staples, most of which went directly into the bin.

The 'Solutions' team had been set up at HQ to encourage staff to offer suggestions on cost-saving opportunities or measures to improve operational effectiveness. Absolutely incensed, I submitted an eloquent report detailing my concerns over this recent misallocation of taxpayer-funded resources. I suggested that future invitations could be more economically distributed via e-mail or voicemail. For my innovative proposal, I was invited to attend an award ceremony to receive a certificate and a gift.

I boycotted the ceremony, opting to go out on patrol instead. My certificate arrived through the internal mail and went straight in the bin. The gift, a leather conference folder, was a useful piece of kit and ought to have been routinely issued. I still have it. The following December, invitations to the carol service were printed on another 4,000 sheets of A4 and stapled to our payslips. I could have screamed.

I was accused of being racist a few times. The first was by Mr Parmar.

He was banned from driving but I caught him behind the wheel on nine occasions inside of three months. If the courts had dealt with him properly the first time, I would not have needed to keep arresting him. He lived on my beat so it was inevitable that I was the officer most likely to spot him breaking the law. I was interviewed by Professional Standards and as good as told to patrol with my eyes shut.

Smith was another. He was an illegal immigrant supporting his stay through sales of crack cocaine. I had him removed on four occasions but he always managed to re-enter through our porous border. He later conceded: "Him not racist but him do him job too well." I personally took that as a compliment.

I found this age of so-called 'equal opportunities' and 'political correctness' very frustrating. Constantly being asked to do more with less, I soon became disillusioned, pessimistic and cynical. Many of us had started out with good intentions and enthusiasm but would eventually succumb to the reality that we were simply pawns in the government's game. Those of us trying to make a difference were overly exposed to internal discipline, in contrast to the small minority of slackers doing a bare minimum. All that negativity caused me to consider returning to the Marines. I went to re-enlist but was dissuaded by the recruiting officer. The Corps was in similar decline and he assured me I was better to stay put.

I arrived at Asfordby Street towards the end of 1995. One of the side streets was called Woodhill. It was a steep slope of approximately 30 degrees and was roughly 100 metres long. I would do sprint training on this stretch. Timing my runs, I would dart to the top then jog back down, compose myself and repeat. I normally made the rapid ascent five times before collapsing at the top. The steep gradient meant I had to work the arms harder and the heel impact was less severe or damaging than sprinting on a flat surface.

I would be bent over on the pavement gasping for air and occasionally the corner shopkeeper would rush out to check on my welfare. He was an elderly Muslim gentleman. He would approach saying, "Sir, sir, are you OK? Do you need an ambulance?" Bless him.

The effect of this exercise was that I was buzzing off endorphins for the rest of my shift. I was at the peak of my fitness and I was actually quite fast. I soon had a reputation for catching those who fled on foot.

1996 was chaotic. At the beginning of the year I injured my calf. I had ran after a suspect along London Road. When I caught him, we wrestled on the snow-covered ground. In doing so I tore my calf muscle in three places. It was shredded internally and there was some horrific bruising. I couldn't walk and was sent home. The problem was, I had no home to go to, so I convalesced at Taff's house in Weymouth.

That April, I arrested a robbery suspect who was high on crack cocaine. He didn't wish to come quietly and we fought in the street. I saw stars after falling backwards and bashing my head on the corner of a wall. My left shoulder was yanked from its socket damaging all the muscle groups and my right hand was broken during the tussle. It was an exhausting battle and I was lucky not to have been stabbed by the knife he was carrying. I got him though, and still turned up for work the next night. With one arm in a sling and the other dangling quite useless, I was ordered home. I borrowed money from the bank and flew to Majorca to recover in the sunshine. I couldn't even slice or butter my bread bun from the in-flight meal but the nice lady next to me kindly obliged.

The shoulder needed many injections before it regained function but would be significantly weaker and vulnerable from then on. It also created further problems with sleeping positions. The right hand still hurts today, especially when cold, and my handwriting suffers as a result.

I was on permanent night shifts throughout the Euro 96 football tournament. I patrolled the city bars in a riot van. There were a few sporadic scuffles but nothing major. Gascoigne scored a wonderful goal against Scotland but we crashed out in the semi-finals to Germany. Déjà vu. Football was not coming home.

'Front line' was the name given to Guthlaxton Street by the local gangsters. It was a well-established focal point for the rebel youth and they considered it to be a 'police no go area'. Operation Wallaby would end that. I was chosen to be one of the regular wandering patrols deliberately targeting that street.

The man who had injured my shoulder and hand that April was once more a wanted individual. He had robbed a service station and struck the cashier on the head with a house brick. There was a warrant out for his arrest. It took me by surprise to see him casually walking down the street. I made the necessary checks and confirmed that his arrest was required. I was quite apprehensive now as I'd got seriously hurt last time. I approached him alone and tried to talk him into compliance. He made it quite clear that he was not going to co-operate and threatened to put me in hospital.

I called for backup and we fought all over again. This one-on-one snowballed into a mini riot. His supporters got involved and even more backup was called. There were scraps taking place all over Guthlaxton Street. My prisoner and three other violent men were eventually secured before we withdrew from the area.

Reassurance patrols were conducted for the remainder of the evening. Back at the station I expected to be in trouble. I hadn't done anything wrong but I had stirred up a right hornets' nest. I was quite shocked to be praised by my inspector. Apparently, this was exactly what Operation Wallaby needed. The 'Front line' was finished.

The issuing of incapacitant spray was still a couple of years away but most patrol officers carried a side-handle baton at this stage. I didn't. The PR24 was too big and cumbersome when running after suspects. I carried my original-issue truncheon instead. I had never hit anyone with it but had smashed a few windows in emergency situations. The modern truncheon was of softer wood than earlier issues and mine snapped in half during a confrontation with a particularly aggressive Pot Noodle.

I filled out the paperwork for a replacement but my inspector, Neil Canham, was protecting his budget and didn't want to finance the reissue. By now close to retirement, he opened his desk drawer, removed his ancient hardwood truncheon and handed it to me. I was shocked but extremely honoured to inherit this heirloom. Canham was a great leader and like a father to me. He would often kick officers out the station and tell them to go and arrest someone. He was the kind of boss you wanted to work hard for. I'm not sure he shared the same sentiment, but to me, receiving that truncheon was like a ship's captain bestowing his sword. I still have it.

Shortly after that, I headed off for the ill-fated bike ride across Spain.

By autumn I had secured a new mortgage on the former matrimonial home. My ex-wife rented it from me while her new house purchase went through. She stayed in the village and I was back in the house by February of 1997. I had two lampshades, an old frying pan, a second-hand microwave and also my old camping stove and sleeping bag from the Marines. I would have to start over.

Things were a struggle. I sold the Golf but kept the veteran bike. I would start to date Leonie that August and life had plenty more drama in store.

I was twenty-eight years old and Leonie was a care nurse in an old people's home. She worked shifts and was quite mature in her attitude. It therefore came as a surprise that she was only sixteen and three-quarters.

She had the best face I had ever seen. She was half-Jamaican and looked a bit like Scary Spice; she dressed like her too. She lived in my policing area and clearly fancied me. I was reluctant to get involved as I felt uncomfortable with her age but I wouldn't be breaking the law if we dated. To my pleasant surprise we got on well and had a lot of fun.

It was an unusual time in my life. Having a house meant the CSA had to take account of my living costs. They also reduced my maintenance because Hannah and Callum could now stay at mine as part of the shared access arrangements. I was coping with that aspect.

I wasn't coping with my work. I was having a lot of success but that was partly down to my crazy 'Mel Gibson's Lethal Weapon' attitude. I was a 'pyscho nutcase cop', completely indifferent to my personal safety and people were concerned about working with me. What danger would I expose them to? At the station I was known as 'Mad Bloke'.

One incident tipped the balance. 'Operation Design' was an anti-robbery initiative in the city centre. Officers were handpicked from the central stations to blitz the streets for three months. There was a detective inspector in charge and a team of detectives for the interviewing of suspects. The uniform officers amongst us were supposed to go out looking for bad guys. My crewmate was Ian Bradbury. He was a well-educated and athletic rugby player. He was confident, competent and capable. We hadn't worked together before but he had been the first to arrive at my TEN NINE with Hagrid some years earlier and we soon got to know and trust each other.

One day on patrol in Highfields, I saw a car being driven by a man who I recognised as being wanted for a shooting eighteen months earlier. I was very good with faces. I told my partner and we intended to play it low key. The suspect apologised for using his mobile phone while driving and for pulling over on double yellow lines. When I told him he was under arrest for the shooting, he denied being the said fugitive.

I was confident that I had correctly identified him, so he was coming in. It was early afternoon on a hot summer's day. He protested at my actions and then started to shout up at one of the open windows of a nearby house. Almost immediately, we were surrounded by a mob that tried to spring his release. One of us called for assistance by radio and within seconds I could hear the sirens. I held on to the suspect with my left hand but had others pulling me away by my right. At the same time, people were pulling him from me. One by one my fingers were prised away and he broke free of my grasp.

Like the winning side in a tug of war, they all fell backwards but the suspect jumped up to flee on foot. My right arm was still being held by his ally so I swung a left hook which took the chap by surprise and he let go.

I gave chase and followed the suspect as he ran through the churchyard and climbed over a barbed wire fence. This same fence would take a chunk of flesh from my right bicep and an even bigger chunk from his arm, but I still had him in sight. He ran through the rear garden of a terraced house, down the side alley and into the next street. I followed but temporarily lost sight of him.

I emerged from the alley to see him run in through the front door of a terraced house on the opposite side. The door was slammed shut behind him. It was impossible for me to cover the front and rear so I charged towards the door ready to kick it in. A young mum was stood outside holding a baby as she spoke to neighbours. She pleaded with me not to break the door as it was her house and she did not know the man who had just run inside. She offered to let me in and fumbled with her keys.

I believed her and I suspected my man would be fleeing via the back door. I ran down the alley and sure enough, there he was, leaping over the wall at the end of her yard. He crash-landed in the vegetable patch of the garden in the next row. The occupant had been tending his climbing beans but the bamboo canes cracked and snapped. Whilst the gardener was shouting at the intruder, I landed like some clumsy paratrooper, apologised and carried on chasing. The suspect knocked over all the bicycles in the side alley to delay my progress. It worked. When I got onto the next street, he had vanished. I looked left and right along the row of terraced houses but there was no trace. I laid down in the road to see if he was hiding under or behind parked cars but there was still no sign.

I cursed my luck. I hadn't been far behind. I had lost my radio, my arm was bleeding, my uniform was torn to shreds and the police van keys were missing. One of my colleagues later said that it looked as though I had smoked an exploding cigar. It was only at this point that I considered my partner. Had he put out a commentary on his radio? My direction of travel? Why had he not joined me on this foot pursuit?

I got back to the original scene. The van was still there and the keys were in the ignition. Bradders was fine and speaking to the cavalry. He had also recovered my radio that had fallen off during the struggle. Before I could speak, the police cars jetted off at high speed with the blue lights flashing.

My suspect had been so exhausted that he had hidden in someone's garden and the occupants had discovered him. He pleaded with the two Asian men to hide him as a 'fellow Muslim'. The men spoke briefly in their own tongue and took him inside. The Asian men were not followers of Islam and while one of them kept him talking, the other called 999. Within minutes our suspect was in handcuffs.

After being patched up at the Royal Infirmary and having a tetanus jab in my buttocks, my crewmate and I were celebrated as 'heroes of the day', but as we debriefed in the bar, the air was cleared. Bradders was quite shaken. I had abandoned him to fight the mob by himself and he had been well outnumbered. I hadn't fled from them, I had pursued what I perceived to be the main danger, but my partner had no idea where I was. The mob had prevented him from assisting me and I had left him in a frightening situation on his own. The results had been favourable that day but we had been lucky. It could have gone horribly wrong. My partner was somewhat smarter than me and intended to get married soon. He did not share my cavalier attitude towards life or death. The incident didn't ruin our friendship, it galvanised it, and we went on to become the most successful partnership of the operation, but I was firmly told that I had messed up.

It was a policewoman, Claire, who told me that I needed counselling. She could see right through my tough guy exterior and gave me a number to ring. It really hadn't occurred to me that I needed help but Claire had hit a nerve and convinced me to make the call. I locked myself in one of the offices and rang the number. I suddenly started trembling as I told the call-taker that I needed to talk. My appointment with counselling was arranged. I didn't know this at the time but I was apparently only days away from being ordered to go by my station inspector.

I wanted to get this over and done with as quickly as possible, so in preparation for the first meeting I started to write my biography. I got as far as Marilyn before breaking down in floods of tears. Where was all this pain coming from? Where had it been hiding all these years? This was a complete shock. I thought I had put all that behind me a long time ago but it had actually just continued bubbling under the surface. Having opened that box, I would now have to confront the dreaded demons.

At the first session, I explained that I was taking too many risks at work. I wasn't suicidal but I wasn't fussed about being killed either. I knew where the problem was. It was my life between four and eleven. I had hoped to deal with this unresolved childhood trauma in one session but Shirley didn't work like that. Her method was to start with where I was now, work slowly back to the beginning and then go forward again. This would mean a weekly visit for the next two months. By the halfway stage I was a total wreck. My insides had been completely ripped out all over again. On one of my days off, I just laid there in bed. I had no motivation to do anything. I was almost paralysed by depression. My heart hurt so much that I had thoughts about getting my old dagger and slowly rolling over onto it. It would mean certain death but at least the pain would stop. That was the ultimate low point. I had hit absolute rock bottom.

I was rescued by Leonie. She was an excellent listener and demonstrated wisdom beyond her years. She recommended meeting up with my dad. I took her advice and got in touch by telephone. Dad was reluctant at first and said he wasn't available. I don't know what made him change his mind but inside ten minutes he had called back and agreed to visit me the following evening.

Dad came over for a cup of tea and we cleared the air. He gave me many answers. My mum had told me that their divorce happened because he would just read the newspaper after work and she felt rejected. Dad's version was different. Mum had been having an affair with a police officer. Yes, my so-called 'Uncle Phil'. That made a lot of sense. He said the key decisions about me were down to child psychologists and Social Services. I told him that their conclusions had been wrong. We parted on friendly terms but would never have a relationship. I have seen him just twice since then, at family funerals.

I saw Uncle Phil at work from time to time. I hadn't realised he was the same person until my dad revealed his surname during our recent meeting. I don't think he knew who I was. Why should he? It was a long time ago and my name was Iain Wright now. It angered me and I thought about killing him. Eventually I gave way to reason. What good would that do? 'It takes two to tango' and my mum was as much to blame.

Counselling had been a revelation and raised a number of issues. How to deal with the past and how to go forward. I had some tough decisions to make. Who am I now? Who will I be in the future? Who is important to me?

It is somewhat ironic that my personality disorder is not derived from Marilyn. Yes, she exposed me to cruelty and I have some sad memories but that wicked behaviour was her flaw not mine. To some extent I can laugh it off. It toughened me up. In reality, I was maladjusted because of my early years in care. Unfortunately, those that meant well did irreparable damage.

My foster carers and Social Services weren't villains but their interventions were so off-target. They had found a cure for my suffering but now I was suffering because of their cure.

The whole 'Iain Wright' identity was fake. I was Iain Hollis. As part of my therapy I decided to change my name back by deed poll. I had no intention of rekindling old ties with a long-abandoned family but I was born a Hollis. That is who I am and will always be.

The mistakes of my past could not dictate my future. Associating with the close and extended Wright family was a reminder of the painful times and I would therefore have to burn those bridges too. That whole family had embraced me as one of their own. I am grateful, humbled and quite amazed by it all really. Inevitably, I inherited some positive characteristics and they can take part credit for the way I turned out. Fostering is not an easy job, especially dealing with damaged goods such as myself. What Lynne and Ivor tried to do for me was very noble. They couldn't save me because my stubborn resistance did more harm, but they were successful with many others. Alas, it remains a period in my life that makes little sense and stirs up a whirlwind of emotions. I gave up trying to unravel the complications and implications because it was making me ill. It was time to let go.

From now on, I would have my work, my home, my children and my name. My new life was very simple and no longer suffocating. I felt much better already but was sent to Flint House for two weeks, convalescing and recovering from my fragile emotional state. Apparently I had suffered post-traumatic stress disorder. I thought that only applied to shell-shocked combat veterans, but I really did need the break. I would come back stronger and a little less crazy.

My close inner circle shrank considerably. Having fewer people in my life meant less complication. I was reluctant to increase the number of friends. I didn't need many as I was still stubbornly independent. I returned to the reclusive loner existence and tended to push away anyone who came too close. I could tolerate company in small doses but preferred low-maintenance friendships. The kind that allow minimal interaction between long absences. I could temporarily be the life of a party but would always retreat to my shell like a hermit.

Just how basic my new life had become can be demonstrated by my BT landline. The phone company was offering discounts for ten numbers of my choice. This was called 'Friends and Family', and the idea was that I should designate those numbers dialled most frequently in order to benefit from the savings. BT wrote to me explaining the details and it listed its recommendations based on my most recent usage. I recognised some of the numbers instantly. They included the Leicestershire Constabulary's main switchboard, my voicemail, my bank, my GP and my ex-wife (child access). Some of these numbers were chosen simply because they had been dialled once in the past twelve months. There was one that I didn't recognise. It was a local number but I couldn't work it out so I dialled.

"Hello! East Goscote!" said the call-taker.

"Sorry, who is that?" I asked.

"East Goscote Chinese!" she replied.

My local takeaway was among my 'Friends and Family'. Quite right too.

Iain Wright had been a cool name for a police officer. Ian Wright was a very successful footballer and whenever he played the fans would chant "Ian WRIGHT, WRIGHT, WRIGHT!" The local youth shouted the same to me when I patrolled.

Hollis is an old English name, meaning 'man who lives by the holly'. There aren't that many of us and even fewer well known. Stanley Hollis was the only man to win a Victoria Cross on D-Day, but the most famous Hollis was Reggie, an incompetent and disaster-prone character in the TV police drama *The Bill*. From now on I would be called 'Wrighty', 'Hollis' and to my consternation, 'Reg'. I left it up to Hannah and Callum to choose for themselves. Happily they jumped ship and joined me.

That December, a cloakroom mix-up at a nightclub resulted in Leonie being accused of theft. It was completely by coincidence that my sergeant and I took the initial report. The full details are complicated but in essence there were three victims and three similar-looking jackets. It was a triangular mix-up where each corner had been mistakenly handed the wrong jacket by cloakroom staff. My sergeant took the witness statement so that I could remain impartial but he did ask me to book in a certain exhibit. Things went wrong when I recorded the existence of this property with a CA prefix. It should have been CS. This was an innocent mistake influenced by the fact I usually wrote CA because that was our area code but on this particular occasion we were assisting on CS territory. The item's very existence proved Leonie was innocent but my error caused it to be overlooked and consequently she was charged with theft. The law specifically obliged me to disclose my error and reveal the exhibit immediately, so I submitted a report to the Crown

Prosecution Service. I invited them to reconsider the decision to prosecute in light of the new evidence. That should have been the end of it. It was… for now.

My old 3 BAS buddy invited me down to Weymouth for New Year's Eve. Taff explained how the whole town partied in fancy dress for the celebration. Potsy, a guy from my shift, would be joining us.

James Potts had been part of a rival partnership during Operation Design. Each pair needed a sensible one, so it was not possible to pair him with me. We were as mad as each other. He was a 6' 7" rugby player and we looked ridiculous stood side by side. Had we teamed up for those three months, there would have been absolute chaos.

We were together on this particular day and had patrolled Highfields since 7am but at 3pm we changed into our costumes. Potsy was to be a poncho-wearing Clint Eastwood-style cowboy and I would be Ginger Spice, with a wig, that iconic Union Jack dress and fake boobs. Finding a pair of size 9 platform boots caused a problem, so I put on my police riot boots and covered them in red masking tape before girls at the station applied the final touches of lipstick and mascara to my unshaven face.

We got a few stares at the motorway services but had a great night. Taff and his wife were Batman and Robin. Literally the whole town took part. I had never seen anything like it. Snowmen, Dalmatians, a police officer chasing a Rastafarian from bar to bar, pirates, doctors, nurses, vicars, monks, nuns and anything else you could imagine.

Men were grabbing my boobs all night and making obscene offers but Potsy had more success (kind of). He was seized upon as soon as we walked into the very first bar. A young female dressed in green army fatigues and a baseball cap, that implied she was a member of some Latin American junta, flung her arms around his neck and they were immediately at it, tongues and everything. We hadn't even ordered a beer.

"Your mate don't waste time, does he?" said Taff.

Potsy later conceded that the Cuban soldier was very, very drunk and he even detected the bitter taste of her burp vomit when they shared that kiss. He was also promptly warned off by her boyfriend. Oh well.

Stranded at the end of the night, Potsy and I hitchhiked. We got a lift off a man in an estate car. "Jump in," he said, "but mind the centurion." We got in to find an armour-wearing Roman spread out unconscious in the back.

1998 did not start well. Professional Standards served me with official papers notifying me that I was being investigated. There had been an outcry over my report. It was suggested that my actions were 'a blatant attempt to pervert the course of justice'. That was ridiculous but I was unable to argue my case at that point and life moved on. I was not overly concerned and went skiing for a week with a gang from work.

Leonie stood trial at the magistrates' court that May. Having heard the witnesses, the court acquitted Leonie, saying that there was 'no case to answer'. She was a victim rather than an offender. That outcome had been inevitable as I correctly predicted in my earlier report. Perhaps now they would drop their investigation into me. The days passed but I heard nothing.

They finally interviewed me in September, some nine months post-incident. They accepted that writing CA was accidental and I was relieved. That was the only thing I had done wrong, but to my astonishment they were still pursuing a case against me and at the end of November I was suspended from duty. My career hung in the balance. I was furious. I had not done what they said. 'My report was false and misleading'. No it wasn't. It was factual and the truth. I was summoned to court but not until January 1999. This cast a shadow over Christmas.

My loyal friend Potsy saw how this injustice was driving me insane and took me up to his folks in County Durham for the festive period. The poor chap had his ears battered all the way there as I stated my defence.

Court was adjourned in January and put back until March. I didn't even have to attend. My defence team had not yet received, let alone examined, any prosecution evidence. This was frustrating for me. I had already thoroughly reflected on my actions and was prepared to justify them. I was a coiled spring but would have to wait.

March was simply a committal hearing. My case would be heard before the Crown Court. I had to attend but only to confirm my name and that I understood the charges.

The first trip to Crown was in early May for my plea. "Not guilty!" I said. It was agreed that I could remain on bail but with conditions of residence. I had to sleep each night at home. The court was told that I was a police officer and the defence team requested that a reporting restriction be imposed, banning the press from publishing my address. The judge agreed. At the conclusion of the hearings he told me to stand up. "Mr Hollis, you will be granted bail to reappear at this court on a date yet to be determined. A condition of your bail is that you live and sleep each night at…" He then disclosed my full address in open court.

The trial would not be until the end of June. I was frustrated once more and suffered from anxiety. I was talking to myself, constantly doing battle with an imaginary prosecutor. My GP gave me some antidepressants. They certainly took the edge off things. I called them 'can't be arsed tablets'. That was their impact. Every time my brain started to overwork, they'd kick in and calm me down as though I couldn't be bothered. They nearly cost me my life.

With some colleagues from work I took part in the Cheviot 2000 fell race near the Scottish border. This was a marathon across various high peaks, each in excess of 2,000ft. I had competed the two previous years, partnered by my last crewmate, Phil Penny, so I knew what to expect.

Phil was a former soldier and with our experience we hoped to get one of the fastest times. We were making good progress but on the windswept high ground the weather deteriorated. I knew that I needed more than just my T-shirt and that I should stop, put on my waterproof jacket from the rucksack and then continue. I couldn't be bothered.

I got colder and increasingly slower. People started overtaking us. What's wrong with me? I needed to cover up and eat. I was carrying bananas and chocolate. "Stop and eat!" "Can't be arsed," argued the voices in my head. So I carried on.

Cold, wet and fatigued, I gradually decelerated to little more than a trudge. I was ready to lie down on the wet grass in the freezing fog and go to sleep. I wasn't cold anymore, the shivering had stopped and I actually felt a warm glow. It would have been such a peaceful and painless way to die.

In the nick of time, Phil had realised. Off with the rucksack and on with the jacket. As I slowly warmed up, I started shivering... a good sign. I couldn't use the can opener to access the Ambrosia rice pudding. He opened it for me and after a few mouthfuls, he dragged me down from the high ground to a lower checkpoint. Sheltered in the safety wagon, we had a hot mug of tea and I recovered quite quickly. I cursed myself for being so stupid, lazy and unprofessional. I would take no more antidepressants thereafter. I was able to continue and finish the course but it would be the slowest of our three races.

I came to realise that I was being prosecuted because of who I was, rather than what I had done. It saddens me to say that the police service has taken its eye off the ball. Management are more concerned about potential damaging headlines than the actual truth. In my case, the issue was that the media could have reported that Leonie escaped justice because of her association with me. The possibility of that potential adverse perception would have to be countered via a trial at Crown Court. This was fundamentally wrong. The June trial date was adjourned until August so my frustration continued.

I spent most of 1999 decorating my house and doing the garden, while preparing for the arrival of my next son. Enforced absence from work enabled more time with Hannah and Callum. We all learnt to play chess but not particularly well. I had started beating the computer but was defeated by John Flynn (my sergeant) every time he did a welfare visit. We had long days playing down by the brook, fishing and playing on a raft that we'd built from junk in our garage. We got to know each other quite well and finally bonded.

One day I decided I would attempt a ride to Skegness and back. 75 miles there, 75 miles return. 150 miles in a single day. Why? Just to see if I could do it. Not much of an adventure, more a physical challenge. I set off at 4.30am from home, riding through Melton Mowbray, Grantham, Boston and finally arrived about midday. I took off my trainers, ran across the sand and dipped my feet in the cold waters of the North Sea. Then I ran back to the bike, removed my Jamaican ginger cake from the panniers and started to eat. I grabbed a 'Jolly Fisherman' postcard, recorded the time, posted it to myself and then started the return journey.

I was never that keen on 'Skeggy'. The new objective was to get home before 7.30pm because it was 'James Bond Season'. Tonight it would be *Diamonds are Forever*. I'd seen it several times before but that wasn't the point. I'd set myself a challenge. My biggest challenge since the failure in Spain. Just outside Skegness the fatigue hit me so I had a fifteen-minute power nap before continuing my journey. The ride was mostly flat. Boring as hell. Made worse by the fact that I was returning along the exact same route as the outgoing. I made it though. On time. It can be done. What next?

Cairo was next. Born in August. The first thing his mother said on seeing him in her semi-delirious state was, "Oh, he's black." He was lightly tanned at most. Certainly lighter than his mum. When he looked into my eyes I knew everything was going to be all right. His middle name was chosen in honour of my loyal friend James Potts (Potsy) who had stuck by me despite being criticised by the area superintendent. The trial was adjourned again. It would now be September.

Naturally I was nervous about being 'The Accused'. There was so much at stake. I could be sent to prison, in which case I would lose my home and my career. I didn't have just any old judge either. Presiding over my case was the famous senior circuit judge, His Honour Richard Pollard. The trial started this time and in a warped way I enjoyed it. Sat in the dock, flanked by a prison guard, I listened to the evidence against me.

By the end of the first day, none of the prosecution witnesses had said anything that suggested any wrongdoing on my part. The judge asked the prosecutor when I would actually be accused of breaking the law. Just because my actions were unusual, didn't make them wrong. He was effectively telling the prosecutor to abandon his case. That advice fell on deaf ears and the second day began. By lunch the judge had heard enough. He cleared the jury, removed his spectacles and then laid into the prosecutor.

"Every witness you call subtracts further from your case. The allegation against this officer simply isn't true. He wasn't perverting justice. I would even go so far as to say he was actually trying to ensure justice was served, and I'm ending the trial now."

The highest authority had spoken and the police were WRONG. This did little to mitigate the bitterness I felt towards my employer but reinstalled my faith in British justice. No matter how inept or spineless the internal policy unleashed against officers, the law and common sense would prevail in a courtroom. Hearing the judge's succinct and eloquent assessment delivered immediate relief and vindication. He banged his gavel and I was acquitted, free to go.

I collapsed and broke down, overwhelmed by almost two years of constant pressure, but I was comforted by my loyal colleagues: Phil Penny, Renno and later Potsy. We went for a beer in The Last Plantagenet. Two detectives were sent to locate me and take me back to Charles Street to be congratulated by that two-faced divisional commander who had once barked at Potsy for remaining my friend. "Just tell him that you didn't find me," I said, in slightly more colourful language.

I collected the kids from school that day. Parents accumulated in the empty playground waiting for the bell. It rang and the children spilled out of their classrooms. Running towards me was my seven-year-old daughter. Hannah had a massive smile on her face and she shouted at the top of her voice:

"Daddy, I'm so glad the judge didn't send you to prison!"

Feeling all eyes gaze upon me I could have died of shame but we hugged tightly instead. Out of principle I went back into work the next day to collect my warrant card and keys. The inspector checked his resources board and asked me to go and join the morning shift.

"No thank you, sir," I said.

I may have been away for ten months but that period had been no holiday. It had been an extremely traumatic time and I was mentally exhausted. I had accumulated a huge amount of annual leave. I intended to use some and adjust to my new freedom.

Chapter 12.

Millennium Marathons

I had always wanted to do the London Marathon. I applied and was fortunate enough to secure a place. I was undaunted by the distance, having once done 30 miles with rifle and kit across Dartmoor. 26 miles in shorts and trainers couldn't be that difficult. I could still run too. Often I would run 8 miles to work, do my tour of duty and then run home again. The thing is, if I wanted a respectable time I would need to train properly, and the variation of shifts at work made that difficult. A strategy slowly unfolded. I wasn't going to train because I knew I could do the distance. To mitigate for a poor time, I would run in fancy dress.

I set about making my costume. I had seen one of Taff Philips' New Year's Eve outfits, 'The Lone Ranger' riding his faithful horse, Silver. I could replicate that. I cut up some old blue police shirts. By then all officers wore white. That made the main uniform. Cardboard boxes made the horse. The rest was pretty much made from masking tape. The thing is, this outfit seemed to build itself and it got better and better. I thought to myself *this costume is going to turn a few heads. I'm going to be asked why I am running. I ought to be getting sponsored.* So at the last minute I became an official fundraiser for the RSPCA.

As part of the process, a media release was made. I was interviewed and photographed by the *Leicester Mercury* and filmed by Midland Asian TV. Then the marathon organisers found out about me and got in touch. They invited me to participate in their fancy dress competition. I had missed the local area heats but they were so impressed with my costume that I was given an immediate spot in the final, to be held in Covent Garden. I had to attend London for the pre-registration in any event so why not kill two birds with one stone?

I met one of my idols, Olympic 400m silver medallist, Roger Black. He was acting as one of the judges. Other contenders included a Millennium baby (who I expected to win), a double-decker bus and a tree but I won.

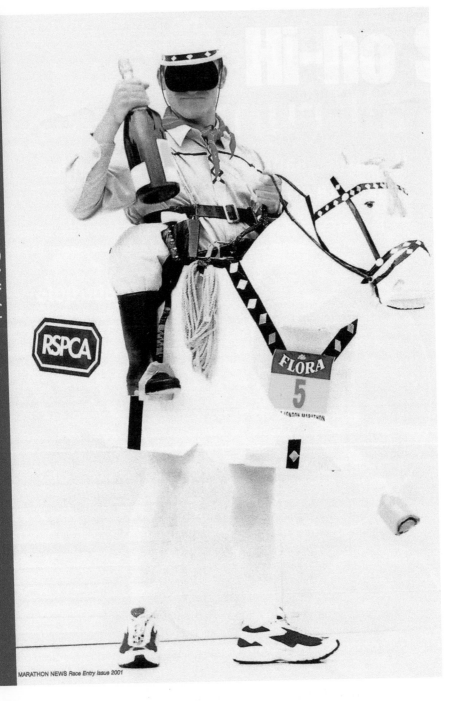

RSPCA

FLORA

5

LONDON MARATHON

With a thunder of hooves and thrilling cry of "Hi-ho Silver Away" The Lone Ranger set off on his 26 mile journey from Blackheath on Sunday 16th April 2000. The Texan lawman, finally unmasked as Iain Hollis from Leicester had taken first prize in the Flora London Marathon Fancy Dress competition the previous Thursday and won £2,000 pounds and a guaranteed entry to the 2001 race. Whether, as Iain crossed the line five and a half hours later, he was that enthusiastic about the guaranteed entry is debatable but with a few months to recover he'll be champing at the bit.

Iain, who ran to raise money for the RSPCA, received his prize at the second Flora London Marathon Fancy Dress Fashion Parade held at London's Covent Garden. The judges included Emma Angel of Angels and Bermans, the costumiers and Roger Black, the former 400 metre runner, who also ran in more conventional kit. Among the prize winners was Jerry Hoare in a Millennium Baby costume. Jerry won first prize in last year's competition dressed as a Millennium Bug - what is it with you and the Millennium Jerry?

Another runner-up, Jeremy Sutton, dressed in a bacchanalian bikini, had only a bunch of grapes to hide his potential. In contrast, Moreton Lloyd was somewhat overdressed in a ten foot aluminium and neoprene tree with a squirrel in it (I'm not making this up!). For sheer size even Moreton could not compete with the Love Bus - six men who ran as a 4.7m long, 2.6m high, double decker London bus.

It is this kind of madness that makes the Flora London Marathon such a fantastic spectacle; the purists may disagree but the highlights have nothing to do with world records or the incredibly strong field of elite athletes - it is the certifiable British eccentric that makes the spirit of the race what it is...

...and remember, next year it could be you.

MARATHON NEWS *Race Entry Issue 2001*

Photograph credit to London Marathon Events Ltd

I think they appreciated my homemade effort more than those which had been professionally manufactured.

My winner's photograph with Roger was to be printed in the *Evening Standard*. Then began my fifteen minutes of fame. A big bottle of champagne was presented before I was whisked off in a limo to the ITV studios. I was on the TV. The interviewer was stunningly beautiful. I didn't know her at the time but I think it was actually Natasha Kaplinski. The media circus wanted me to appear on Channel 4 the next morning, so they put me in a hotel for the night and paid for my rail fare home. The limo driver took me to pre-registration and I gave him the bottle of champagne for his service.

I couldn't believe what was happening. It turned out that the millennium year had special funding. As winner of the 2000 Flora London Marathon Fancy Dress Competition, I received £2,000 prize money. I had also won a one-week holiday for two at Hotel Club La Santa in Lanzarote. I had also secured a guaranteed entry to the next year's marathon. The annual holiday that I had booked in order to participate was reimbursed as my actions were good PR for the police. Is this really happening to me? What a turnaround. Seven months before, I was the bad cop in the dock and now Leicestershire Constabulary was celebrating me as one of its own.

The London Marathon is not just about running 26 miles and 385 yards. It is a must-see carnival. The crowd is the real star of the show. Many rows deep, those at the front offer Jelly Babies, boiled sweets, slices of orange or banana. The kids try to high-five every runner who passes. The crowds cheer and clap encouragement. Live bands entertain from roadside balconies. It is fantastic. The discerning support would shout, "Hi ho, Silver!" or "Who is that masked man?" but the less savvy would say, "Ride em, cowboy" and "Go sheriff!" One even asked if I was Zorro.

Hazel Irvine interviewed me on Tower Bridge. I think I was supposed to stop and smile for the TV cameras but continued jogging. I wasn't deliberately snubbing the BBC. I still had that deluded mindset of pursuing a respectable time and couldn't afford the delay. Anyway, I ran it, finished, collected my medal and came home. It was hard work. I had hoped to do it in under four hours but it took me five and a half. Constant pounding with an altered gait to compensate for the costume saw me bruise both big toenails. They fell off eventually but grew back again.

Using some of the prize money I rounded my fundraising effort to £1,000 and then Leonie and I went for a well-deserved and long-overdue break in the sun.

I took the opportunity to run the 2001 race. This time I aimed for a more respectable time but two events would disrupt my practice. Tayna arrived in February. Born at the LRI like her brother, the first thing her mum said was, "Oh, she's just like Cairo."

Tayna was named after Tayna Lawrence, a Jamaican 100m sprinter who ran in the 2000 Olympic final. She finished third but positions one and two would later be disqualified as drug cheats. Yes, it is TAY- NA and not TAN -YA. She would be regarded by her siblings as Daddy's favourite.

Absolutely no truth in that. They're all unique and each has given a classic contribution.

Hannah:

"Some people are pretty, some people are smart. I can just burp loud."

Tayna:

When asked to name an animal beginning with the letter Q. "Cute little kitten."

Cairo:

Modelling a new England shirt on his birthday. "How old are you, Cairo?"

"FOUR!"

Anticipating that he'd announce his footballing ambitions, I asked, "What are you going to be once you're older?"

"FIVE!"

Callum:

In the corner of our kitchen, there is a gap between the wall and the side of the fridge. This is where I store the spare plastic bags. I took all the kids to the cinema to see *Indiana Jones and the Kingdom of the Crystal Skull*. A spaceship lifts off and vanishes at the end of the film. One of the characters said it had gone to 'the space between spaces'. Hannah asked where that was and Callum replied: "The side of Dad's fridge."

It was quite spontaneous and we all erupted with laughter. It wasn't intended as a funny line in the film and I doubt the audience understood our humour, but if anyone needs a plastic bag now, they go to the 'space between spaces'.

Returning to the marathon. I had also been ill just before the event. I'd had all four wisdom teeth removed in one appointment. With my gums stitched up and with swelling and bruising to my face I was unable to train. I had to rely on my basic fitness. Four hours forty. Not happy. It was an hour quicker than last time but I had no costume. I could do better. I applied again. I was accepted again.

My 2002 training was disrupted by another injury. On duty we had entered an address on a missing person's enquiry but there saw a man that I knew to be on the run from prison. His arrest meant an immediate incarceration, so he tried to escape. Head first, he rolled out of the kitchen window. The back door was locked so I followed in hot pursuit via the same window. By the end of the alley he was safely detained in handcuffs but then the adrenaline wore off and my groin started stinging. My jeans were torn and blood staining was developing in a sensitive region. It seems that I had caught my scrotum on the spike that secured the window latch. Five stitches later I was sent home. This injury was in a very awkward place. I couldn't have my legs together, so walking, driving and riding my motorbike were almost impossible for about ten days.

Despite this minor mishap, I entered the race once more. Most of us running that year wore a black ribbon to mark the recent passing of the Queen Mum. Paula Radcliffe was the first to finish in the women's race and I achieved a personal best of three hours forty, with an impressive finishing sprint race down the Mall. By now though, I was addicted and couldn't wait to improve. Originally I only wanted to run once but so far I had competed three years in a row. I applied again. I was accepted again. Hopefully there would be no injuries next time.

Chapter 13.

My Left Foot

'Scientia Potentia Est'
(Knowledge is Power)

-Sir Francis Bacon
AD 1597

2003. I was properly training for the marathon this time. 8 miles twice a day. Then disaster struck. I broke my ankle while making the arrest of a drug dealer. He didn't want to give up those twenty-three rocks of crack cocaine in his hand, not to mention be deported for being an illegal immigrant, so he struggled. Adding insult to injury, this was another man that I'd had removed only eight months earlier, yet like Smith, he was able to re-enter through our lacklustre border controls and continue plying his lucrative trade.

I heard the snap but the adrenaline blocked my pain until we had secured the drugs and our prisoner. Then I went to stand up. I couldn't. I started to shiver as the shock took over. The adrenaline cleared and then the pain arrived, taking my breath away. I didn't appreciate how serious it was at the time but my life would never be the same again. Things would be different now and I would not cope very well.

The initial medical opinion of three professionals was that I had simply snapped a ligament and that it would be six weeks before I could run again. It shouldn't be a major issue and I ought to be able carry on as normal quite soon. The marathon was just ten weeks away. Would I make it? I was advised against running that year and the event organisers agreed to hold my place until the 2004 race. Despite many sessions of physiotherapy, it would be thirteen weeks before I could run again, not six, and even longer before I could operate the clutch on my car. Being the left ankle meant I could not support the weight of my motorbike. I dropped it several times causing expensive repairs and that prompted me to invest in an automatic Honda Civic.

Weeks turned to months. The ankle hurt every day. It was aggravated by running, standing, walking, driving and in fact even simply by gravity. Consequently I was unable to train properly.

2004. I set out to pound the streets of London once more. I checked my time on Tower Bridge. Halfway. I was well behind schedule and unsure of whether I would make it to the finish. The foot was agony. The pain domino rallied to my knee, hip and back. Glutton for punishment and with a marine mentality, I finished having walked most of the second half. I wouldn't be doing that again. I suddenly felt old and that life was too short. I had always been invincible. Now I had found something I couldn't do. I hated this new experience.

I refused to give up running entirely. The 8-milers twice a day every day shrank to 3-milers once a day twice a week. I needed to find something else. Kayaking to work would fill the gap for a few years.

2005. It was impossible to not have feelings for Leonie. We had been through a lot together and I enjoyed her company as well as her great sense of humour and heart-warming smile. The stigma of the age gap had long been left behind and I thought we might go the distance but unfortunately, her often unnecessarily chaotic and disorganised lifestyle was beyond my level of tolerance. The early symptoms from my injured ankle may have been a contributory factor, as I was becoming increasingly frustrated and agitated through pain and impaired abilities. We had lasted almost eight years, which was a record relationship for me. She left behind Sabre, our loyal blond German Shepherd who looked like a lion. He would only last another year before his back legs went. Letting go at Chine House Veterinary Surgery was heartbreaking. He had been with us for nine years.

2006. When my ten-year savings plan matured I had enough spending money, but it would need a seven-year loan to take us all to Disneyland Florida for two weeks. It had to be this year. Any sooner and Tayna (now five) would have been too young. Any later and Hannah (now fourteen) would be too old. With no girlfriend but needing another adult to assist with four kids, logic said take Leonie. She was loved by all four and her presence would enable me to take my elder two on activities that were off limits to the younger ones. The money was well spent. Their faces each day said this was truly the trip of a lifetime.

There is no fairy-tale ending to my story, but there nearly was. I had long held a flame for a girl I knew at school. I had registration class with Mala twice daily for five years. We shared some lessons too, including French. She was an Indian, who in my mind looked similar to Whitney Houston, only slightly better looking. We had managed to stay in touch when school ended and met a few times in the late 80s to catch up. She was at university studying to become a dentist and I was globe-trotting. I had last seen her in 1989. Having joined me for a drink in the city centre, I escorted her back home. She kissed my cheek at the corner of her street before running back to her parents' house. I never saw her again and always regretted it.

It was a Christmas card in 2006 that ignited our reunion. Her husband's name was absent. They had separated and weren't getting back together. I was single but not for much longer. Things were bliss… for a while.

2007. When the police rang me at home with an urgent message to contact Andrea, I knew my mum had died. Andrea was Mum and Paul's only child. She had been my bridesmaid in 1992 but I hadn't seen her or my mum much since then and not at all after my bridge burnings of 1997. That was almost ten years ago.

The news was confirmed and the funeral would be the next week. I also had to deliver the message to Tony. Like me, he had withdrawn from the family and no one knew where he was. Getting hold of me had been easy; Andrea just had to call the police. I knew where Tony lived completely by chance. I had seen him coming out of his house on occasions as I travelled to and from work. Death messages are something that police officers do quite routinely. They were usually distressing and this one wouldn't be any different. Tony's reaction was similar to mine, shocked, a little subdued but not devastated. We had a chance to catch up and had a beer in his kitchen.

The next day I went to tell my dad. On arrival, I found that he already knew but we had a chance to catch up too. Stood talking in his kitchen, I heard a voice shout from upstairs, "Is that my long-lost brother?" Sarah ran downstairs to greet me, followed by Stacey. They were different now. No longer little girls. They were grown women and getting ready for work. From their faces, I could easily tell that they were my dad's daughters. Tony and Andrea looked like my mum. I hadn't seen Amanda since she was a few weeks old and her brother, Wesley, was just a name.

I looked like neither my mum nor my dad. I do have an uncanny resemblance to my Uncle Melvin in New Zealand. He went over there when

I was four. I write to him once a year and still have the boomerang he gave me all those years back, but in response to the obvious question, he insists I am not his love child. It transpired that Dad was again single. By now he had six kids, two from each of his three wives.

I would see Dad and Tony at the funeral the next week. Cairo and Tayna had never met my mum and she hadn't been much of a grandma to Hannah or Callum. They had seen her a few times but that had been many years before. My elder two were always eager to meet their wider heritage and decided they'd come along. Their only regular exposure to my side of the family was, well, actually, just me.

Mum arrived at Gilroes Cemetery in a horse-drawn carriage. First to exit from the following cortege was one of Leicester's most prolific burglars. Are we at the right funeral? He then helped a tearful Andrea from the car. "Oh no!" I sighed. The others looked at me as though I had suddenly succumbed to grief. He was Andrea's partner. He'd later recognise me as I'd arrested him once before. He told me that people could change. He hadn't. He was on one of my station's 'wanted' posters a few months later.

I learnt a lot during the eulogy and they said some nice things. My mum was only in her late fifties but had been ill for a while. Tony and I were mentioned briefly. That came as a shock. I felt like a gate-crasher rather than a son of the deceased. They played two Queen songs: No One But You (Only the Good Die Young) and Days of Our Lives. The distinctive style evoked memories of Bohemian Rhapsody and my eyes welled up. I noticed Aunty Do was there too, sobbing. It had been such a long time since I'd seen her and I wanted to go over and give support but I was in danger of losing it myself.

By April 2007, I had to stop my running full stop. I was suffering constantly. I started each day with mild symptoms but developed a progressively worsening limp until by the end of my shift I was hobbling round using a broom handle or piece of wood as a crutch. My colleagues drew faces on these items. There was 'Brenda the bald-headed broom handle' and 'Paul the plank'.

My dilemma was whether to seek a new medical opinion or soldier on. Advice from well-meaning colleagues was that if I honestly presented my symptoms to HR I would be medically discharged. I wasn't ready for that but soldiering on wasn't an option either. I simply couldn't do it anymore. I revealed my limitations and was put on light duties until I could be seen by a specialist at the QMC.

"That is a very grotty ankle," said the doctor examining my X-ray. Then came the new diagnosis.

"In 2003 when you snapped your ankle ligament you also chipped off a small piece of bone. The bone has been floating loose and causing inflammation and pain with every ankle movement. Your overall ankle joint is lax due to the non-functioning ligament. Consequently the bones have been rubbing against each other and at the sites of friction, spurs or osteophytes have started to grow. We can remove the loose bone fragment and shave the spurs but cannot repair your ankle."

2008. Surgery in October had limited success. Partial relief of symptoms while on crutches but a return to similar amounts of pain once weight-bearing. Surgical scarring would cause more nerve damage and further reduced the joint's flexibility. So after seventeen years of operational service, it looked as though I would end my police career behind a desk. Me? That cannot be right, surely?

I asked my GP for some more Co-codamol but he refused on the basis that they were addictive. With a now raised voice, I protested that I needed them in order to get through my long list of tasks but the good doctor soon lost his temper. In his opinion, I was trying to do too much and that was the main reason for my pain. I disagreed. I was doing no more than usual and ought to have been able to manage.

"Look! It's over, you're a mashed-up useless cop. The life you knew before is finished!" he shouted.

He then went on to express the view that I would be better off having my lower leg amputated. I wasn't ready for that blunt and honest assessment. I trusted my doctor, he had always been right during the last fourteen years, but I was still horrified by his suggestion. The truth hurt. I didn't want to hear it and stormed out of the medical centre, holding back tears. They can't have my leg. I'm a runner.

Having had time to consider that avenue, I sought the opinion of the police medical officer, himself a former paratrooper. He saw no reason to medically discharge me for having a prosthetic. He agreed with me that I would be faster and fitter with one. Hey, I could even do another marathon if I had the limb removed. It was simple. A no-brainer. Take the bloody leg off.

My surgeon however, disagreed. Amputation would not necessarily get rid of the pain and my general movement and function, although limited, was still better than any prosthetic could offer. Running marathons and prolonging an active police career was a short-sighted approach. My long-term interests would be better served by 'lifestyle changes'. In other words, a medical discharge.

I refused to accept that proposition. The job sent me for hypnotherapy but that failed because I was too mentally stubborn and focussed. I was put on synthetic opiates. They blocked the pain but messed up my brain so much that I could literally have killed people if they said anything that irritated me. I nearly attacked three men in the cinema because they were making too much noise. I was there with my kids and they were using some bad language. I tolerated it for about two minutes before I snapped and leapt directly over rows of empty seats to confront them. They apologised and left minutes later. The film hadn't even started. I was normally quite placid. What was happening to me? I gave up on that medication and moved on to whisky. Glenfiddich was effective in large amounts and didn't cause a hangover but it was not available on prescription and was very expensive.

At home I was sleeping downstairs in the conservatory and using a bucket to pass water. The stairs were an extra burden. Getting to sleep was a problem unless I was completely comatose from alcohol. One night poor Callum came downstairs to change TV channel via the Sky box. He could watch programmes in his room but to alter Sky he needed to use the remote on the box downstairs. He turned on the living room lights which then shone into my sleeping area. He changed channel and then left the room. He also left the light on. This tiny task was a massive irritation to me. Enraged, I jumped up, ignoring the pain, and not even realising that I had been in bed naked, I charged up the stairs and burst into his room. He sat up in his bed, puzzled. "What, what? What have I done?"

That naked grown man approached and punched him, screaming and shouting at the sixteen-year-old for his complete ignorance and disregard. My poor boy. Sorry.

To say I was short-tempered is an understatement. On occasions I'd smash a sink full of pots in the kitchen just because someone had made it necessary for me to walk further than I needed. I was becoming a complete asshole.

Shopping at Asda would be done at about 6am on a Saturday. With an empty car park I could pull up just short of the main doors and speed down each aisle without obstruction and there'd be no queues. I'd be home again and back in bed for a rest before anyone else was awake.

Quite often I would randomly just fall over. I could get back up but would sometimes fall over again after a few paces. I really had to concentrate when walking and slow the pace. I was in danger of ruining my suit trousers but this was also quite embarrassing.

2010. I needed help but no one was listening to me. No one understood, no one was helping. That's not actually true but it is how I felt. After my formal request for amputation was denied, I decided to do my own operation. I planned it for about six months. I researched where the bones were and which veins to consider. I needed a period when I could take extended leave, which was difficult because of my specialist post.

I hadn't deliberately set out to become an 'expert witness' but that's the way things happened. By 2004, I already had more exposure to drug investigations than most officers, and courts allowed me to express my opinion rather than just sticking to the facts. I was successful at this because I practised constantly and did everything I could to ensure a jury would understand the relevant inferences. On my debut, I had been forewarned of a need to demonstrate the construction and use of a crack pipe. It was one of those 'here's one I prepared earlier' moments. Having explained and assembled the various components, I lifted the pipe, placed the mouthpiece between my lips and flicked the lighter. The response to this unfolding spectacle was cheers and applause from the public gallery. It appeared that there was a cop on crack in the witness box. As my reputation developed, so did the demand for my opinions and attendances at court. It reached the stage where I was commenting on more than 200 cases a year and was on court standby for 75% of my duties. I didn't want to let anyone down by not being available but the earliest window of opportunity for DIY surgery was April 2010.

I booked time off for the Easter break. I bought some surgical scalpels, new jigsaw blades and sterile dressings. I packed my hospital bag, withdrew some money from the cashpoint and bought three big bags of ice from Asda. I had a bin liner and tourniquet at the ready so that I would not spill blood all over the taxi. I shaved my leg and then froze my foot in an ice-packed cool box for two hours. At this point things went wrong.

There had been so much to do at work before my longer than usual absence and consequently I finished later than originally planned. I had hoped to be at the hospital before my daughter returned from college. This delay meant that Hannah came home while I was still freezing my foot. I knew that I would struggle to mute my screams once the cutting began and even if I could, she would walk in once she heard the jigsaw in action. No time to lose then.

With a wooden spoon in my mouth for biting down, I lined up the blade. The view was strange. Surreal. It caught me a little unprepared. The leg was smooth, hairless and pink. I didn't recognise it as my own and could feel nothing when I prodded it. This was not my leg or was it? Suddenly I started to question my actions. It was as if I was outside looking in at someone else about to make a mistake.

When I had originally devised this plan, my appointment with the pain management clinic had been six months away. That was too long at the time, but waiting for a gap in my diary had eaten up the calendar. Now that appointment was only ten days away. "Just wait, Iain. See what they say at the hospital. If all else fails we can do this another time," said the voice of reason in my head. Some might say I chickened out. Others that I made the right decision. I don't know.

What I do know is that all of a sudden I had two weeks off work with absolutely no plans. I felt relief that I did not have to be in hospital or hide from the children that I had chopped my leg off. It was a massive burden release. Then my boss rang. He was suspicious that I had not attended the leaving do of a respected colleague. I had been vague in explaining my intended absence and he was checking in to see if there was any gossip. A new lady perhaps? I had no answers prepared, so I came clean.

"Well, actually, I was going to saw my own leg off, but don't worry about it. I've decided against it now."

What on earth was I thinking? I've just said that to my boss. Yes, he's a close friend but he is also my supervisor. Off duty, he suddenly became my inspector. He rang his wife to tell her he would be late home AGAIN. My house was surveyed like a crime scene. As a former army medic, Dave Purvis recognised my make-do surgical theatre. Next thing he was on the phone for the emergency doctor to come and section me under the Mental Health Act. Oh fuck!

Our conversation revealed that I was absolutely broken and at a very low point. As an invincible former Royal Marine, I could not live like this. The doctor arrived and I got a surprising boost. Instead of agreeing to section me, he actually took my side. He completely understood what I was trying to do and why. His report described me as 'intelligent and rational' (ought to get that framed) and he was generally sympathetic but advised against any further DIY surgery attempts.

The pain management clinic offered very little. First they tried a TENS machine (electric pulses). I couldn't feel the low settings through nerve damage and the higher ones either electrocuted me or made me dizzy and nauseous. I was taught to do self-acupuncture. That would give improvement for about an hour but couldn't be done frequently. An hour of relief two to three times a week was hardly beneficial. Physiotherapy and hypnotherapy had been tried. Amputation and a return to opiates were ruled out. That left just paracetamol and ibuprofen.

It didn't end there though. Back at work I was sent for counselling. Lifestyle changes! Have you considered giving up your career? Why do you need to carry on? Have you not done enough?

I couldn't give up. I wasn't programmed that way. When the going got tough in the Marines, the lesser men would be thrown into the back of the safety wagon. That was never the place for me. As a commando, I was expected to keep going when everyone else had stopped. I would never stop.

Despite my determined stance, I couldn't do a straight eight-hour shift. The occupational health department had sanctioned me doing just five-hour days but in a bid to justify my continued employment, I would carry on working full-time. In order to clock up my weekly forty hours, I was working in frequent short bursts with rests in-between. I would spread this over seven days, instead of completing just five shifts of eight hours each.

Much of my work involved reading case material and compiling written reports. I could perform these tasks from home on a police laptop but working inside pain thresholds meant a few hours Saturday morning and a few more Sunday evening. Sometimes I would be typing late at night and my working days were overextended.

2012. Everything outside of work had to be abandoned or neglected to achieve my forty-hour weekly targets. The garden was overgrown, the house was becoming rundown and the excessive drinking was pushing me towards an early grave. The system was simply unsustainable. My life was just work, rest, work, rest, work, sleep. Those who knew me well had made allowances but my new boss made a fresh assessment. He took one look at my fatigued face and bloodshot eyes and made the decision. It was time. From September there would be no more working from home and I would be barred from commenting on any future cases. I would have to allocate that workload to my protégés.

He was right, of course. Who had I been trying to kid? Doing half-days created a much healthier work/life balance but I didn't know how much longer I could remain in the police. Work kept me busy and I was bringing in the results at court but my role did not require police powers and with cuts to budgets and changes to conditions of service, it seemed inevitable that I would be released.

2013. That's exactly what happened. They broke the news in February. I had twenty-eight days' notice. My last day was 25th March. After almost twenty-three years, I was gone.

I had started at Charles Street in 1990 as a general duty officer on foot patrol around the city centre. Then to St Matthews as a community policing officer. After that to Asfordby Street in a variety of roles. From 2000, I was all over the county with drugs enforcement and surveillance jobs. Much of that detail cannot be published but I worked with some outstanding officers. By 2004, the CPS regarded me to be an expert in drug dealing and from 2008 until I finished that was my main role, to examine case material from others' investigations and offer my opinions. I commented on hundreds of cases and gave evidence in person on 57 occasions at various Crown Courts around the country, including the Old Bailey. My contribution helped to secure the convictions of 589 drug traffickers with a total prison sentence of 1,530 years. Not a bad tally for someone who left school with just three O-levels. The government's latest brainwave is that future officers should have minimum education standards equivalent to a university degree. Why?

For my efforts I had two crushed discs in my neck, broken ribs, black eyes, a lacerated bicep, a broken hand, a dislocated shoulder, an internally shredded left calf, a life-changing broken ankle and five stitches to my scrotum. Does the government seriously believe that cops are going to be fighting crime and chasing after bad guys when they're sixty years old? Well, I certainly won't be. I think I have done enough. I was a pensioner at just forty-four.

I have never been one to celebrate being a police officer. It is one of those jobs that immediately alters people's perceptions and makes them wary but if I had a pound for every time I heard someone say:

"I don't normally like cops but you're all right..." Most of us were like that.

Many of my close colleagues remain in covert roles and can't be named but I was very fortunate to work alongside such a bunch of skilled, dedicated and motivated professionals. It would be very hard to present a gold medal to the most outstanding or influential individual I ever worked with, but I can easily name my perfect relay squad: Wardy, Harding, Renno and Big Mac.

Simon Ward wasn't my official tutor, that role belonged to Russ Johnson (who did a great job, by the way), but my first shift sergeant, Ron Grantham, recognised my potential and said I could learn a lot from him. Wardy was a fearless officer and regularly got injured as a result (evidently, I mastered that aspect). He was also very keen-eyed and his stop and search success rate was second to none. I remember one Sunday evening, the control room dispatched us to a report of a shed break-in. We headed out of the station, but with Wardy setting pace in the wrong direction, I asked where we were going.

"We're not going to a shed break-in, we'll have a prisoner before that. They can send someone else."

We soon reached a side street next to the cinema and promptly arrested someone in a stolen car. I couldn't believe it. I shadowed Wardy for the next six years and it paid off.

Renno was the new boy on my first shift. I had done all right since joining, my raw talent and enthusiasm got me noticed, but Paul's arrival had soon earnt him the title, 'Golden Balls'. He was like a magician and could pluck criminals out of a hat. It was quite remarkable. Perhaps being a former taxi driver had something to do with it, they know *everything*.

I have already alluded to Harding. He drove the immediate response vehicle (IRV). He drove it fast too. I had every confidence in his ability but when he switched on the blue lights, I just hung on for dear life and closed my eyes.

Fraser Macintosh was way junior in service to me but you would never have known. Almost single-handed, he dismantled a cocaine-dealing network. I was effectively employed as his bag man for the protracted enquiry. It was a brilliant piece of policing, which in my opinion should have won him 'Investigator of the year' but the job was generally reticent about our line of work. Drug success exposed an inconvenient truth.

I definitely aspired to be as good as the first three but by the time it came to Big Mac, I knew I was getting 'too old for this shit'.

Looking back at my time in the service, I was bitter in places and frustrated in others. It was a difficult job. You'd get paid for most of the hours you worked but, by law, you were never off duty. When it was time to act or exercise power, often you would be damned either way. The police don't always get it right but they usually try their best.

Overall, Leicestershire Constabulary represented a force for good and I am quite proud to have been part of that team.

Chapter 14.

Irie Mon

'When I was at work, life was about yearly highlights
When I retired, years were about lifetime highlights'

- Iain Hollis

I wouldn't be sharing my retirement with Mala. We had been on and off constantly over the last six years as our interracial relationship caused problems on her side. That was a pity because we were well matched in so many ways. C'est la vie. Au revoir.

The residual effect of my expert evidence was that I would be required to attend further court trials post-retirement, pro bono. I didn't get paid for these attendances. There was usually compensation for loss of earnings, but I was a pensioner who had no earnings, so they simply paid my travel expenses.

With regular warnings to be on standby for weeks at a time, finding a new job would be awkward, so I discussed this with a barrister who agreed that in future cases, suitably qualified people could review what I had written and agree, or comment otherwise. I was not an eyewitness and other opinions were available. They were definitely available because I had helped to train twelve protégés before I left. My last day in court was that July and then I walked away from it all… *permanently.*

Next stop… JAMAICA.

Two weeks with Cairo and Tayna at an all-inclusive resort. They loved it. They saw some of their inherited culture and walked tall with pride. We took a catamaran to Dunn's Falls, a raft ride down the Rio Grande, and they swam with dolphins. Tayna was fearless at the latter. She was the youngest and smallest in a group that included Cairo and a load of adults. I was very proud. We did some mountain biking in the Blue Mountains and visited a rather disturbing slavery museum. The cruelty and suffering caused by man is quite shameful.

We visited Bob Marley's house. Cannabis is illegal in Jamaica but the government turn a blind eye at this particular attraction. You could openly buy it on arrival in the car park. By one of the boundary walls was a serving hatch. On the other side sat a dreadlocked Rasta. In front of him were bags of weed, rolled spliffs and a large tray of cannabis cake.

The kids were really keen to give it a try. The guide said it was OK but the cake was strong with a delayed reaction. "Just nibble it," she said. I was quite relaxed about this. I wasn't a cop anymore.

"OK, let's do it. Two spliffs and a slice of cake please." I handed him the US dollars. "Irie mon," he said.

We would share the first spliff between us. Tayna had one puff and didn't like it. Good result. Cairo, being a big man, overdid it. As for me, well, I was a little lightheaded too.

Next stop on the guided tour was a bar for a shot of Jamaican rum. If you finished it, you could keep the souvenir shot glass. There are now three of them in my cupboard. We took a look at Bob's old bedroom. Cairo was in fits of laughter and couldn't stop. He had the giggles. His laughing was infectious and soon everyone from our group was in hysterics.

After leaving the gift shop, we were driven to a restaurant for a typical meal of rice, peas and chicken or goat. Tayna slept all the way there and missed the stunning landscape. Cairo simply had a vacant stare. I was nursing broken ribs at the time. I had fallen off my push bike returning from the pub after a few too many beers a couple of weeks before. The pain was now gone, albeit only temporarily.

Back at the resort, Tayna did not want any cake and was straight into the swimming pool. She could have been a mermaid as she hardly left that place. Cairo and I sat nibbling the dope brownie on our sun loungers like a couple of giggly kids. It had no effect and didn't taste that nice. Cairo wanted no more and joined Tayna in the water. I went back to our beach hut and finished it off.

I laid on the bed and shut my eyes. Then I sank into the mattress. The ceiling lowered. The whole bed descended slowly too. Then playing cards started to rise from the gaps between the floor tiles. My eyes were still shut but I could see all sorts of things happening in my room. There was a front door of a house with a white-faced banjo leaning against it. I zoomed in and the banjo transformed into the Starship Enterprise. I saw my silver Honda Civic. I zoomed in on the front wing. It was no longer silver metal but instead layers of overlapping silver-coloured fish. I saw Mala in her bikini and she turned into a zebra. Wow. I'd eaten too much cake and this was the delayed reaction.

We kept the second spliff for a fitting occasion. A few days later the birth of Prince George was announced. That was ideal. Again, Tayna didn't wish to partake so it was Cairo and I who went into the bathroom to inhale. I turned on the shower, set it to cold and closed the shower curtain. We would both exhale into the shower so that the smoke and smell would be sucked down the plughole rather than set off the smoke alarms or linger outside the window. We were jolly. Hoorah for Prince George! God save the Queen!

Next morning I went into the bathroom. Smiley faces had been made on the toilet seat and mirror. I shouted to the kids, asking who had been drawing with the toothpaste. They said it was me. I have no recollection.

Kids, DON'T DO DRUGS!

Chapter 15.

All Rivers Run

My fighting weight as a sixteen-year-old was 11st 7lb. Lack of exercise and excessive drinking saw me balloon to 14st. I gave up drinking for a while but still struggled to lose weight so I joined a gym. Swimming aggravated my symptoms. I enjoyed the circuits class once a week but in order to cope I would have to be almost dormant all day waiting for the class to begin and spend the next day recovering in pain. It seemed that there was little for me to benefit from my membership, so I ended the subscription. What could I do instead?

Maybe it was a midlife crisis but I did a rerun of the 1999 Skegness ride. Took me a bit longer this time because I had to stop for breaks more frequently but yeah, I did it. Jolly Fisherman postcard sent. 150 miles in a day. Three days to recover though. I won't be doing that ever again.

I always fancied the idea of kayaking from home to London. There was a map on display in the bar/restaurant at Foxton Locks. I followed the blue line with my finger. From here I could get to London by canal. From my house I could get to Foxton by canal. That meant that I could paddle from home to London and back. It was just a matter of planning.

I bought a British Waterways map from Amazon and packed my boat with supplies. I kept a diary. It was just a piece of A4. I don't have it any longer but I transferred the contents into an e-mail in order to recount the details to friends. Below is an edited version of that original e-mail.

Sunday 22nd September 2013

15:40 departed East Goscote on foot with my fully loaded English-made SAGA Kayak. The sun was shining and the walk to the River Wreake at Beadles Golf Course was quite difficult. By 16:15 I was on the water and the journey officially began.

What would follow included 155 miles of paddling, one weir, 142 locks, four tunnels, four nights in the field, one capsize, one train journey, one coffee, one Twix and one bus ride home.

The kayak was much slower than I had been used to, owing to the stores being carried. 4 mph was reduced to nearer 2.5 mph. It was dark before 20:00 and what should have been a six-hour leg (24 miles) to Foxton Locks reached seven and a half hours with the destination still a long way off. Night one, 00.15, was spent under an arched bridge in Blaby, close to the A6. I only needed my slug and roll mat as the location was dry and sheltered.

Monday 23rd September

Up at 05:30 for Ambrosia rice pudding breakfast. Pushed on from 06:00 to Foxton. First negotiating Saddington Tunnel, 880 yds. This was hardly demanding. On entering I could already see the light at the other end. Made Foxton by 08:00 meaning I was well behind schedule. What was supposed to take me six hours had taken nine and a half hours. Weather was fine but hauling the heavily laden boat uphill past the ten locks was tiring. The constant immersion in water saw both wooden toggle ends crack and break off that morning.

At bridge 57 – 09:00 – I stopped for morning tea and stashed my first cache of supplies in bushes. I hoped to reach London on Wednesday. I would collect these supplies on the return journey and hopefully be back home by Saturday. The boat was immediately lighter and increased pace slightly. Husbands Bosworth Tunnel had a sign forbidding kayaks. The emerging longboat captain pointed this out to me but I denied that my intention was to enter. Once alone I advanced. Mini torch in my mouth for the 1166 yds. No drama. Continued on a slow meandering section and past the Welford Arms. Stopped midday for Super Noodles at bridge 34.

Crick Tunnel was 1,528 yds (1 mile). No signs but I had to give way to an oncoming light at the halfway stage. I stuck to the right and clung onto a guiding rail and chain as the big boat passed. Its lights gave significant illumination for much of my remaining time in the tunnel. Emerged close to 15:00 and downed a tin of fruit cocktail. Next stop was Watford followed by Norton Junction which had a sign stating that Leicester was 41.75 miles behind me, so adding 8 miles to East Goscote, I was by now 50 miles in. The lock at Norton Junction was very awkward for passing kayaks as they have to negotiate a staircase. Advised by a longboat captain that Blisworth Tunnel – 3,057 yds (2 miles) – was not open to kayaks and I would not be allowed through. Pressed on regardless. The canal is sandwiched. Port side heading south is the M1 motorway. To starboard the Midland mainline with high-speed Virgin trains every few minutes. Very long stretch. Dark by 20:00 yet still no sign of the tunnel. Almost pitch black by 21:00 and need torch to simply paddle as high banks, trees and no moonlight to reflect on water. I cannot tell what is sky and what is canal. This is quite disorientating. Eventually I see tunnel entrance. Entered and cleared after forty minutes. Emerged to immediate shelter of an old stable. Hot chicken and vegetable soup and luxurious night. Feet starting to smell so washed in the river.

Tuesday 24th September

Very tired and didn't want to get up. Important to clear tunnel site. Ambrosia breakfast 05:30 and on the water by 06:00. Cold foggy start but became brighter around 10:00. Over aqueducts very high up and crossing over A-class roads. Cleared picturesque Milton Keynes mid-morning before tea. Then on to Leighton Buzzard ignoring a convenient 24hr Tesco (good for resupply on return).

Reached Marsworth Junction 19:00. Averaging just 3 mph. It seems that the impact of negotiating seven locks is the equivalent to 1 mile's journey time. On this day I have cleared twenty-seven locks. Sign reads Brentford 38.5 miles. High tide at the Thames is 11:00 tomorrow (sixteen hours away). My dilemma. Such a journey would be possible but involve paddling right through the night and tackling no fewer than fifty-seven locks. An immediate return looks unfavourable as outward journey will have been at least one day longer. Early night on canal bank. Light rain but under bivvy. Full relaxing twelve hours' rest but site within earshot of railway with steady flow.

Wednesday 25th September

Tired. Contemplating staying in bed till midday but cannot be sure of tomorrow's tides. Up at 08:00 for Ambrosia and tea. On the water by 08:30 for attack on the locks. First twenty completed by 11:50 and stopped for noodles. Had passed a Safeway supermarket earlier. 14:30, completed thirty-five locks but only 14 miles in six hours. Dragonflies and kingfishers everywhere. 16:30, now completed 20 miles in eight hrs. Passing boat captain advises tomorrow's tide is 07:30. Share the canal for several miles with fellow kayak paddler, Michael. He gave good advice and tips about the Thames. 20:30 is 35 miles in twelve hours (fewer locks). Too dark to continue. On the final leg but getting closer to M4 motorway (noise) so bivvy in woods at Osterley Lock. Unfortunately in direct flight path of jets taking off from nearby Heathrow. Abated through the night.

Thursday 26th September

06:00 up and onto water. Breakfast can wait till the Thames. High tide is 07:30. Cleared the unmanned lock at Brentford. Staff just arriving at the Thames gate. Watch is twenty minutes slow and it is already high tide. Straight onto Thames. AWESOME. Peace and tranquillity at this stage. Young athletes training on the river in their rowing boats. Gentle pull of the current. Banks already showing significant recent drop in water level at 07:50. Grey day. Some rough water around nature reserve islands and small waves but not getting wet. Spray deck advisable perhaps. At 09:50 backside quite sore from constant sitting (no locks). Pulled over to north bank to readjust and munch on some Jelly Babies. Back onto the water. See the Shard, and London Eye in the distance. Sun is beginning to shine brightly. Selfie photos galore, even at 'The River House' (MI6 HQ). Ignored by police patrol boat.

At Millbank Pier the London Eye reappears as does Union Jack at Westminster. I have done 15 miles in approximately two hours with little effort which means the current is approx 4-5 mph in addition to my 3. Decide to switch banks without taking into account the effects of current. Turning angle not met as Millbank landing quay approached with haste. Forced to abort for fear of capsize but now thrust against the side and being crushed by tidal waters. Pushed back towards pipeline but no grip and capsize. Buoyancy aid is superb, water not too cold. Kayak upturned but swim to bank. Witnesses do not raise alarm after my thumbs-up. Camera is an obvious casualty. Wheels are gone too, and my sunglasses. Everything else has survived due to waterproof storage bags. Bail out one bridge before Big Ben. Continue wet. Advice from passing boat to cross to southern bank. Calmer waters in terms of shipping lane and tidal flow. Large waves from the wake of passing boats – quite hazardous. Pass HMS *Belfast*. Selfie on mobile at Tower Bridge 11:04. Depart Thames on northern bank after St Katharine Docks.

Kayak looks clean after its wash. Left with sponge and paddle. Someone will enjoy this boat I'm sure. Goodbye, old friend. On foot to station via St Katharine Docks. The Diamond Jubilee Galleon moored close by. Quite impressive.

Wet but drying. Reach St Pancras 13:50, Ticket £56. Train departs 13:55. Sat in corridor because I stink. Trolley maid, Starbucks coffee, two sugars and a Twix. The train only takes one hour. I'm going home.

Job done.

I had originally intended to paddle back home. I had my younger children stay with me most weekends. On the day of departure I had just dropped them back at their mum's and with no time to lose, I set off.

Falling behind schedule and missing the Wednesday morning tide meant a whole day had been lost and therefore I would struggle to get back in time to have my kids that next weekend. With the wheels attached I could possibly drag the boat through London and return by train. That became the plan. There was a point in the Thames that led to another canal route which would take me to within a very short distance of St Pancras.

The capsize scuppered everything. My wheels had gone so I had no chance of pulling the heavy boat behind me. It was impossible to carry along with two loaded kit bags, I was soaking wet and cold, and the kayak needed hull repairs too. They weren't critical but would become so had I continued much longer. The boat itself was of very little financial value although with a small amount of TLC it could provide many more years of fun. Abandoning the craft in a car park seemed to be the best thing to do.

I was satisfied with this adventure. I was buzzing. It was one of the best things I had ever done.

Chapter 16.

The Girl from Ipanema

Brazil is an enormous country but for sightseeing it has to be Rio de Janeiro: the iconic 'Christ the Redeemer', Sugar Loaf Mountain, Ipanema and Copacabana beaches, as well as the famous carnival and Maracanã Stadium which would host the FIFA World Cup final.

I had long wanted to go but violent crime was a serious concern. Being on the world stage would bring increased security and therefore be an ideal time to visit. The question was, should we go during the 2016 Olympic Games or the 2014 World Cup? It was put to a vote. Unanimous. 2014. We chose the World Cup for two reasons. Firstly, Brazil is synonymous with football. Secondly, our trip would coincide with Callum's twenty-first birthday. I had spent mine freezing cold on exercise in Norway but my son would have something much more monumental.

I knew that if England qualified the prices would be hiked. I had the money already set aside from my pension lump sum. We decided that we were going regardless of whether the England team would be joining us. That way we could book early and go for less than half price. England had one remaining qualifier. At home to Poland. A win, and we would be packing our football shirts and flags.

Hannah, her boyfriend Chris, Callum and I went to the game at Wembley. It finished 2-0 and we were ecstatic. We few, we happy few, were going to Rio and we were already booked. Bring it on!

The wait from October 2013 until June 2014 was frustrating but eventually we were on the plane. Our little outing had already tripled in value but I had not been tempted to cash in. This was one of those occasions where I wanted to say, "We were there!"

British Airways to Madrid and then on to our final destination. Never flown with BA before but it was a different class to Ryan Air. Even had a camera on the tail section which relayed images to our headrest TVs. We watched as the wings dropped below the clouds and the compact buildings below us came into sharp focus. A perfect landing followed by nervous energy and childish excitement. We're here!

A hotel transfer was included or at least that is what the ticket said. No sign of our name on any of the chauffeur or taxi boards. I left the group to make enquiries. I returned to an excited Callum. We'd only been there five minutes and already he had bumped into Louis Figo (Portugal's most capped player). They had shared a selfie which Chris had managed to photobomb.

Obrigado, Figo. Cheer up, it's only a game.

We hailed a cab and left the airport. Hitting the main highway we closed up behind an army truck. The flaps of the canvas canopy were open to reveal rows of seated armed police. Pistols were drawn. I sank in my chair and discreetly fastened my seatbelt. Well, that would've been my natural response in England.

Our hotel could not have been in a better location. It was on the corner, equidistant from the two famous beaches. Hannah and Chris had their own room and I'd share with my son. We were only there for eight days. England had its training camp in the shadow of Sugar Loaf but its matches were many miles away.

We had attempted to buy tickets from the FIFA website as soon as they were released; in fact, I had logged on and waited in the queue from about 3am until 7am but the England and Brazil games were immediately sold out. It didn't matter anyway as all of the games would be shown on massive TVs on Copacabana beach. The area would be packed and have tonnes of atmosphere.

We were there. England was there. It was our year. Come on. We headed out to sample the world's most delicious steak. We'd been on the go for about forty hours by now, spurred on by euphoric adrenaline. Chris was ill at the time and it was touch and go as to whether he could travel with us. He and Hannah turned in sensibly but for Callum and me the night was still young.

We started a bar crawl along the Copacabana. Only little huts selling cans of Brahma lager, they were all the same. The opening ceremony was not until tomorrow but we spotted a few England shirts. There were far more Argentinian'. We weren't wearing football shirts and were indistinct until we spoke.

Across the beach road were the hotels and bigger bars. One in particular, The Balcony Bar, had loud and rowdy singing. I'm a little deaf but Callum could definitely here 'England' chants. We headed over. It was packed with our lot. Women outnumbered the men and most looked stunning but some were quite clearly blokes. I made sure Callum realised. Getting our first beers from the bar, we were groped repeatedly. Pecs, buttocks and groin. "Don't lose your wallet!" I said.

We were offered cocaine, and then marijuana, both of which we declined. In my experience, you simply cannot risk taking cocaine. Too many rip-offs and it tends to be mixed with cheaper powders such as dental anaesthetic, caffeine, glucose or paracetamol. It's a game of Russian roulette and really isn't a worth it. But what an amazing bar. It was buzzing with pre-tournament excitement.

We moved back outside and stood on the front patio drinking our beers. "Wow, look at her," I said.

Then she winked at me. Oh my god. Tall, with legs that went up into the clouds. I might just live out my retirement here. "Callum, we're going to have to keep moving, otherwise I'll be leaving with her."

We drank up and kept exploring. On the side street an old grandma offered us marijuana. We declined once more and kept walking. It soon seemed that we had left the main zone but we already knew where to party in future. We found a quiet bar. Had a glass of English beer, Old Speckled Hen, and then caught our second wind.

Straight back to the Balcony Bar. Callum found some English lads and I started chatting to a friendly Argie who freely conceded that they weren't getting the Falklands back. Then there she was again. Stood right next to me. We both knew what was going to happen next. I bought her a drink and nature took care of the rest. Patricia was a twenty-six-year-old, beautifully tanned Brazilian and I couldn't keep my eyes or hands off her. I was so blessed to have been born male.

I approached Callum. "Son, sorry, I am a weak man. I will see you later."

It was nearly 7am before we both got back in. The tournament opened later that day. The Balcony Bar remained closed for the rest of our stay. The police had closed it down for some reason. Things were much tamer thereafter.

From the rooftop pool you could see Jesus. In fairness you could see him from everywhere. He was on a high mountain and illuminated at night. We took a sightseeing tour which included a visit to the massive statue. It was winter in Brazil but temperatures were still in the high 20s. Clouds enveloped Christ's head so selfies were a problem, but we got one eventually. Overcrowding at the top and with poor visibility we headed down the cascading stairs. Coming up from the opposite direction wearing his iconic glasses was Dutch superstar, Edgar Davids. I recognised him and turned to call Callum.

A random bloke suddenly shouted, "All right, Royal!" This was a standard greeting or acknowledgement that I was a Royal Marine. The man had seen my shoulder tattoo and introduced himself. He was a former Royal Marine too. He was now employed as Edgar's bodyguard and gave me and my group a personal introduction. Great photo.

The Maracanã Stadium looked impressive. Hannah and I posed for photos in extravagant carnival costumes and then we all took the cable car up Sugar Loaf.

For England's first game we had to walk through approximately 4,000 Argies who were blocking the road and camping on the beach. It was quite daunting but my lot held their nerve. Shame about England.

We had watched the game from the designated area known as the 'Fan Zone'. This was a security patrolled fenced area on the beach with a massive TV screen above a stage, from where dancers and singers entertained before games. We saw no violence and even the fiercest rivals were partying together. It was almost Utopia and I remember thinking how marvellous it was that football could bring so many different people together as one.

We watched other games from deckchairs on the beach. My gang discovered that it didn't like mojitos so I had to finish all four. Sat there in the sun was heaven. The others bought watermelon, beers and ice creams from the constant procession of beach vendors.

Mexico v Brazil was interesting. I was single at the time and on the lookout for a new lady in my life. I was keen on Patricia but having agreed to meet again at the Balcony Bar, I had lost contact already. Who would be the most attractive, Brazilians or Mexicans? It was a close call but the Mexicanas got my vote. I will have to go there one day.

I saw Robbie Savage (former Leicester City) strolling down Ipanema and said hello. Saw Rio Ferdinand (former Man United) on Copacabana and I didn't bother. Martin O'Neil and Andros Townsend were in front of TV cameras one day. We gathered to watch and my tattoo prompted more former marines on bodyguard duty to say hello.

We would be flying home after England's second game. Another defeat and we'd be out of the tournament already. It was raining that last day. I didn't want to fly home soaked, drunk or covered in sand and made the early bid for a quiet bar. Callum had other ideas and dragged me back to the Fan Zone. This was the last night and he was really going for it, two pints to each of mine, and he'd taken charge of someone else's unwanted cocktail. We all stood like fools in the rain, singing, 'God Save the Queen' and 'England Till I Die'.

Having a plane to catch and with England losing again, we started to make our way out of the crowd towards the exit, periodically looking back and praying for that sudden roar of an equaliser.

As we were leaving we encountered a group of Mexican lads. They wanted to swap shirts with an Englishman. Callum had bought his T-shirt out there off the market and it had cost about £3. It wasn't official merchandise. It had a number 10 on the back but the three lions looked like goats. The

Mexican's shirt looked genuine enough, but I knew Callum's was fake and this would not be a fair trade.

I tried to dissuade him from being a rotten ambassador but slightly drunk he wouldn't listen. He made the exchange with a straight face and then there were the mutual shoulder slaps of international trade and friendship before we parted.

Getting a safe distance away we both erupted with laughter. A most audacious shirt swap had taken place and we started to run before the error was realised. I couldn't run that fast and we were a bit wobbly from drink. Onlookers must have been confused. Callum, still draped in the flag of St George and me in my 1998 England Umbro, were rolling with laughter, yet the final whistle had blown and our team was out. Crazy English!

Under the street lighting, Callum inspected his new garment. "The bastards!" he said. "They've ripped me off; it's fake."

All is fair, I suppose. We rejoined Hannah and Chris, got changed and caught a cab to the airport. Then disaster. Callum had lost his iPhone. We started searching bags and repacking suitcases in vain. Where was it? On the beach, back at the hotel, in the cab? Hundreds of photos. Some really good ones from this trip but many others. He was distraught. Much more distraught about that than England's failure. Fortunately they were all backed up on his 'cloud' and were retrieved once he got a replacement phone. We boarded the plane with Tony Pulis (then Crystal Palace manager). We were coming home. Once more, football was not.

Chapter 17.

Acrop-Hollis

I had been to France for a few booze cruises but had never seen the real country. I wasn't that fussed about it, to be honest. I had a kind of tongue-in-cheek love-hate attitude towards the French, having never truly forgiven them for killing Nelson at Trafalgar. Just when I was about to let bygones be bygones, they boycotted our exports. Two can play at that game. You won't catch me eating their apples or drinking French wine.

I actually wanted to get to Athens and see the Parthenon, or Acropolis as it is more commonly known. Joanna Lumley had done a TV show about Greece and it looked amazing. I had time on my hands but not much money because I was saving for a three-week holiday in Thailand. I had already paid for my flights and accommodation but needed to save some spending money. Then it came to me. Why not ride my bike to Athens? The Thailand trip was not until January and it was now the end of August.

I researched a route on Google Maps. Approximately 2,200 miles. That was a serious challenge. Almost twice as far as the planned ride in 1996 that ended so miserably. I would split this ride into three phases, each with a specific objective.

Phase 1 – Bronze medal would be to reach the Eiffel Tower in Paris.

Phase 2 – Silver would be to ride up and over Great St Bernard's Pass in the Swiss Alps.

Phase 3 – Gold would be to finish at the Acropolis in Athens.

I was quite apprehensive about this trip. I was a bit older now and I had taken a few knocks since the last time when I was just twenty-seven. Following on from the kayak trip to London, I intended to keep a diary. A proper notebook this time which included a photocopy of my passport, next of kin details, ferry timetables, train times, airlines that did return flights from Athens, and the opening pages included a day-by-day route plan. I was scheduled to arrive at the 'Gold' objective on day 26.

There were a number of key dates to monitor. England would have two Euro 2016 qualifiers, the Scots would hold their referendum on independence and the Oscar Pistorius verdict would be announced. On the last page, just to keep me sane, I had a picture of Cheryl Cole.

I also wrote down a kit list. These items would be stored in a large sports holdall and loaded onto my rear parcel rack. I neglected to include one very basic item. See if you can guess.

- Sleeping bag
- Bivvy bag
- Bivvy sheet
- Roll mat
- Small Union Jack flag
- Gore-Tex jacket
- Fleece jacket
- Ron Hill tracksters
- Woolly hat
- Gloves
- Reflective jacket
- Camera & tripod
- Sunglasses
- Map & compass
- Money and bank cards
- Passport and train tickets
- EHIC card
- Travel insurance documents
- Head torch
- First-aid kit
- Needle and thread
- Pen, pencil, sharpener & eraser
- Knife
- Candles
- Lighters × 2
- Spare batteries
- Camera & mobile chargers
- Plug adapter

- Ear defenders
- Condoms (have various uses)
- Painkillers
- Tweezers
- Insect bite spray
- Mosquito repellent
- Shaving cream and brush
- Razors
- Mirror
- Shower gel
- Toilet paper
- Muscle rub
- Sun cream
- Vitamins & cod liver oil
- Toothbrush & toothpaste
- Puncture repair kit
- Bike pump & spare inner tube
- Swimming trunks
- Knee braces x 2
- T-shirts x 3
- Running vests x 2
- Boxer shorts x 3
- Socks x 2 pairs
- Allen keys
- Adjustable spanner
- 2 bags of Alpen
- 3 Cup a Soups
- 30 teabags
- Asda powdered milk
- Bluet gas stove + spare canister
- Metal mug
- Scotchbrite
- Mobile phone

The total weight was 15 kg. I also carried 2 litres of water. One litre weighs 1 kg.

I did a road test on Sunday 31st August and made the necessary final adjustments. I set off from home at 11.25am on a bright, sunny Tuesday, the 2nd September 2014.

I had picked up the bike second-hand from eBay. It was a bit too big for me but I'd manage and at just £80 it was a bargain. The 'Marin San Rafael OVATION' had twenty-four gears but I'd never get higher than the eighteenth. The kitbag was so big that occasionally my heels would brush against it as I worked the pedals and the weight would cause a destabilising pendulum effect if I stood up out of the saddle to push hard.

I reached Syston Station in just ten minutes. With hardly any effort I had averaged 12 mph. The train arrived on time but boarding was difficult. The bike was heavy and I struggled to lift it. A fellow passenger assisted and I took my seat. Then came the questions: Where was I going?

"Greece! Ferry from Dover to Calais. Ride to Paris to see the Eiffel Tower, then south to Lake Geneva, over the Swiss Alps into Italy and then follow the coast to Slovenia, Croatia, Bosnia, Monte Negro and Albania. Cut in cross country through Macedonia and fly home from Athens after a selfie at the Acropolis."

The man was amazed. "Really?"

This seemed to stir his spirit of adventure and he quizzed me for more information. He then, with great enthusiasm, recounted the details to the guard and ticket inspector. They were fascinated too. I felt like a fraud. I was getting all this attention yet hadn't done anything yet. The train arrived at Leicester, I was assisted to the platform and wished good luck.

The train for London arrived five minutes late but I hoped to make my connection on time. Sitting down I noticed that there were 3-pin electrical plug sockets for charging phones and laptops. That was handy and I took advantage.

The late arrival at St Pancras meant I had just minutes to find platform 12 and board for Dover. Apparently, bikes aren't allowed on the escalators and I should have used the elevator. No time for that.

I just made it, running down the platform as the final whistles were blown. Stood in the aisle with my bike, I noticed blood trickling down my right ankle. I must have caught myself on one of the metal pedals. It had removed chunks of flesh and my ankle was starting to sting.

I reached Dover Priory and rode quickly to the ferry port. I bought my one-way ticket but the next ferry was leaving in ten minutes and the boarding gate was already closed. All that rushing around and now I would have to wait

for an hour until the 4.40pm crossing. I sent a text to Hannah. Next stop…
FRANCE.

The P&O *Spirit of France* was delayed and that annoyed me. I did not intend to do night-time riding and I considered it vital to clear Calais as quickly as possible. I would be sleeping in woods or fields and did not wish to be stumbled upon by gangs from the refugee camp known as the 'Jungle'.

I got myself a glass of Stella Artois and found a comfy chair by the window. Oh look, another charging point. I plugged in my gadgets to ensure I was fully loaded and then relaxed.

I had been the first to board but would be the last to disembark. I was choked by all those lorries initially but then the road was clear. I had about an hour of daylight remaining. Let's get moving!

From the very beginning, I found the French signs annoying. Google and my printed maps gave me numbered roads to follow. When I was on those roads the French had given them completely different numbers. This was very frustrating. Was it some sort of security measure to confuse the Germans if they invaded a third time?

It was still warm but getting darker. With an abundance of energy and first-day enthusiasm, I was not ready to stop. The more miles I clocked today, the sooner I could be out of France. Against my initial plans I found myself riding into the darkness. Heading west I could see the English Channel over my right shoulder. The busy shipping lane was lit up by vessels going in various directions. In the far distance I could even see the lights of the southern shores in England.

I picked up signs that read 'Boulogne par la cote' and followed that coastal route. I stopped about 10.30pm and camped under a tree on a small track off the main road. My head torch seemed to act as a magnet to lots of little spiders. I quickly fell asleep but was awoken by noisy cockerels. Was it morning already? NO! Just 3am and they were already competing with each other.

Wednesday 3rd

By 7.10am I was back on the road and at 9.25am I stopped for a drink in the town of Samer. No SPOON! I nipped into a local supermarket to purchase the utensil. I had to buy a pack of three. That was too many. I definitely needed one, but decided that two would provide me with a spare and they could have a dual function as tyre leavers in the event of a puncture. I discarded the third as it was unnecessary excess weight. I bought a pack of chocolate biscuits and then found a bench to have a rather civilised and typically English morning tea.

Dotted along the coastal road were various museums of the D-Day invasion. A Sherman tank outside one and massive concrete gun emplacements outside others.

I had cleared Boulogne by midday and rode on through glorious sunshine. There were many wind turbines. Many more than I had seen in England. There wasn't much traffic. I was typically overtaken by campervans, motorbike tourists and HGVs. I didn't see many cyclists.

At 2.30pm I stopped at McDonald's for a 'Big Tasty' meal. That would prove to be my regular diet on this trip. I needed the carbohydrates and it was easier than cooking. I reached the cathedral city of Amiens just before 7pm and had a quick look. I wanted to be out of the built-up areas soon though because of my standard night-time routine.

I was camping for free. That meant I needed to sleep somewhere safe, preferably secluded, quiet, away from the road and where I was unlikely to be disturbed by passers-by, dog walkers or drunks returning from a bar. This wasn't that difficult and usually meant somewhere out in the countryside surrounded by trees. My logic was that people were unlikely to stumble across me if I camped when it got dark and moved on at first light. Sleeping in cities or built-up areas was to be avoided.

For this second night I found a gated orchard. In it was an old wooden dining table. I camped underneath thinking it would be quicker than erecting my bivvy. As I shut my eyes in the silent still night, I could hear a faint crunching sound. I searched for the source. Something was gnawing away from inside the table so I abandoned my den and set up a bivvy between two trees.

I estimated that I had done close to 100 miles on this first full day. I was very dehydrated though. The hot end of summer sun was still powerful and I wasn't drinking enough. I had finished my original 2 litres. I had bought 1.5 litres from a supermarket for just 35 cents. The same size bottle in a service station cost €3.80 but I had been desperate.

Thursday 4th

My second night was awful. I had been sweating heavily and my sunburnt face had been reflecting heat off my arms (used as pillows). I checked the mirror. There were white tidemarks where my sunglasses had been and my bottom lip was shrivelled. Fortunately, today was overcast and grey. I made good progress in this more favourable weather but had to divert near Creil as the road was off limits to cyclists. My road map did not include many of the smaller routes so I headed on a loose compass bearing towards the capital.

By mid-afternoon I had joined the D316 and followed that into St Denys, Paris. From there I meandered through the city and came to the Champs Elysees. Had a selfie at the Arc de Triomphe before arriving at the Eiffel Tower about 5.30pm. I sent a text back home. In reply I received the welcome news that England had beaten Norway 1-0.

Soldiers patrolled with rifles drawn and the traffic was chaotic. The skies were still grey but I had made it. This was the BRONZE. I had ridden to the Eiffel Tower. I was buzzing with excitement and satisfaction. I was one day ahead of schedule but had no time to lose. It would be dark soon and getting out of Paris for night number three would take a while. First, a victory celebration. I found a French restaurant, cleaned myself up in its bathroom and then ordered a steak, French fries and a couple of glasses of vin rouge.

That wine went straight to my head and I needed to walk it off a bit before I could risk getting back into the saddle. I followed the Seine south and continued on a loose compass bearing towards Melun. The navigation went wrong from thereon. I ran out of roads. It was motorways in all directions and I had nowhere to go. Most of the place names weren't even on my map. I needed a bigger scale, an A-Z or street map. I was exhausted from going in so many wrong directions. There was a nature reserve just on the edge of an industrial park near Combs-la-Ville. I found some high ground away from the croaking frogs and soon fell asleep. But for the sound of lorries on the nearby motorway, it was a comfortable night.

Friday 5th

After yesterday's achievement, the Swiss Alps seemed so far away. I was tired and frustrated. My priority now was to find a decent map. I moved into the residential zone. On the bus shelters were local street plans and these helped to pinpoint my location and ascertain the most appropriate direction to travel. I was soon riding along the D306 into Melun. I stopped for a much needed McDonald's breakfast. I think that I had overexerted myself in order to reach Paris a day early but now I was fired up and ready again.

I bought a detailed atlas from a service station. The new map was awesome and I couldn't go wrong now. Any redundant pages were torn out to reduce weight. Another Big Tasty with extra salt on the fries kept my engine burning.

By 9.15pm I was camped in a treeline at the edge of a field outside St Florentine. I had a full bird bath. My bum was getting saddle sore. It was uncomfortable to sit but standing was aggravating my ankle, hip and back. I started popping the ibuprofen and padded my seat out with my woolly hat.

Saturday 6th

After a good night's sleep I hit the road at 7.40am. There was a McDonald's at Tonnerres but it was not yet open so I headed for a picnic area and had a big mug-full of Alpen. I figured that I should eat that from now on and lighten the load. It was not necessary to keep as emergency rations. They made Alpen in Switzerland and I'd be there soon. The terrain was already changing. It was getting higher and I had to do a lot of hill climbing which was harder than I had anticipated.

The D905 made navigation easy and was my companion for much of that day. I passed an impressive renaissance chateau and large dam which locals used for swimming, and the upper banks like a beach for sunbathing. The lower banks were lined with anglers. Little geckos dashed out in front of me from time to time and I swerved to avoid them.

This would be the day that I ran out of water. The situation became desperate. Villages were few and far between. If there were local shops, they were all closed for the weekend. France is not a 24/7 nation like Britain. By 4pm the sun showed no sign of cooling and my 0.5 litre bottle was almost empty. But then there was a long downhill stretch that would soon take me into Dijon. Right?

Wrong. What followed was a series of steep climbs with hairpin bends like an Alpine road. My water was all gone. I found a discarded roadside bottle and there was some clear liquid in it. Should I take the risk? No option. It tasted like water and I downed it.

I eventually reached the town of Genlis on the outskirts of Dijon. All the shops were shut. I cursed the place but 'Royal Kebab' was open. Like a scene from *Ice Cold in Alex*, I quaffed my first 0.5 litre bottle from the fridge. It cost €1.50 and barely wet my mouth. Water is so undervalued. I had not been this thirsty since the jungle in 1987. I bought another four bottles and a bottle of cherry coke before feasting on a large chicken kebab with salad and chips.

I slept that night in a hedgerow on the village outskirts behind some sheds.

Sunday 7th September

It was another night of excessive sweating and I decided that my Gore-Tex bivvy bag was responsible. The bag was supposed to be waterproof yet breathable. I would put my sleeping bag inside then climb in. Doing up the bivvy bag zip meant no insect bites. Unfortunately I think my Gore-Tex was beyond its sell-by date. I had owned it since 1985 and it still displayed my details: MNE WRIGHT IDH P044793K. It was like sleeping in a bin liner. I was soaked and my sleeping bag was too. I slashed and discarded the old and now useless piece of kit.

I rode on to the town of Parcey. There I bought 3 litres of the precious liquid and a couple of apples. I stopped mid-morning for a rest and to lay out all my kit for drying and airing as I dined on more Alpen. Not far to Switzerland now. I sent a couple of text updates back home. My nose was starting to peel.

At Salins-les-Bains, I bought some more water and a delicious custard-filled croissant. I spent the rest of the afternoon riding and pushing uphill. This was quite arduous and I was concerned over exactly how much there would be. The steep gradients and hot sun were taking my breath away and I had to climb in frequent short bursts, taking rests under shade whenever or wherever available. If it was this bad in France, what would the Alps be like?

The road signs were still contradicting my google directions but my new atlas was serving me well. Many of the cars that overtook me were Swiss-registered and the cows in the fields had bells round their necks. I knew that this would be my last day in France.

As the daylight faded, suddenly there was a sign for Switzerland and the road started to descend. The steep incline saw me accelerate with no effort. I was freewheeling at great speed. Ahead was the border post. All lanes were open, no guards, no passport inspection, just straight through. I am in Switzerland! YES!

It was cold. Wind-chill factor during the descent had frozen my insides. I had zoomed past a Chinese takeaway during the downhill stretch and really wished I'd stopped to order a Fu Yung and egg fried rice.

By 9.30pm I had gone further than I'd intended. I was tired and it was dark. I made a hasty camp at the roadside near Croy and got warm in my sleeping bag.

Monday 8th

Had the best night's sleep. The cooler temperature helped and there was no sweating. Light car traffic commenced around 5.30am and gradually roused me from my comfortable slumber. The air was crisp and it was quite breezy too. I needed to use my kitbag as a windbreak in order to make tea.

At over 500 miles, this was by now officially the longest bike ride I had ever done. My French atlas covered parts of Switzerland so navigation was not yet an issue.

With it being 100 years since the beginning of the Great War, I dedicated my ride through France to the memory of all those who suffered or fell. The landscape was too beautiful for fighting.

A different kind of conflict would happen today. Switzerland v England. Coincidentally, my destination would be the Swiss town of Bex.

I reached Lausanne about 11am and dived into Lake Geneva. The sun sparkled on the warm crystal-clear Alpine water. Fully submerged I felt as though I could swallow large gulps.

I cleaned as much kit as I could and after using plenty of soap, put on a fresh set of clothes. I discarded my first well-worn T-shirt and boxer shorts to make the load lighter. I didn't shave as I was unsure of the climatic conditions higher up. My back tyre was looking bald. Carrying all that weight meant it was working harder than the front one which still looked like new. I swapped them over and then rode clockwise around the lake towards Villeneuve.

I grabbed a McDonald's at Rennaz. Much more expensive in Switzerland. I purchased some more water, milk, Toblerone, apples and lip balm from a supermarket and then pressed on. I came to realise that nearly everyone in this place drove a Porsche, Ferrari, Mercedes, Audi or BMW.

I picked up signs for Great St Bernard's Pass or Col du Grand St Bernard and pedalled on. It wouldn't be long until I started climbing again.

The map suggested that Orsieres would be a convenient place for tonight. Any higher and it might be too cold. An early night and an early start would hopefully see me complete the ascent before the midday sun became intolerable.

Tuesday 9th

I woke up after a decent night. My Bluet stove had run out of gas but a complete mental block descended upon me. I knew how to change the canister and had the spare out ready. Of course replacing the canister was simply the opposite of removal. I had forgotten. It wasn't like that at all. Compressed liquid gas hissed out of the punctured canister. I tried brute strength to make the connection but in doing so I froze my hand. How stupid of me. I'd carried that spare for nearly 600 miles. Excess weight for nothing and my hand would now be sore from a cold burn. I was going up into the mountains with no cooker and that meant no hot tea until I was down the other side.

The ascent was hard work. At one point I was topless, pushing my bike up the steep winding roads, hairpin bend after hairpin bend until I reached Bivouac de Napoleon. The French emperor had once marched his army this way and stopped here. I doubt he would have seen all the souvenir shops though. A coach-load of tourists clapped a round of applause as I trudged on through. It would have been a lot easier to have taken the ski lift but I pressed on to the tunnel which would run for 6 km.

At one point the view to my right from the tunnel was a picturesque dam holding back very blue water. On reaching the exit there was a second tunnel for motor vehicles but my only option was to veer off and head towards the famous pass.

The weather deteriorated as I went higher and the rugged terrain reminded me of Dartmoor or Snowdonia; cold, windswept, low-lying clouds with freezing rain falling. There were cliffs, massive boulders and short brown grass. Waterfalls and many small streams trickled towards me. Why was I carrying so much water? There were some lower patches of white. They were sheep. Higher up those patches were snow.

At regular intervals there were large concrete bandstand-type constructions. Avalanche shelters. There'd be no danger of that today. Not enough snow. The pass is only accessible from June till September. The rest of the year it is covered. Sometimes as deep as 8 metres. I used each shelter as a food station and munched on chunks of my Toblerone.

At times the ascent was close to 45 degrees. Easy for the 4x4s, campervans and motorcycles that overtook me. There were no other cyclists or pedestrians; I was the only one working hard. I reached the top by 1.15pm. At the summit there was a restaurant, a hostel and a border checkpoint. In the car park was a Dutch couple with their St Bernard dog. I tried to get a selfie with the beast but he was awkward and kept moving. I couldn't stay there too long as the rain was coming down and I needed the warmer temperatures of the valley below.

Right there, on the border with Italy, was the sign I had been seeking. I had just bagged the SILVER.

With no passport inspection or guards, I was straight through into the Aosta Valley. Below me lay approximately 10 miles of steep descent via hairpin bends. I put on all of my clothing layers and gloves before commencing the rapid freewheeling. My brake pads took a beating.

Halfway down, I turned a corner and there in front of me was the opening scene to the 1969 *Italian Job*. I was awestruck. This was an amazing bonus and I started to sing Matt Monro's 'On Days Like These'.

I was completely buzzing now. This trip was officially a success even if it had to end prematurely. By the time I reached the plaza in Aosta I was frozen to the core. There was bright sunshine in the main square and people sat outside under parasols with cold beers. I was shivering with a dripping nose and was more appropriately dressed for the Arctic. I found a camping shop and bought some replacement gas for my stove. Then it was time to celebrate. A hot Italian pizza to warm me up and a cool Italian beer to wash it down. I had certainly earnt this meal but my appetite was insatiable. I ordered a second pizza and two more beers. I sent text messages to announce my success. I was very pleased with myself. To make my day even better, the news from home was that England had won last night, 2-0.

I was back on small-scale maps now but at least the Italians hadn't changed the road numbers. The weather deteriorated and just south of St Vincent, I came across a roadside derelict. This provided a dry night and adequate shelter from the constant downpour.

Wednesday 10th

On the road by 7.05am and made good progress. I had company for a short while, an elderly Italian man wearing full Lycra and exercising on his racing bike. He spoke no English but could do German, French or Spanish. We communicated via the latter. Hablo un poco Español. As a result of his advice and directions, I stopped mid-morning at Lago (lake) di Piverone for another bath and my first shave. It was a beautiful spot so I did my laundry there too and made a mug of tea.

I reached the outskirts of Milan around 4pm and dined once again at McDonald's. I noted how long, smooth, flat and perfectly straight the Roman roads were. There were plenty of signs too. Cycling in Italy was easy so far but my lack of language skills caused a problem. How was I to know that 'frizante' meant sparkling carbonated water? I bought a 2 litre bottle and was covered in froth and spray when I opened it.

I had a couple of encounters that afternoon. Which sounds the more credible? That I stumbled across the San Siro Stadium or that I strayed into the red-light district? Well, both were true.

Just 12 km from Milano, the main road suddenly became a motorway and I was prohibited from continuing. My map was useless at this stage but I knew that I was west of the city and consequently took the next available right turn. This road took me into an industrial unit. It was only about 5pm. There stood in one of the car parks was an attractive young lady – very short skirt and wearing Italian flag knickers. As I got closer it dawned on me that she might actually be a man, a transsexual. I couldn't help but stare. Was this an office fancy dress party? The woman/man stared back with a smile. She can't be, I thought and quickly looked elsewhere. Down a side alley was another scantily dressed woman and in the trees sat on camping chairs were two slightly larger and older women. Yes, this was indeed the vice zone. I turned around and went back the other way.

Then I saw a silver-coloured VW Polo driving around a muddy grass field. I laughed to myself, suspecting the driver had been having some fun with a prostitute behind the trees. I continued but noticed a man sat on a fence at the roadside. He was well hidden back in the trees and texting on his mobile phone. A pimp perhaps? As I cleared him, I was overtaken by the Polo. The driver almost immediately slammed on the brakes just in front of me. I was a little startled by this. Did he want to speak to me? No. He was looking back in his mirror. I overtook him and then he reversed at speed to where the suspected pimp was sat.

Memories of my old job returned. I had seen this type of unnatural behaviour before. I suspected this was the prelude to a drug deal. Let it go, Iain; way out of my jurisdiction and not even my job anymore.

With this type of activity happening, I decided that Milan would not be a safe place to sleep rough and with a renewed sense of urgency I pressed on.

The traffic in the city centre was lawless and chaotic. Italians do whatever they want. Horns tooting, scooters weaving in and out, the cars drive, turn or park wherever and whenever it suits and often without warning. Others were ignoring the traffic lights. Complete madness.

Heading through the city on a compass bearing I literally rode by the football stadium. The home of both Inter and AC Milan had to be worth a selfie. Then it was a determined effort to clear the built-up area and rest for the night. Eventually reaching the outskirts of Melzo, I camped in a field. There was an electrical storm that night but I managed to stay dry.

Thursday 11th

I would need to take it easier today. Pushing hard yesterday made my knees ache. I struggled to get back on the right road and wasted a couple of hours going round in circles. My compass invited me down a gravel track which became a dead end. I then had to scale a fence and climb a steep embankment. This had to be done by instalments. First a reconnaissance of where to go, then carry the bike and finally carry the kit bag. This was tiring and the mini-operation saw my front mudguard break off. Oh well, a bit less weight.

To my relief I picked up signs for Brescia and followed the SS11 after a welcome McDonald's breakfast. I would need to ask for a café latte in future as the espresso was too strong and very small.

Roadworks caused me to divert onto the SP185. There were many more large lorries on this route and these new hazardous conditions encouraged me to ride quickly. The Alps were visible once more over my left shoulder and I took a lunch break by a beautiful river. With the sun shining brightly, it was an opportunity to dry my kit after last night's deluge. I also bathed in the clear waters.

I had not had a proper sleep for more than a week and it was starting to show. I noticed that I was suffering fatigue-induced concentration lapses. Minor ones, such as forgetting things that I had just done. This would cause a paranoid response. Before moving off, I routinely checked various things. Was my load secure? Were my passport, wallet and camera stowed safely? Had I left anything behind? Despite knowing I had done these standard practices, I would be unable to remember doing them and have to stop to double-check. Sometimes I even triple-checked. This was slowing me down.

A big supermarket in Brescia enabled me to replace my frayed bungees, drink some milk and end my salt craving by munching on a large bag of crisps.

By 7pm I had reached Lago di Garda. This scenic lake was a popular tourist resort but also quite exclusive. All of the lakeside beaches were privately owned and fenced off. With black clouds looming and flashes of lightning I would need to find or make shelter very soon. On the road out I came across a wooded area and had just enough time to build a perfect bivvy. The heavens opened but the trees reduced the impact and I would stay dry. I had a wonderful night's sleep.

Friday 12th

Awakening that next morning I needed to address an itch on my face. As my hand scratched my cheek, it dislodged the culprit: a big fat juicy slug. They were everywhere. All over my sleeping bag, my kitbag, my bike tyres and my trainers. It took a while to pack so as to reduce the number of passengers but I would be finding stowaways for a couple of days.

By 9.55am I had reached Verona. I was kindly allowed to charge my gadgets in McDonald's. The camera battery was completely flat. It seemed that I had been badly bitten by insects last night, despite wearing repellent. I considered purchasing a mosquito net and decided to keep a lookout. The afternoon was difficult as I rode through wind and rain for about four hours. Being cold and wet encouraged me to ride for longer in order to stay warm but it was exhausting. I cleared the city of Treviso and headed southeast towards San Dona di Piave. By 9.30pm I was about 7 miles short but a derelict farmhouse beckoned me over and I had a comfortable night sleeping on a flat bed that I made from an old wooden door.

Saturday 13th

I hoped to see the Adriatic Sea today and make Trieste for a last-chance Italian ice cream. I would not be disappointed. The sea came into view about 1.30pm and I reached the frontier city by 3pm. Trieste looked worthy of a longer stay. Perhaps I might return some other time but having spent five days in Italy I was keen to press on. I had a huge ice cream and then pedalled to the border. A bicycle lane took me directly into Slovenia. Again there were no guards or passport controls; indeed, so far, I had only once needed to show my little red book and that had been before boarding the ferry in England.

I had no map of Slovenia but my Italian one covered the relevant area. I headed to Koper where I had another McDonald's meal. Then I got a decent map from a petrol station. After that it was a steep climb into the mountains. I found a gated track just outside Sveti Anton (St Anthony) and laid out my roll mat on the flat tarmac. I had a good peaceful rest.

Sunday 14th

I was awoken by constant church bells at 6am and after just two hours of riding I made the border with Croatia. There were plenty of guards here. They looked me up and down. The reader of my passport took it away to his supervisor who scrutinised it further, but it was returned quite quickly, no questions asked and I was waved on. Others in cars were being thoroughly searched.

I was excited about having made it this far. Rijeka this afternoon would be the halfway point. I liked extending my number of countries visited. My five years with the Marines totalled twenty-five. I would add only six more over the next twenty-three years but since leaving the police I had done Jamaica,

Brazil, Switzerland, Slovenia and now Croatia. Altogether that made thirty-six. 'Dobrodosli' was the greeting on the first sign. Welcome to Republika Hrvatska.

I had entered near Grad Buzet and spent most of the day climbing into mountains and forests. Truly beautiful countryside. Motorcycle tourists and campervans were overtaking me and I was quite jealous of the effortless ascents. It was too hot to climb at midday so I took a break by a mountain stream. Good place to have a wash, shave and do my laundry too. The wet clothes would dry over my handle bars as I pressed on an hour later.

The quickest and shortest or direct routes were subject to toll charges and off limits to cyclists. For me it would be long, meandering mountain roads, but these were so peaceful and once I reached the high ground, the coastal views to my right were spectacular. The Croatian mountains provided me with free water. Firstly from a fountain, secondly from springs and thirdly from the streams. It was a comfort to know it was available and meant I need not carry so much. I cleared Rijeka and then rode over an impressive bridge from Crik Venica. The crossing was high up and the winds made me a little unstable. It was a very long way down to the valley below.

A baguette, bar of chocolate, carton of milk and tube of paprika Pringles satisfied the appetite that evening before bedding down in a lay-by near Novi Vinodolski. I was immediately attacked by mosquitoes. The repellent failed. It was very hot in my sleeping bag with clothing garments wrapped around my face and any other exposed skin. I had a terrible night.

Monday 15th

The traffic started early and I was ready to join it at 6.30am. Following the coast was fantastic. The sun came up to shine on the mirrored sea surface. Croatia was stunning. Dubrovnik was over 350 miles away so I would be in this country a long time. The riding was difficult though. The sun was very hot and the undulating mountain terrain massively reduced my average daily mileage. The uphills normally involved walking. Firstly because they were so steep and secondly because my bike was in need of servicing by now, particularly the gears. They didn't enjoy being changed and I did not dare do so in case that broke my drive chain, leaving me stranded. Navigation was easy though; I just had to keep the sea to my right and for part of the way I could use the overlap detail from my Slovenia map.

Snakes! Little ones the size of a peperami wriggled out in front of me.

Many had been run over but I was trying to avoid killing them. I thought it funny how I was completely calm about the geckos yet concerned about these slithering things. They were after all just geckos without legs.

At Karlobag I resupplied – bought some apples, milk, water and Croatian Jaffa cakes. I came to realise that much of this coastline's beauty was fake. It was man-made. The cliffs descended to the clear blue sea waters. The road had been carved through the living rock and the rubble had been dropped into the sea to make foundations and artificial but natural-looking coves. Each time I rode around a bend I would see a similar landscape. It would be spectacular but unnatural. There was no sand either. I would say that I preferred Scotland but this place had guaranteed sunshine.

I noticed that many of the road signs had been used for target practice. They had holes from shotgun blasts and bullets.

I rode until nightfall and came to a huge bridge with signs indicating that it was a venue for bungee jumping. There I took a photo of a large tourist information map which gave me an indication of my current location. This map revealed that my plan to simply keep the sea on my right was flawed. There were so many offshore islands and the views were intermittent due to mountains. I couldn't tell what was coastal water or inland lakes so I just had to keep pushing south.

I camped that night on a track just off the main road. I had just got comfy when I had to move. A car towing a trailer full of logs for a wood-burning stove was heading towards me on its way to a nearby cottage. I moved slightly off the track but was conscious of the snakes. It was cooler up here. Too cold for mosquitoes, right?

Wrong. The silence was interrupted by a buzzing sound that circulated my right ear. I swiped it away. Then it was in my left. I swiped it again. Then it returned to my right ear. And so it went on, that tiny predator persistently looking for a way in to feast on my blood. I stretched my woolly hat down over my ears and buried myself deep inside my sleeping bag. The buzzing stopped. Then the crunching started. What was that? I looked up but could see nothing. The crunching sound continued. Something close by was eating and I could hear the vibration in the soil. Was it a grub in one of those apples? Or something in my kitbag? I checked it but no signs. It was a clear starry night. The temperature was dropping. Despite being tired, these noises were keeping me awake. It was several hours before I dropped off.

185

Tuesday 16th

I woke up soaked. An icy dew had descended. I had been sleeping out in the open as there were no trees from which to suspend a bivvy sheet. 5.30am and I either had to get moving or stay shivering in my bag.

By 8am I had cleared Benkovac and ridden into Islam Grcki. This was a battle-scarred village, an almost ghost town. There were shrapnel marks on the road surface, possibly from grenades or mortars. Some of the houses were peppered with bullet holes around the doorways and windows. This place had clearly seen some heavy fighting. Many of the houses were now unoccupied and any of them would have given me a better night than I had just had.

Some die-hard residents had remained with a few roaming chickens and goats but otherwise this was a sad and sorry place. On the village outskirts was a memorial decorated with candles and floral tributes for those who fell in 1993.

By midday I had reached Krka. This fjord was indeed an area of outstanding natural beauty. Small ships could sail deep into the mainland. There were campsites, sandy beaches, beautiful bridges and scenic waterfalls. A wonderful place.

My route in had been interesting. Mostly downhill I had seen sheep with bells round their necks, vineyards and several roadside memorials. It seems that where someone was killed, be that in conflict or a road collision, a marker would be placed. That might be a mini-shrine or a marble headstone featuring an engraved image of the deceased. It seemed to be very Christian-orientated.

The route out was perhaps the steepest climb of my entire trip. From sea level right back up into the high ground and National Park region. Signs advised motorists to beware of wild boar. Aha! Last night's crunching sounds were finally explained. Dried carcasses on the road indicated that the snakes were getting bigger too.

Some of the cars took me back to the 1980s. There were Vauxhall Astras, Chevettes, Cavaliers, Ford Escorts, MK1 VW Golfs and Renault 4s. Hardly any rust. Must be climatic. In England we put corrosive salt on our roads to prevent slippery ice conditions. Out here they probably didn't need to.

By late afternoon I had cleared Split and ended my day on the outskirts of Podstrana. At night-time, the illuminated high cliffs and coastal water reminded me of Gibraltar. Getting out of town seemed impossible. I was tired and in danger of falling over. There was no proper footpath or indication of where the road ended. I could easily fall over the edge of a cliff or down a hole. After a few near misses, I decided to dismount and started walking. I cannot physically walk far before developing a progressively worsening limp. I soon began to struggle. Fatigue was one thing. Ankle, knee and back pain were something else. I urgently needed to find discrete sleeping quarters.

I don't know how I spotted it. There was a concrete embankment over to my left. I could see there was a hole in it. Above the embankment was a row of terraced houses. I examined the hole. It led into a service chamber with some kind of boiler or plumbing machinery installed. There was a raised flat platform that could serve perfectly as a table and bed. I lit a couple of candles and moved in for the night. I was completely sheltered, wind and mosquito free.

Wednesday 17th

Had the best night of my trip. I really needed that place to catch up from all those nights of disturbed sleep. Headed out into an overcast morning that brightened up around midday. By 2.30pm I had reached a scenic viewpoint with a car park. Tourists spilled from their coaches to take photographs of the lake below and surrounding mountainous countryside at Bacinska Jezera. I joined them.

I set my camera on a timer and holding it at arm's length by the tripod, I posed for my selfie. A voice in English called out, "You want me to take that?" I checked the quality of my snapshot. It was OK. "No, I'm fine but thanks anyway," I said.

The volunteer was shocked that I was English and was very pleased to see a fellow Brit. Andy and Ann were a couple in their fifties. Not yet retired, they had simply taken a year out to go touring Europe and North Africa in their campervan. I was invited to join them for a mug of coffee. A real mug, not that metal monstrosity that I was used to. A real mug didn't need masking tape around the rim to prevent my lips burning. Ann went to put the kettle on while I sat on the bench overlooking that magnificent scenery.

I was quizzed about my journey and I disclosed the adventure so far. They were fascinated. Andy spread out his map to show me exactly where I was, about two hours from Neum. The coffee arrived and so did the chocolate biscuits. This was a truly welcome break and it was good to have a proper conversation. The couple were from Taunton and that of course held a mutual interest because it was my old home with 40 Commando. They said that the unit was still there and that marines regularly ran by their address. Andy inspected my transport and decided that my chain needed some oil. Quite a bit actually.

I could easily have given up at that point. Stop too long and the motivation to get moving again would diminish. I had to keep going. I thanked my superb hosts and we wished each other luck for the rest of our journeys.

Well-lubricated, my machine was a much smoother ride; silent too, no more creaking. It didn't take long to reach Bosnia. I passed through this narrow section of the country inside thirty minutes before returning to Croatia. I then rode through a large valley full of crop plantations and roadside markets selling the locally produced fruit and vegetables including pomegranates, grapes, lemons and garlic. They also sold their own brands of jam, fruit juice and alcohol. Unfortunately, I had no local money and was therefore restricted to card purchases at supermarkets or service stations. I stopped when it was dark just south of Sloan under a picnic bench in a roadside lay-by.

Thursday 18th

On the road at 6am. I wanted to be out of Croatia today. My regular roadkill included moths, butterflies, caterpillars and large crickets. Sometimes they'd go under my wheels. Sometimes they just hit me in the face. Those large crickets were quite painful.

By 7am I had stopped at a very convenient waterfall which provided me with a full shower, an opportunity to do my laundry, give all my kit a thorough clean and fill all my bottles while boiling up some water for a hot mug of tea.

The ride to Dubrovnik was tough. Undulating terrain with more ups than downs. The hot sun made this even harder and my water was disappearing fast. By 9.20am I had arrived. Cruise liners were moored in the harbour but diverting to the main town would involve a steep descent. Coming back up again would be a real challenge. I decided against it. "Stick to the objective and do not get side-tracked," I told myself.

Just a few miles from the border with Montenegro I was overtaken by a cyclist. He was obviously touring like me but his bike and kit looked far superior to mine. He waved his hand in a friendly gesture as he rode past but I was in no mood for a race and couldn't go that fast anyway.

With the border post in sight I quickened but then a huge snake appeared in the road. It was about 1.5 metres long and as thick as the cardboard inner of a toilet roll. I swerved as it was in striking distance. My words were: "Oh ya fucker!" It had given me a fright but instead of attacking me it slipped away into the long grass.

I was through the border by 12.20pm. Montenegro was one of those countries that England usually hammered at football. Were it not for this trip I would have had no idea where it was. A pity really because it was a beautiful place.

I was straight into the first supermarket to top up my supplies and buy some lunch. Bought a Twix and some caramel wafers. I also bought a carton of milk. I started to gulp it down but to my shock it was plain yoghurt.

Once fed and hydrated I set off again. I came to the delightful Rissan Kotor Bay. A very impressive sight. Surrounded by high mountains this natural womb-shaped harbour was a popular tourist spot. Bars and restaurants lined the shore. There was a ferry across the narrow inlet but I would opt for cycling the long way round. For part of this I would be joined by a German.

The same cyclist who had earlier overtaken me before the border reappeared, he was taking a photo of the view. I wanted a similar picture and by way of co-operation we used each other's cameras instead of taking selfies. I cannot recall his name. I probably never even asked. But he was retired and in his late fifties or early sixties. Still looked young and very fit. He had cycled from Germany and was heading for Corfu. From there he would get a ferry to Italy and cycle back home. I was very impressed. He was travelling much lighter than me as he was spending his nights in hotels. Consequently we were at odds in terms of cruise speed but we shared part of that journey. When we reached the main moorings he wanted to go and take photographs of the ships, so I wished him well and carried on solo.

Rissan Kotor Bay

After a further resupply at a supermarket, where I purchased real milk, I found an abandoned garage workshop. There were some holes in the roof, but it was dry and insect-free.

Friday 19th

Another great night's sleep. Today was bright and sunny as I headed towards the town of Bar. I wanted to take a selfie at the welcome sign. I found an old beer can as part of my preparation and carried it for many miles. When I finally arrived at the sign, my camera died. The battery was flat.

I headed into town and found a pizza shop. I don't speak Montenegro and the young lady who served me spoke no English. I thought I was ordering a single slice. It transpired I had ordered all six. This would be more than I could manage. The lady let me charge my gadgets in the shop and I sat outside gradually filling up with the heavily loaded bread. I don't think washing it down with Sprite was a good idea. Buying a second can was definitely a mistake.

For €6 the pizza was a bargain but with a 60 cm diameter (24 inch) it was as big as a bike wheel. I took my time as my gadgets would need at least half an hour. Helicopters whirled high above and periodically people would jump out for some recreational parachuting. It was quite entertaining.

I should perhaps have stopped at two but went on to complete five slices. My insides simply could not cope. My stomach had obviously shrunk due to the daily exercise and limited food intake. When I started off again I could hardly walk. That heavy dough base was absorbing my body moisture and making me thirsty but drinking was almost impossible. I felt as though my insides were ready to burst and I thought it would be many days before I would need to eat again. I managed to clear the outskirts but then had to stop and lie down.

I set off again about an hour later. As it turns out, I had taken the longer route and this would add an extra 10 miles to my journey. I enjoyed the ride though. Montenegro was lovely but I was disappointed by the amount of roadside rubbish and general discarded waste. Some of it had been thrown in the rivers and this included disposable nappies; consequently, I would not be drinking from those natural sources.

I found a convenience store just short of the border and bought some apples and water from there. I picked up an Albanian map from a service station and made my way through the frontier checkpoint.

Montenegro officials stamped my exit but there were no Albanian border guards. No welcome sign either. I was definitely there but perhaps they didn't need border guards because no one ever visited. People only left. First impressions were not good. The place was clearly poverty-stricken. Shanty towns, and an obvious increase in discarded rubbish. The road itself was little more than a dirt track. The crisp clean air of Montenegro was replaced by the stench of stable dung and ammonia. There were horse-drawn carts on the road and the occasional car driving without any lights. How much of this would there be? Would it get better soon?

No. I had only been there ten minutes before I was overtaken by two teenage youths on a moped. The passenger was brandishing a semi-automatic pistol. He aimed it to his right but did not fire. Would he turn to point it at me? I think the saying is something like, "I shit myself." I really thought my time was up. I was going to be robbed or murdered for a battered phone, camera, second-hand bike, dirty sleeping bag and about €10.

The gunmen continued out of sight. I was still alive for now but were they planning to ambush me further up? It was getting darker. As a tourist I would be vulnerable but how could I look like a local? I hid my maps, turned off my bike lights and removed my reflective jacket. *Look confident and pretend you know where you are going,* said the voice in my head.

I got out of the fields and onto the main carriageway. Not much by way of street lighting and massive cracks or potholes on the roads. The worst roads so far. I did not feel comfortable in this place. This was the equivalent of an A-class road yet vehicles were travelling in both directions without lights. I wasn't taking that chance. The reflective jacket went back on as did my bike lights. I rode as hard and fast as I could to get as much of this stage of my epic journey completed. I'm not sure what time I stopped but the night air was making me cold and the wind chill factor made things worse.

There were no safe places to sleep. Every piece of land seemed to be guarded by noisy dogs. Some were obvious guard dogs, others were just wild or strays. Oh please, get me out of this place, I am not enjoying it. To be honest, I was quite afraid. Perhaps I was still in shock from the gun incident earlier.

I came across a construction site. There were plenty of local guard dogs but none specifically at this spot. There was some ambient street lighting and a roofless new-build. It was four walls and an open doorway. It would give me some protection if I could sleep with one eye open.

I sent a text home and was delighted to hear news that the Scots were sticking with the Union Jack.

Saturday 20th

The dogs barked continually and my heart never stopped racing. I couldn't sleep and at 3.30am I gave up. Time to move. I checked the map and took a B-class road away from the built-up areas.

I would soon approach a village. The first guard dog started to bark. He wasn't chained up and began chasing me, so I accelerated as fast as I could go. By the time I reached the second house a new guard dog joined in the chorus and this turned into a relay event. Each new house alerted the next dog and so on. Most were only barking and chasing me away from their territory. Once I was sufficiently clear they would back off. I didn't know that at the time. In the otherwise peaceful early morning it seemed as though the whole neighbourhood would be awoken by this constant barking and I would be surrounded by suspicious locals.

I had been checking back to make sure no gnashing teeth could get my ankles but then further up in front, caught in the glare of my lights, were two more pairs of eyes, reflecting the beams back at me like small torches. I couldn't stop, slow down or turn around. I simply had to pedal faster and go for ramming speed. As I got nearer, the dogs got braver and more aggressive, snarling and snapping at my legs. Please make this nightmare end.

Out of breath and with my heart pounding I was finally clear of the town. I consulted the map once more on the edge of an industrial unit. I couldn't risk that again. Were there any alternative routes? As I sat on the ground with my torch, a man approached to offer assistance. It was about 4.30am. I told him I was OK and sped away before he could get close. Returning to the well-lit built-up area I went on to a service station forecourt. The map painted a grim picture. It was mountains in all directions. I was stuck. The only road available was a motorway and that would obviously be illegal.

The attendant approached and seemed friendly enough. I pointed to my destination on the map. He fingered his way along the big red line. "That is the motorway, and I am on a bicycle," I said.

"In Albania, no problem," he replied.

Could I trust him? He seemed genuine enough. What choice did I have? I'd have to risk it. Motorway it is then. I set off towards the capital, Tirana.

This road was 'the motorway', but it wasn't 'a motorway'. For the most part it was a single carriageway, lined with shops and businesses. The road condition was shocking. Sometimes large sections of surface were missing. Sometimes there would be huge splodges of dried concrete making crusty scabs. There were no kerbs either, so if I veered off course I could end up in a ditch.

It would be terrible in a car. On a bicycle I could swerve around some of these obstacles. Horse and carts just rode through regardless. The attendant had warned me to take a detour at one point to avoid the worst sections of road but that would have added significant extra mileage and I was in a hurry.

I reached Tirana by 8am and then began an afternoon of almost constant ascents. During one of the longer ones, I was joined by a friendly local cyclist in his Lycra racing gear. He rode along giving my kit bag gentle pushes in support and propelling me forward. He spoke very little English but having consulted the map and knowing my destination, he invited me to follow him on a shortcut. There was daylight by now and I was slightly less worried about my predicament. In any event I felt I could trust this chap. He led me through a mountain tunnel. It was still under construction and not yet open to cars. The road surface was brand new and perfectly flat, black tarmac. We cycled through before he waved goodbye. Then came the rapid descent down the other side. Half an hour of freewheeling on a perfect yet deserted road.

Reaching the town of Elbason, I rode through the centre. Sat around the traffic island were people selling dead chickens. They were holding the birds upside down with all the feathers still attached. A police van with about four officers inside drove by. I remember noting that the blue light on the roof was held in place by Sellotape. The children spotted me as a tourist. They smiled, cheered, waved and high-fived me. I was sorry that I had no treats to hand out. I noted also that mosques and churches co-existed here, literally side by side as next-door neighbours. How refreshing.

I had perhaps been unfair to Albania. Most of those I encountered were friendly towards me. Even the traffic cops with their speed guns had smiled and waved. With so many water springs fed by the mountains, there were dozens of hand carwash sites and they all sought my custom. But first impressions last and the roads had punished my bike. Both of my wheels were buckled and one of my pedals was loose. I'd have to go slower from now on.

The climb out via hairpin bends took several exhausting hours and on reaching the summit there was a massive line of cars waiting to cross the border. I joined the queue. I would be in Macedonia tonight, not a moment too soon, and I exhaled a huge sigh of relief.

By 7pm I was in Kalishta. I bought Pringles, chocolate and a local beer to celebrate my new surroundings. I was on the shore of Lake Ohrid. The shopkeeper was a friendly and helpful chap. He only had one hand yet was skilfully able to navigate his mobile phone to Google Maps. He then plotted my best route and translated those directions onto my own map. I sat down on his bench and relaxed. It had been a stressful twenty-four hours but now I felt safe again.

I rode down the pitch-black country lane and decided to camp off road in the treeline. I would be fast asleep within minutes.

Sunday 21st

At exactly 6am I was awoken from my deep slumber by a very loud muezzin. Across the field there were two tall minarets flanking the domed roof of a mosque. I couldn't sleep through that and decided to move on early. I had just 360 miles remaining. The end was in sight. It seemed I was the only one up. This holiday resort was perhaps at the end of its season. I had worked very hard yesterday and perspired heavily. I really needed a bath. Viagra Beach looked inviting but the sun was not yet warm enough to act as a towel and the water was too cold in my fragile state. My urgent need of a wash would have to wait. At 7am the church bells started but all the shops were still closed.

Macedonia was cleaner than Albania, with much better roads. It was equally as mountainous though and I would be climbing for most of the day. Unfortunately the high roads were used by fly-tippers and once again there was litter in the rivers and streams. I needed water but could not get it from there.

By midday I had reached the summit and came across an abandoned restaurant. It was boarded up at the windows and doors, and the rear car park was now used as a dump. Fortunately, at the back of the property was a dripping water pipe. It had been a tap but the handle was missing. By carefully balancing my bottles I could fill up here, while at the same time drying out all my kit after last night's drizzle. I could also have a bird bath and shave.

Once freshened up, I freewheeled back down to the lowlands. This was not at high speed though. The impact of a fast and heavily laden bike going over potholes or blistered tarmac could destroy my already damaged wheels. Drying my kit had been in vain too. The clouds burst and it rained for much of the afternoon. I warmed up at a bus shelter by drinking a hot Cup a Soup.

On the road towards Bitola I was stopped by a couple of lads in a car.

They wanted directions and we consulted my map. In return they offered to give me a lift. I was tempted but couldn't accept. I had come this far unaided and that assistance would invalidate my intended achievement. They fully understood my sentiment and parted, leaving me to press on through the rain.

The turn-off for Bitola was announced by a large road sign. This same sign also gave directions for Greece. It was a semi-euphoric moment. I was inching closer to my destination. The sun came out at Bitola and I restocked at a service station. The border was just a few miles away.

By 4pm I was there. I was ecstatic. A huge Greek flag flew over the border post. Wow; I had ridden my bike to Greece. I couldn't quite believe it. I wanted to savour the moment. I was clicking away with my camera trying to get the perfect selfie. I got it, but wanted another, just to be certain. A Greek soldier shouted a rebuke. Photographs were prohibited at this site and I apologised.

Clearing the checkpoint, I rode into the first village and shouted a hearty "Hello!" to everyone I saw. I was so happy. I sent several text messages back to England but nobody was interested. More important things were unfolding. Leicester were beating Manchester United 4-3 and minutes later 5-3. Double wow!

Greece was paradise. I was back in more familiar modern surroundings for the first time since Italy. The roads were perfectly smooth and a man at a garage allowed me to fill my bottles from his outdoor tap.

I found a brick outhouse which contained an electric switchboard for irrigation equipment. I was on the edge of a very large orchard. I bedded down for another cosy night and went to sleep with a beaming smile on my face.

Monday 22nd

I was up about 7.30am. I didn't want to be caught trespassing by an angry farmer. I had expected Greece to be constant sunshine but this first day started with grey skies and light drizzle. The road signs were easy to follow but coming across one warning about grizzly bears caused me some concern.

By midday the sun finally came out and I was cycling topless. I came across a stranded motorist. She was Russian — quite beautiful and she looked amazing in those tight white jeans but didn't speak a word of English. We communicated by way of charades. Her car was low on fuel and the dashboard advised she had sufficient for another 30 km. She wanted to know whether she would come across a service station inside that distance. I had just come from that way and assured her she'd make it. There were several for her to find and I would have quite happily pointed them out.

Just south of Kozani was a big lake. I had hoped to bathe there but the shores were swamped by bird excrement. Ducks and swans owned that place and I simply couldn't access or exit the water without getting covered in muck.

Later that afternoon I heard a grizzly bear barking away. I was initially alarmed until I realised I was cycling past a fenced-off bear sanctuary. I spent most of the afternoon climbing and it was hard work. When would there be a downhill stretch? I came across a herd of goats with bells round their necks. So, in Europe, that was cows, sheep and now goats. Roadkill indicated there were still many large snakes in these parts.

The constant sun was starting to burn me now. I smothered myself in sunscreen but my right shoulder was developing tiny blisters as I rode by

Mount Olympus. On reaching Elasona I was waved in by a kebab shop owner. He persuaded me that I needed one of his delicious chicken-filled pitta breads and a plate of chips. All washed down with a can of beer. The second portion tasted just as good and then I continued my journey.

I found myself climbing again, constant uphill, but high ground meant cooler temperatures and stronger breezes which meant less chance of mosquitoes. Unable to ride up the steep incline I was on foot again. My bike started to make music. There was a tinker, tinker, tinker sound like someone drumming glass bottles. It was the spokes on my back wheel. Two were broken and were tapping a beat with each revolution. At the summit was a war memorial with several large Greek flags. I took shelter behind it and had a windy but cool and comfortable night.

Tuesday 23rd

Only 225 miles to go. Up at 5.35am meant a chance to do more miles before being baked by the hot sun. My typical diet was muesli for breakfast, two apples throughout the morning and then whatever I could buy later. Emergency rations consisted of more muesli. Whenever possible I liked to use fresh milk but would use powdered the rest of the time. I didn't particularly need hot food or drinks.

I had breakfast at a bus stop in Larisa. It was raining again but not cold. I would enjoy riding in this light shower. I stocked up at a Lidl in Farsala. All that muesli had made me constipated so I bought plenty of chocolate. I had been collecting water from discarded roadside bottles. It seems that out here, people bought water and drank a few mouthfuls, but once it had become too warm, they would toss their bottles out of the window. Plastic bottles littered the gutters in scenes reminiscent of the London Marathon. It was quite disgusting. I had soon collected 3 litres and that was enough for a full-body cleanse. I stripped naked behind some trees and had a bird bath. I put on my last set of clean clothes and threw away most of the old. I kept my woolly hat to act as a saddle cushion but the contents of my kitbag were getting lighter.

I was able to refill my bottles at a freshwater fountain and the sun was out in force once more. Morale was high but so were the mountains. On my way up I came across a cotton field. I had never seen one before. Rows of chest-high trees with branches supporting soft white clusters. I took some as a souvenir. It felt just like cotton wool. There were many cotton fields here.

Some were being harvested by tractors but others by hand. I couldn't tell if these cotton pickers were slaves or peasants but it looked like hot work.

After the intense uphill there was a plateau stretching out for miles. That was a welcome sight. I could see vehicles in the distance crawling up a slow meandering hairpin bend-type road. Was I destined for that route or would I be turning off? What a silly question. It was uphill again for three hours. It seemed to be never-ending. Shirtless again, I had taken to frequently dousing my head with water from those discarded bottles. My sun-bleached hair was so soft and clean from continued washing with mineral water.

As I neared the summit I got a rear tyre puncture. The steep incline would not be an ideal pit stop so I continued on foot until it levelled out at Domokos. Out with the tools and 'French spoon tyre levers'. To my dismay and frustration, the spare inner tube I had been supplied with at the bike shop was the wrong size. I had carried it all the way across Europe for nothing. A rubber patch repair would have to suffice.

It seemed a good time to service the bike in any way that I could. The front tyre was now completely bald and smooth to the touch. The tyre walls were cracked and full of holes. The back tyre was in a similar condition. With much less rubber, both would be prone to punctures from now on. My seat was torn after a fall in Verona. The front mudguard was missing. The pads were severely worn from excessive braking on the steep descents. Both wheels were buckled and had spokes missing or loose. The rear was the worst. It would knock against the frame with each revolution. To correct this, I had to stamp on it repeatedly and bend it back. The offside pedal bearings had gone and it grinded and creaked. If I pedalled too hard it would fall off for certain. The handlebars creaked. In terms of maintenance, there was little I could do other than tighten a few screws and bolts.

Another fountain in the village provided me with a free refill and enabled me to wash off most of the black oil smears from my fingers. At 4pm I cracked on.

I reached Lamia by 7pm but didn't stop to eat. I had the bit between my teeth and was spurred on by the thought of the finish line. I was tinged with sadness though. I had enjoyed this adventure and it would soon be over. It felt as though life really was too short. There was so much to do and see in such precious little time.

Unable to locate my intended route due to roadwork diversions, I strayed onto a new section of motorway. It wasn't fully functional but there was a smooth surfaced hard shoulder. I could race along for 10 miles to the next exit and join my road from there. It was a good plan. I burnt up the distance in no time and then started the long steep climb from the slip road. When I stopped for a mug of tea, I had an annoying sharp pain developing in my right arm. I looked down at my elbow to see a greedy mosquito sucking away, his straw buried deep in my flesh. I smacked my left hand down and the blood splashed in all directions.

I had to walk up this steep incline. I was still walking as night fell. Looking back I could see all the lights of Lamia. It was an impressive sight. I turned a corner near the summit and suddenly it was pitch-black. No ambient lighting, only darkness and the occasional glare of headlights from a passing vehicle. I bedded down on some roadside waste ground just before 11pm. It had been a very long day and the climbing had exhausted me. I was at Elefttherochri. This place name amused me. I pronounced it, 'He left the rockery'.

Wednesday 24th

Another early start, 6.30am. The sleep wasn't great because sporadic traffic flow kept breaking the silence. I was travelling light now. I had dumped a lot of kit, lost a lot of body weight, I had got used to riding and my fitness levels had increased. I had renewed enthusiasm and motivation for the final stages and this combination resulted in my being three days in advance of schedule. An easy ride today would mean I could casually cruise into Athens tomorrow for a selfie at the Acropolis around midday.

It wasn't long before I began the descent. I was entering a valley. Flanked by wedge-shaped cliffs on either side, I was heading for the low-lying flats. That was a refreshing change. A very easy ride but I was almost out of food and running on empty. I used my last Cup a Soup and finished an apple. Eventually I came to a small village called Heronia, where I bought some new supplies including chocolate and vanilla custard-filled croissants. By 2pm I had reached Thiva. That had been my intended target for the day but I was already there.

I took a break. Found a coffee shop. Had a large latte, a baguette and some ice cream. The counter staff asked where I was from. "England," I said. They then asked me whereabouts? In my experience, few foreigners knew of anywhere in England other than London, Manchester or Liverpool. I would normally have to explain that Leicester was a small city near Birmingham in the centre of the country.

"Leicester," I said, preparing to elaborate.

"Ooohh. Leicester City FIVE, Manchester United THREE," came the response.

I was quite proud of my team. They had put Leicester on the map. Well done, the Blue Army.

In a positive mood, I set off. Any distance completed from now on would mean less to cover tomorrow. Just 65 miles to Athens. I didn't need to get there today. The sun would be down before I could arrive so I would just take my time and nurse the bike towards the finish.

The riding was easy for the next two hours but there in the distance were layers of mountain peaks blocking my route. The jagged triangular features looking like rows of shark teeth waiting to chew me up.

I had used my last tea bag at 3.30pm so I was ready to tackle the obstacles. Fortunately, having climbed to clear the first hurdle meant the hard work was over. There was then a small drop followed by another rise and another small drop. Four hurdles in total but ancient man had carved out the most economical route. By 7.30pm I could see the Aegean.

A fresh wave of enthusiasm lifted me. Why stop now? I followed a flat coastal road and could see ships and large tankers just offshore. By 7.45pm I was at Dafni Monastery at the outskirts of the city. I was not thinking straight. Common sense said I should have stopped way back at Elefsina but now I was in the built-up area and riding along the ring road. My first rule was to avoid camping in such places. Perhaps I could find a cheap hotel.

I stopped at a Lidl and bought a bottle of local wine for celebrating. Then I realised I had no corkscrew. I asked for directions but I did not speak Greek and my potential guide had no English. Then I remembered that in my diary was a picture of the Acropolis. I had included it in order to bridge the various language barriers and show people where I was heading.

I came across a newspaper kiosk, presented my diary picture and asked which way to go. The vendor exited the small booth and joined me at the roadside. He pointed to an illuminated yellow structure high on a hill in the distance. "Acropolis," he said. I was looking straight at it. I could see it. I was nearly there.

It looked a lot closer than it actually was and it would take another hour to reach the tourist spot. There were busy night markets and overflowing bars. The place was throbbing. I walked about looking for the entrance, finally finding it about 9pm. It was closed until morning. I'd have to come back, but now it was time to celebrate.

I found an outdoor restaurant and grabbed a table. There was some live

Greek music being played. My table gave me a view of the illuminated temple and I was quite awestruck. I told the waiter I wanted two Greek beers. One to be drank quickly and immediately, and a second to be drank more slowly with my meal. I hadn't realised that the bottles of 'Mythos' would be so big.

I ordered a sizable banquet. A mixed meat grill for two. Half for me and the other half for... ME. I had earned it. 2,200 miles had taken me just twenty-two days and I was four days early. Those figures suggest an average of 100 miles per day but in reality it was far less. The final days in Greece were like double shifts on pure adrenaline and the fatigue would soon hit me.

The bread basket was empty before the hot food arrived. I was ravenous. It took me about two hours to finish my dining experience. I even had a dessert of ice cream and fruit. It was about 11.30pm before I left the restaurant. There seemed little point in paying for a room now as I would need to be up early and first in the queue for sunrise at the 'Gold' objective. Where could I rest?

I patrolled the streets looking for a quiet spot. There weren't any. The place was still buzzing and the party noise would last until 4am. Eventually I found a car park and concealed myself behind a pile of building materials. Confirmation that this was a bad idea came when two returning partygoers walked by. The female needed to take a leak. Her choice of lavatory was my choice of bedroom and I startled her. Perhaps thinking I was a tramp she apologised and ran back to her boyfriend. I had to sleep with one eye open but was quite relaxed.

Thursday 25th

I was up at 5am and walked around the main sites gathering my bearings. By 6.30am I was having a latte and a chocolate muffin in a coffee shop. I also took the opportunity to charge my gadgets. I then moved up to the tourist hotspot and joined the queue. The gates opened at 8am. The coaches of Chinese were spilling out and Greek soldiers were holding a parade which kept the crowds entertained while I sneaked towards the front.

Once through the barriers, I jogged past all those before me. They were reading notices and taking photos but I knew the shot I wanted and didn't want to have to share it with anyone else. Many staircases later, I reached the upper plateau and stood at the front of the ancient temple.

Shock and horror. It was covered in scaffolding and undergoing major renovation work. I was so annoyed. I started to walk round the structure. Fortunately, the rear aspect looked similar to the front. Better still, it was illuminated by the rising sun. I set up my tripod for the perfect selfie. On my first attempt at 8.14am I had the coveted picture.

Gold!

That's it. I've finished. I took another picture just to be sure. And another to be doubly sure. Then I realised that I was so skinny that a topless picture was called for. I stripped and took on the pose.

Then there were whistle blasts and screams from one of the staff. She ran over berating me. I had to cover up, this was holy ground. She was very serious. She inspected my photos and insisted I delete the semi-naked shot. I did as she asked. I didn't mind. My skinny appearance was not something I wished to savour nor indeed would want to share.

I went to use the toilets for a wash. I did not recognise the man in the mirror. My arms and chest had wasted away. My face was tanned but gaunt. I needed to put on a few pounds.

I watched the soldiers raise the Greek flag and sing their national anthem. I laughed to myself. I was actually there. The train and ferry totalled about £40. I had come all this way to Greece and it had cost almost nothing. From this high ground I could see the whole 360 degrees. Athens in every direction. Where was the sea?

The ancient history was not that important now. I intended to take a dip in the Aegean then race to the airport. After reclaiming my bike, I set a compass-bearing and zigzagged through the streets. I bought a souvenir T-shirt for the flight home. It displayed a warrior helmet and the words 'This is Sparta'.

With the sea in sight, I picked up another puncture. The bike was about dead so I'd ride on the flat tyre and get a taxi to the airport.

I reached the beach, stripped the bike of anything salvageable and dived into the warm sea. I was still chuckling to myself. There on the beach was a shower. I grabbed my soap and took full advantage. I would be clean and fresh for the airport but needed to replace my smelly trainers. They were offensive.

I said goodbye to my bike and raised a salute. I half-expected it to disintegrate like a two-wheeled equivalent of the Bluesmobile. The machine had done well and carried me for many miles across eleven countries. He could now retire in Greece. I hailed a cab and we headed off. The warm sun through the windscreen and the rocking through the driving motion made staying awake extremely difficult.

We reached the airport where my frustration with the French was reinforced. Owing to their industrial action, there was a shortage of flights. Consequently, what should have been a £120 ticket was suddenly quadrupled.

I managed to secure a last-minute cancellation that day but would have to hurry. They were boarding already and baggage check-in had to reopen just for me. I was told to run down to a gate and pass my bag to a handler and then run back the other way to the boarding gate. I was out of breath but I had made it. I hadn't managed to replace my trainers though. Perhaps the cabin crew would lend me a plastic bag. Suddenly I was pulled from the queue by security.

"Mr Hollis, come this way please. There is a security concern with your baggage," said the supervisor and I was led away to a police van.

What risk? I am not a terrorist. I am one of the good guys. My hand baggage included a camera, phone, wallet and passport. My kitbag had some camouflaged items and bike spanners. Was it my combination tool with a small blade? No, it was my Bluet gas stove. I had neglected to consider this owing to the rushed check-in. With no time to lose, I signed a disclaimer and was allowed to board. A massive relief.

It was a no-frills flight with Ryan Air but I was happy to spend what was left of my euros on two small bottles of red wine, a tea and a Twix. I was celebrating. I had the window seat in a row of three. Beside me was a young lady from Colombia sat next to her English boyfriend. I buried my feet as far as I could under the seat but the air conditioning was doing a good job and the smell was hardly noticeable.

I chuckled to myself as I browsed my photographs. Memories came flooding back. My neighbours' curiosity got the better of them. I would soon have to recount details of my expedition to this enthusiastic audience. The young man had once ridden across France. What were the chances of that? The lady told me that I should visit Colombia one day. She said it was not a bad place.

By 6.30pm I was on the way to Leicester. I had landed at Stansted, cleared immigration and headed down to the on-site railway station. I had just enough time to grab a BLT sandwich and a large coffee before my transport arrived. After another coffee and a Twix on the train I was there. I walked out of the station and got straight into a black cab. I was going home.

Friday 26th

The house was empty on my arrival. I was greeted by a sink full of dirty pots, but at least my plants had been watered. Using a corkscrew, I opened my wine and relaxed.

When Callum came home, he took one look at me, screamed and ran away. I had been 12st 5lb when I began. Now I was just 11st 3lb and my appearance was quite a shock.

I was satisfied with my achievement. This was the biggest and best thing I had ever done (at that time).

Chapter 18.

Per Mare Per Terram

It took a while to regain the weight but the freedom to eat anything was a luxury while it lasted. I was soon back to a healthy 12st. My time away had been fantastic but the overpriced flight home meant I had been unable to save any money for Thailand. Still, it was only September and that trip was a long way off. I debriefed myself and asked what I could have done better?

Navigation, gadget-charging, water-carrying, insect-bite prevention and catering were all areas for improvement. It didn't matter though. I wasn't going to do it again. I didn't even have a bike.

My tally of countries visited now totalled forty-one. I'd bought flag fridge magnets and set them up in chronological order on my fridge door. It was quite an impressive haul. Each flag represented cherished memories but there was room for a lot more. I consulted my world map. I was already going to Thailand via Dubai but before then I had nothing in my diary. What to do next?

I made provisional plans for the 'BIG ONE'. Portugal and Iceland would be excluded on this occasion but with a bit of careful planning I could ride through all the remaining countries in Europe. It didn't look that far on a map. If I could reach Athens, I could reach the Black Sea. If I could get that far, I could certainly reach Sweden.

I started my research. Russia, Belarus and Turkey were initially considered but they all required entry visas, and political tensions caused me to reject those countries. To do the rest would be close to 4,000 miles.

Bit by bit I started to prepare. First a replacement bike. Thank you, eBay. This time I would take a bicycle trailer to enable me to carry more water and kit. I bought a mosquito net, later superseded by a two-man dome tent with a mesh-lined zip-up entrance, a replacement Bluet stove and spare canisters, and a detailed road atlas. Was I really going to do this? Well, it would put an additional eighteen flags on my fridge. Of course I was going to do it. Definitely. I think. Maybe. Perhaps.

The cost of equipment started to pile up. There would be no move before the spring. "Stop for now and start saving for Thailand," I told myself.

I chose to test my new bike by riding down to the Tower of London. There was a ceramic poppy display around the castle's grass moat. One poppy for each British or Commonwealth serviceman killed in the Great War (888,246 poppies).

I headed down on the 10th and made it in time for the two-minute silence at 11am on the 11th. The event was televised and there was a huge attendance at the site. My knees had not recovered from the Greece trip and it took me much longer than I had anticipated. The strong headwinds had taken their toll as well so I decided to come home by train.

As winter approached, I became increasingly restless. I hated it here in the cold. It accentuated the pain from my old injuries, forcing me to remain indoors like a prisoner in my own home. I found myself trawling for deals on Expedia. Two weeks' bed and breakfast in Malta, flying from Birmingham, was just £220. The same deal from East Midlands was £1,200.

If I went, I could fill up on breakfast each morning, do some snorkelling and read my book. It would stop the boredom, I would be warm and it would be cheaper than being at home.

It was a no-brainer and I instantly fell in love with the place. I took a boat trip to Comino and the Blue Lagoon, did some snorkelling there before being shown the sights of Gozo which included the spectacular cliff arch known as the 'Azure Window'. As a movie location that place staged Khaleesi's wedding in *Game of Thrones*. I took another boat trip around Valetta and also an excursion to Sicily where I went up Mount Etna for a look inside the volcanic crater. For transport around Malta I used the Arriva buses. For €1 you could get unlimited all-day travel. In the first week I had been everywhere and taken about 200 photographs.

On the second week I lost them all. I had taken a coastal walk. I came across a cliff arch like the Azure Window but much smaller. In order to get a perfect selfie I had to step down part of the crumbling cliff. There were rocks and waves below so I was very careful with my footing. I paid less attention to my camera. It fell off the tripod and bounced down the cliff, bang, bang, bang, plop.

My camera and pictures were at the bottom of the sea. I cursed my carelessness. Had that really just happened? All those pictures. They were good ones; the bad ones had been deleted. These were the 200 I wanted to keep. The camera would be ruined but what about the memory card? There was a chance that that could survive the saltwater corrosion if I retrieved it quickly but the froth and swell looked treacherous. I was on my own and couldn't take the risk. Or could I? I went down the cliff to the water's edge for a closer look. No, it's a bit too hazardous. Disappointed, I climbed back up.

At the top I met two surfers in their wetsuits. I told them of my loss and they said I'd be all right to attempt a salvage. They agreed to act as *Baywatch* with their surf boards if I wanted to start the underwater search. That was good of them.

I stripped naked and dived in. I immediately realised I shouldn't have. The current was too strong and I was soon tired out. It washed me into the search zone but the rise and fall of the waves were buffeting me against the rocks. I couldn't even see underwater because of the froth. I'd tried and given it my best shot but failed. Now it was time to swim back. I couldn't. I was like a spider, fighting against a draining plughole. I started swallowing water and considered it highly likely that I would drown very soon. Struggling and fatigued, the survival instinct kicked in and told me to stop swimming for the shore in that turbulent trough, but instead head back out to sea. Reaching calmer waters would enable me to get my breath back and ride in on a wave to a more favourable exit.

It was a decision that perhaps kept me alive. My two lifeguards were shouting instructions but I couldn't hear. Eventually I was well-positioned for beaching. The waves catapulted me forward and caused me to crash heavily on the rocks. As the waters receded, I was swept out again. My rescuers' outstretched arms were only inches away but I didn't want to drag them out with me. On the second attempt I landed further up and they were able to pull me out. My legs and feet were cut, grazed, bruised and bleeding but miraculously nothing was broken. My two rescuers were very apologetic that they had encouraged me to even attempt such a foolish and futile mission. I laughed it off and thanked them.

I was in a state of shock for the rest of that day. My heart was thumping and the whole world seemed to be moving in slow motion. I wasn't ready to die but had come so close to death. That night I was unable to sleep. Every time I closed my eyes I was drowning under the water. I was so lucky to have survived. I got out of bed, got dressed and headed to a corner shop for a big bottle of wine. That did the trick.

I could get a decent second-hand replacement off eBay for £30, but out here even the cheapest and most basic camera would cost £60. I couldn't leave this place without some snaps even though I fully expected to return one day. The Malta experience took me well over budget and now it was Christmas. There were two more flags for my fridge but I still had no spending money for Thailand.

I would have to borrow from my bank. I was only going for three weeks. Couldn't be that expensive, could it?

Pattaya was superb. Non-stop partying. By the end of the first week I had met Noi. A tiny forty-one-year-old single mum with a twenty-one-year-old son. Noi was very pretty and fancied me until she realised I was English.

"England man clazy, dink too much whisky," she said and refused to date me. Eventually my persistence paid off and we were inseparable for the final two weeks. Something started eating my leg during the second week but Noi acted as nurse during my stay and really looked after me.

She was a good lady and even came to the airport to bid me farewell. Before my flight she tied a piece of string around my wrist, something to do with Buddha, and she said it would bring me good luck. It did. I was on one of those double-decker aircraft. At the boarding gate I was ushered upstairs and shown to my seat. This can't be right. "Am I in the right seat?" I asked. "Yes Mr Hollis," said the flight attendant. I was in Business Class and had received a free flight upgrade. Cheers, Buddha, and thank you, Noi.

I would return to Noi that September and December. We rode elephants and I tried eating scorpion, crocodile and jellyfish. We visited sections of the Thai-Burma Railway, including Hellfire Pass and the bridge over the River Kwai. We climbed the Erawan Falls which were an absolute paradise. We travelled to Cambodia and visited the temples at Siem Reap. We visited her family in Bangkok as well as the Grand Palace and Reclining Buddha. Thailand is an amazing country and there is so much more to see. Noi left a lasting impression on me and at the time of writing this I consider that I may have a future in that fantastic country. Who knows?

Chapter 19.

Wandering Star

'A man may climb Everest for himself, but at the summit he plants his country's flag'
                                    - *The Rt Hon Baroness Margaret Thatcher*

With debts from the first visit to Thailand and a return trip already booked, this next expedition would need to be treated seriously as a money-saving opportunity.

As with the earlier ride, I would have to set myself military style objectives so as not to become distracted or side-tracked. That said, this was not to be a race or record attempt. It wasn't even that much of a challenge. 40 miles per day for 100 days is not difficult. In some ways calling it a bike ride was a misnomer. I would be in a tent more than in the saddle, so this was really a camping expedition.

The ultimate aim was to put eighteen more flags on my fridge by visiting the outstanding virgin territories inside Europe. France, Belgium, Germany and Switzerland I had visited before but it would be my first time in the others.

Mission A. You WILL arrive in Austria via Luxembourg and Liechtenstein. You WILL then test the waters of the Alpine Lake at Zell am See.

DAY 1. 16th March 2015

It was only 3 degrees on our windswept island. The continent would surely be warmer. I was fighting the early signs of fever and a throat infection. Too much stress and overexertion would run me down, so I needed to relax and take things easy.

I had deliberately plumped up to a flabby 13st. My freestanding bike was 15 kg. It was a lightweight Carrera Gryphon. Very fast. It had a gelled seat but I also bought a gelled seat cover for added comfort. The loaded trailer weighed 49.5 kg. This included 5 kg of basmati rice, 4 kg of Alpen and six cans of fruit cocktail at 500g each. Wearing my first set of mostly disposable clothing, I set out from home. It was 10.45am and thirteen minutes later I was at Syston train station. The trailer felt heavy but I had managed approximately 8 mph on this first leg, despite denting the trailer chassis by hitting a concrete bollard.

The train was empty but on time. I was the only new passenger and the guard helped me aboard. Minutes later I arrived at a packed Leicester station. I waited on the busy platform anticipating the next potential hurdle. How was I going to get both the bike and trailer onto the carriage? Which carriage?

The next train on the platform had a designated bicycle storage area at the rear. Perhaps my train would be the same. I positioned myself accordingly and waited for my transportation. It arrived on time but where were the bike racks? Oh no, this time it was at the opposite end of the train. Nine carriages away. Weaving through the crowds I reached the front but got stopped by the platform manager.

"Hold on, hold on, hold on, you can't take that on there," he said.

I showed him my ticket but he told me I was supposed to reserve a place for my bicycle and there was no such facility for a trailer. That was ridiculous. Other passengers were taking massive suitcases and my load was not much bigger. I had booked online and had received no such prompting from Trainline.com. I pleaded with him to let me board, as I had a connection and ferry to catch. He was anxious that the scheduled train depart without delay.

"How fast can you unhitch this trailer?" he asked.

I pulled out the retaining pin and the towing arm crashed to the ground. "Is that fast enough?" I said.

He slid open the mail-sack carriage. "In there, quick as you can!"

I loaded up and then ran to the first passenger carriage. I walked down several aisles as the train started to roll. I found my seat, 43C, and sat down to catch my breath. I was supposed to be taking it easy.

The transfer at St Pancras was flawless. This time I knew exactly where platform 12 was and I used the elevator. The train to Dover was empty. Just me, José and Wilson.

The ferry charged me extra for the trailer but altogether it was just £28 for the three of us. With £19.50 for the train I'd be in France for less than 50 quid. We sailed promptly out of 'Blighty' at 3.30pm and I went to lie down for an hour, hoping that the rest would reduce my temperature. I knew I would be the last to disembark, so I relaxed and avoided most of the lorry fumes.

Hello France, I'm back. I rode out of port. It was just as cold there as in England. I took a left turn to ride east. Hooded refugees lined the streets and gathered round burning oil drums. One man started to chase me and I prepared to fight. I wouldn't be able to outrun him with this heavy load and didn't bother trying but I was rather annoyed by this confrontation so soon after arriving. I glanced back with a frown but he had already stopped running and smiled. He was only pretending to chase me.

"Hello English!" he shouted.

I rose my open palm as a casual gesture and pedalled on to the unexpected dead-end. Of course, I was back in France. The land where navigation is impossible. I took the next available turn. I knew that I was heading onto the motorway, but didn't care. The first French policeman to give me a hard time was going to get a right mouthful.

I pedalled a short distance along the hard shoulder. More refugees were running across the motorway into the wooded areas, and overhead was a road bridge leading to the east. I climbed the steep embankment and confirmed the route. That'll do. Then I descended the steep embankment to collect the bike, 'José'. I repeated the journey to transport the heavy trailer, 'Wilson'. I hitched everything back up and then sat down. I had no energy. I was ill. This evoked memories of Spain.

I had all the time in the world. 100 days was ample for this task. I had found the right road. I just needed to get out of the 'jungle' zone and grab an early night. Pop a few pills and I would be fine tomorrow.

I reached the open countryside by 8pm and pitched my dome tent behind an old warehouse. As expected, the first day had been stressful but I had made it through. Tomorrow would be much easier. Now it was time for bed.

DAY 2. Tuesday 17th March

It was a very cold night and my sleep was broken. My mind was doing battle and I had entered a nightmare. For some reason this expedition had been suspended. I was back in England but my kit was still in France. I had great anxiety all through the night arranging new flights and timetables. I woke up completely disorientated. It came as a great relief to see a bright pink sun rising as I stepped out of my tent at 7am. I was still in France. Everything was fine. It was just a bad dream.

I had morning tea and Alpen on the outskirts of Gravelines. Checking my load I noticed that the carbon fibre poles had slipped from their bag and were missing. With poles, the tent could be erected anywhere. Without poles, it would become a luxurious mosquito net that needed external supports. I was annoyed by my early incompetence. Maybe I would find a camping shop in Dunkirk.

My search was in vain and to make matters worse the trailer linkage between the towing arm and the bike-frame bracket was buckled. It was in danger of imminent separation and would certainly not last much longer. I used some paracord as a binding but that was inadequate. My speed dropped down to about 5 mph. Now I needed a camping shop and a bike shop too. Not a very satisfactory state of affairs.

I paid my respects at our Dunkirk cemetery. So many headstones. I passed numerous concrete gun emplacements and pillboxes along the coastal road. The sun came out about midday and I was able to strip off to just a T-shirt. By 2.30pm I was in Belgium. Not my first visit; I had been to Bruges with Mala. This place was very cycle-friendly though. I stopped about 6pm in some woods by the side of the road. Paracord and bungees stretched out the pole-less tent and using my camouflaged military bivvy sheet, I made my accommodation both water-resistant and invisible.

I then cooked my first meal. I had some basmati rice, a bell pepper, garlic, an onion, eggs, a tin of mackerel, a bottle of mixed spices and some extra virgin olive oil. All healthy ingredients and very filling, washed down with a big mug of tea made with Asda powdered milk.

It was 7.15pm. The map said I was 10 miles from Ypres. I'd be there tomorrow but it was dark outside so now was time for bed.

DAY 3. Wednesday 18th March

A comfortable night with a little rain but no bad dreams. Unfortunately, I had slept on top of a warren and could hear the furry friends scurrying around below me. The cockerels and woodpeckers created a racket about 5.15am but I'd already had ten hours in my sleeping bag by then. Fresh air, good food, a few pills and plenty of rest were beating my ailments and I was getting better.

It was a foggy start so I stayed in bed till 8am. I reached a very picturesque

Ypres (Leper) by 10am and rode through the spectacular Menin Gate. I had seen it before on TV. It was dedicated to the British Empire forces who had fallen in the Great War. The walls were inscribed with individual names and regiments. So many guardsmen, Canadians, Australians, Indians and Pals battalions too. Liverpool took an absolute pasting. It was very sobering and poignant. There were fresh floral tributes and I believe that they hold a service there every single night with a bugler playing 'The Last Post'. There were many war memorials in this town and massive cemeteries on the outskirts. The largest of which was German near 'Hooge Crater'. A bloody conflict not forgotten but sadly we didn't learn.

I passed three bike shops. One was closed, one abandoned and the third was only open from 4.30pm to 7.30pm. I couldn't hang around that long. I had a tin of Prince's fruit cocktail for lunch. I had forgotten how good it tasted. I got a free water refill from an outside tap at a garage. Heading almost directly southeast towards Luxembourg, the border would overlap and by lunchtime I was temporarily back in France.

I stopped for Alpen and tea. My navigation was assisted by my 'tablet' and Google Maps. For this little expedition I had invested in portable solar panels. They could charge my tablet, camera and mobile phone. A truly awesome piece of kit. The sun was shining but I'd be happier in Belgium.

I found another bike shop that afternoon. SHUT.

By 7pm I was just outside Tournai in Belgium. I ran out of water during the sunny afternoon. I couldn't find any open shops and even resorted to knocking on a few doors. I got no replies so I helped myself via someone's garden tap. My route planner led me to an impressive canal. In places it was as wide as the Thames at Westminster. Some of the boats and barges were like mini oil tankers. In England a canal boat might carry a bicycle on the roof, but here they carried cars. Following the canal made navigation simple and the flat, straight waterways were easy riding. I later made a comfortable shelter in the treeline beside the canal towpath. By 7.30pm, after more home cooking, I was snuggled up in my bag.

DAY 4. Thursday 19th March

A cosy night but the cockerel's chorus started at 3.30am. It was a chilly start but I managed to get the bike repaired in Tournai. €20 for a brand-new linkage was money well spent. The weather was cold and grey and my solar panels did not perform. Without power, I would soon lose Google Maps and the GPS. I could use the road atlas but there were further pending incursions into France. Where was the sun?

As I passed a farm field, a large, white, thick plastic sack blew out in front of me. That looked as though it could come in handy and I stopped to give it a further inspection. Labels suggested it had previously stored chemical fertiliser but I had other intentions for this item. Firstly, it was an ideal size to act as a tarpaulin to cover my trailer load. Secondly, it could be used as a reflective rear fascia board and make my trailer more visible to following traffic, and finally it could form half of my tent's groundsheet each night. The other half would be made from a similar-sized clear, heavy-duty plastic sack that stored my sleeping bag. I liked it when kit had multiple purposes; it felt economical and well-planned but often it was just convenient coincidence. This bag would prove to be an outstanding acquisition.

I had cleared Mons by 4.30pm and headed for Beaumont along the N40. I stopped about 5pm. It was getting very cold and uncomfortable. I took shelter in a small copse. The trees were tall and leafless so they provided little cover in the daylight. I had just got comfy when two farmers headed towards me. Was I trespassing? Probably. I sank a little lower and covered my equipment with branches and fallen leaves. The men were chatting away and not particularly paying attention. Fortunately they walked on by and I remained undiscovered. I just hoped my tablet would not go PING and announce an incoming message.

DAY 5. Friday 20th March

It had been a freezing night and at one point I had to get up to put on more clothes. The raisins in my Alpen were as hard as stone. I was up at 7.15am but today was the same as yesterday. I soon found out why. There was a solar eclipse. It ended mid-afternoon and I was able to recharge my tablet. I bought some fresh supplies from a supermarket before dining and sleeping in the woods outside Philippeville around 7pm.

DAY 6. Saturday 21st March

It was a cold foggy start but after tea and biscuits I was on the road for 7.45am. I got water from an outside tap by a barn. The weather didn't improve much and I was a little disappointed about this trip so far. The nights were cold, the days were cold and I'd been going for almost a week with no new flags to add to my fridge door. I had deliberately set off in early spring to avoid the mosquitoes of summer. I knew my situation would improve as the seasons progressed but at this particular moment I was rather downbeat.

Seizing an opportunity I topped up my water bottles from a hosepipe left running on someone's drive. I think they had been cleaning the car and had forgotten about it. The sun came out at 4pm but black clouds loomed. Soon it would rain and hail so I took cover in the Ardennes Forest. With plenty of dead wood lying around I was able to cook on a natural fire and save some gas. The fir trees provided great cover from weather and onlookers. It was a very comfortable location.

Saturday in the Ardennes

DAY 7. Sunday 22nd March

It rained heavily through the night but I stayed dry. It was quite cosy in the forest and very peaceful. I even saw a red squirrel. I hit the road about 7.45am and made good progress. It was only 4 degrees but the sun came out about 1pm and fortunately I was riding towards blue skies.

I had enjoyed cycling in Belgium. Far easier to navigate there than in France and much better cycle routes. Unlike back home, cyclists seemed to be revered in Belgium. Car drivers would give me plenty of room and even stop to wave me forward when they had right of way. That would be quite confusing for me. Why is he letting me through? What a nice man. I would regularly shout, "Merci beaucoup!"

By 3.30pm I was in Luxembourg. Hallelujah! One down, seventeen to go. At last a new flag for the fridge. I celebrated by buying a hot sausage roll, a Toblerone and a packet of hot and spicy Pringles from the service station. All the shops were shut. Europe doesn't seem to have the English Sunday trading policy.

I camped about 5.30pm just outside Steinfort, in the woods again, and cooked on an open fire. I had been without power for a while but sun was penetrating the trees and I was able to plug in my tablet for a partial boost. I wasn't euphoric but morale was certainly lifted by this first success. I made a note in my diary.

'Loving the jungle routine', which had nothing to do with sleeping in the woods. It was a reference to the long static nights spent in Brunei. Under the trees we could only march tactically during the daylight, so there was plenty of rest each night. This trip was similar in that way but it was no longer a bike ride or a camping expedition. It was a way of life.

DAY 8. Monday 23rd March

Up at 7.55am. There had been a frost overnight and my water had iced over. The sun was rising but I'd have to wait a while longer before my morning tea.

Luxembourg is not a very big country and it didn't take long to reach the capital. There was nothing particularly impressive about this place. It was similar to its neighbours of France, Germany and Belgium so I wasn't going to hang around. The sooner I could get to the sunny countries, the better.

In order to exit the city I had to cross a deep valley. I had expected a long freewheel descent but there were roadworks and I had to divert to a pedestrian bridge. This branched out from the high cliff before a square tower staircase took me to the ground below. This was a particularly tiring time as it had to be done by instalments. First carry the bike down a few flights, then run back up to collect the heavy trailer and repeat the journey. This shuttle-run on the multi-tier staircase took ages. Once I was done, it was a short ride to the river crossing before a steep climb back up the other side. As the crow flies, this distance was less than a mile but it took a couple of hours.

I refilled my bottles at a leaking fire hydrant and continued riding towards the sunshine. Soon I came across a Harley Davidson showroom. I had been overtaken by several motorbikes already and it occurred to me that future trips would be better executed by that mode of transport.

When the full warmth of the sun encouraged me to ride in just a T-shirt, I stopped and demolished my last tin of fruit cocktail. That was 3 kg off my load. I rested by a tree on the grass verge. Then I started feeling a stinging sensation on my buttocks. I was sat on an ants' nest. Not ordinary ants either. Massive ones. Black and red in colour with a powerful bite. Reminded me of the last *Indiana Jones* movie.

The final stretch was a gradual descent towards the natural border created by the River Mosel. I passed petrol station after petrol station. The whole stretch was occupied by busy pumps and crowded forecourts. Was there a fuel shortage? Perhaps it was a tax arrangement or a reduced price. There were none on the German side.

I marked the border crossing with a selfie on the bridge and feeling quite pleased with my progress, started looking for a place to sleep. Close to Remich, the main road cut directly through a forest so I had options, left and right. It was only 4.55pm but I made luxurious sleeping quarters. I had still not found any replacement tent poles but had mastered this handicap. Using two forked sticks as spacers with paracord and bungees attached to two trees, I was able to expand the tent to its full size and function. My bivvy sheet acting as the waterproof and camouflage flysheet, made my improvisation better than the original tent.

The sun was still shining but the midges had started to bite, so I entered my zip-up apartment and had another early night. I had taken a book with me but it was hardly used. The dim light made reading difficult and the head torch was a magnet to tiny creatures that could penetrate the mosquito net. I would send a few messages and updates via my tablet and unwind listening to music on my MP3 player.

DAY 9. Tuesday 24th March

It was a chilly start but had been a dry night. It had been a noisy one as well. A constant owl finished his shift only to be replaced by a constant woodpecker. I was up at 7am and immediately disturbed a bright red fox which ran away across a field. Then I scared a German hedgehog which scurried away into the leaves. I hit the road without breakfast and pedalled for two hours until the sun came out.

I stopped for tea and Alpen at a peace memorial in tribute to the American 94th Infantry Division which had fought battles around the Saar-Moselle Triangle region during the winter of 1944-45.

There was a long, arduous and energy sapping climb. Fortunately there was only the one. I resupplied at a supermarket in Dillingen and cooked around 3.30pm. It had been my intention to camp but the location was not ideal and it was far too early. I then pressed towards Saarbrucken via more impressive canals. Folk were very active around there. Many people were jogging or cycling and on the water were various rowers. Graffiti artists quite openly sprayed their paint in my presence.

I camped in the trees just off the path. The same path that would lead me back into France tomorrow.

DAY 10. Wednesday 25th March

Up at 7.45am. It had rained heavily but I'd stayed dry. It wasn't a particularly bright day but the flat canal towpath meant I was in for an easy morning. I strayed freely over the border and came across an impressive weir at Sarreinsming in the Vallee de la Sarre. On one of its banks was a watermill and the big wheel was turning with the current. It was very picturesque, prompting a selfie.

I would end today having ridden exactly 40 miles. That was slightly below average because it had been bitterly cold and I'd had to put on extra layers of clothing. By 7.10pm I had taken shelter in a fir tree plantation about 3 miles from Ingwiller. Pine needles and soft peaty soil make the most comfortable mattress. I was tired and ready for sleep.

DAY 11. Thursday 26th March

My rest had been refreshing but another cold day lay ahead. Fortunately, most of it was by canal towpath. I headed out at 7.45am and by 1.30pm I had reached Strasbourg. It was the EU Parliament building on the opposite bank that provided confirmation of my arrival. All those flags. I zoomed in on their detail and tried to recognise as many as I could but that was difficult without a strong wind to unfurl them.

Strasbourg meant I was close to crossing the River Rhine into Germany. That was an exciting prospect. It also meant I would be leaving France for the last time. Needing no further encouragement, I picked up the pace and crossed the bridge an hour later. Au revoir, la France.

I found a camping shop in Offenburg and bought two new gas canisters for my cooker. I was no longer concerned about replacing the tent poles. I was managing just fine without. I also resisted the temptation of a Burger King or kebab. It was welcome canals and cycle lanes for my return to Germany but there was nowhere to sleep. There were barns and farm houses but everywhere I considered stopping was occupied. Sleeping in people's gardens was breaking the protocol.

As the darkness fell, I would have to take a chance. There were some bare trees near a footbridge. It was a bit exposed but I reassured myself that I was unlikely to be seen if people weren't looking for me. It would be pitch-black soon and I could be gone early next morning. I moved in for the night. Joggers and cyclists moved by my position but I remained unnoticed. Why did the Germans have to be so active?

DAY 12. Friday 27th March

I was up at 6am but getting packed was problematic. I was on an arterial route. Dog-walkers, joggers, cyclists and pedestrians were all in my vicinity. I packed up discreetly and casually emerged from the inadequate thicket.

I hit the canal path and soon after found myself contemplating German efficiency. To my right was the autobahn. Alongside that was an A road, the railway line, a B road, a cycle lane, the canal and finally another cycle lane going in the opposite direction. Everything running parallel. Initially I thought this was quite splendid but later I was annoyed by German 'over-efficiency'.

It seemed that the default setting for German cyclists is 'blind obedience'. The cycle routes were in good condition and well signposted but so convoluted. I might ride up to a small hazard such as crossing a minor road junction. The task would be simple enough. Stop, look in both directions and wait for the opportunity. When there was a gap or no traffic, I could leave the cycle lane, cross the narrow width of road and rejoin the cycle lane on the other side.

In Germany, however, the signs would direct me to turn right, right again, then left, down an alley and left again to a marginally more favourable crossing point several hundred metres away. Then there would be the additional distance to travel back in order to continue on the original heading. There was no common sense. It was a bit like the council painting double yellow lines on a 6 inch stretch of road. Someone had been paid to plan and implement this unnecessary health and safety policy. I liked Germany though; overall, it was a nice place. They call their ambulances 'Krankenwagons'. That made me laugh.

I rode through some spectacular scenery. I found a wonderful fountain for a free top-up and made a mug of tea. Ahead of me were high mountains and valleys. By the time I reached Wolfach, it was looking like Alpine Switzerland already.

Google Maps had served me well up to this point but today they would fail. The car route involved a very long and severe climb. The cycle route involved a much shorter but equally severe climb. I opted for the latter. Fortunately, I had just stocked up at Aldi.

My tablet led me between two houses and towards a wooded area. I started up the steep dirt track. This couldn't be right. I went back to the road and walked either side of the alley monitoring the blue dot on my GPS screen. I was definitely in the right place and returned to my bike. There was no way I could push it with the trailer attached so this would be another 'obstacle by instalments'.

It was a severe incline. There was certainly a track but no one had used it for some time. This was taking forever. I tried to calm myself down. What was the rush? There was no rush; I just didn't like expending all this energy on a fool's errand. Where was the road? Where was this track leading? I was going up all of the time and there had to be a summit eventually, but I couldn't see where that was. All I could see were trees. One of the biggest trees had fallen and was blocking the track. I had to work even harder to climb around it.

Eventually the track became a dirt road that led even higher up into the mountain forest. Under the trees it got dark quickly and by 8pm the visibility was too poor to continue. I had been climbing since 4pm and was exhausted. I camped on the road. It was cold at this altitude and the night was uncomfortable.

DAY 13. Saturday 28th March

I pressed on at 6.45am and came to a break in the trees. I could see how far I had come. Not far at all but, wow, it was steep, almost 45 degrees.

Reassuringly, I also spotted a sign offering a route for mountain bikers. I followed it. Still too steep for a hitched trailer so the instalment routine continued. At the top of this section was a tarmac road. At last!

I had never been superstitious about the number thirteen. I was born on the 13th so I was exempt but Day 13 was plagued by bad luck. I picked up a puncture on one of the trailer wheels. It was just a thorn and my repair kit could sort that. I removed the lid to my rubber glue and squeezed the tube. Nothing happened. It had dried out. I had ample patches but no adhesive. In desperation, I sliced open the glue tube and removed what was left of the dried-out compound. There was just enough to smear over a patch and it still had some sticking ability. It would hopefully hold for now.

Then my boots gave out. They weren't expected to survive the entire trip but I had hoped they would last a bit longer. The sole had completely worn through. I removed the laces as emergency string and added the old footwear to my bag of rubbish. On went my fresh socks and trainers. I checked the GPS. It indicated left. OK. I made a tea and pumped up the tyre.

A pair of local Nordic walkers passed and waved. I didn't need to ask directions. I knew exactly where I was now and where I was going next. I just hoped the tyre remained inflated.

Refreshed and confident I hitched up the trailer and started cycling again. We were going left but the road would obviously bend right soon, wouldn't it? Why are we going down and not up? At the hairpin I could see the left turn would take me back to Aldi. I could have cried. I had just freewheeled the equivalent of my recent four-hour uphill shuttle run.

This was now a test of character. The GPS kept telling me to turn around as I began the slow trudge back to my earlier pit stop and beyond. Eventually the tarmac ended and the road became a dirt track once more.

I took out my compass and set a bearing. Whatever happened I would be heading southeast. It became steep again and that meant doubling the distance from now on. It felt like I was part of the Royal Navy Field Gun Race. It was so tiring. By 9.30am I had reached the top. I stepped out to a green field with commanding views over the surrounding countryside. I needed a rest and stopped for another tea.

The GPS did not want to admit being wrong. It was spot on now and my road atlas concurred. Of the fifty-six photographs I had taken since leaving England, seven were on this high hurdle. I was at Schramberg. The sun was now warm, the road was good and I had time to make up, so I cracked on.

My luck changed. The very first shop I came to was selling bikes and I picked up a new puncture repair kit.

By 1pm I had reached the ancient town of Rottweil which is the origin of the similarly named breed of dog. Rottweiler means 'butcher's dog'. I cooked lunch from a roadside bench and basked in the spring sunshine. The warmth prompted me to have a full bird bath which was much needed after the morning's exertion.

It was a good feeling to be clean, fed and watered, with inflated tyres, lubricated bearings and chain, and fully charged gadgets. I knew exactly where I was and where I was going. In this new simple life, everything was perfect.

I headed for the junction but the road sign was strange. It seemed to suggest cars only but it wasn't a motorway. I cycled on. It was an excellent road and I really picked up speed. Occasionally someone would blast a horn as they overtook me. Just being friendly, I thought, and waved at them.

Then I got yelled at by a rear-seat passenger of a car that had slowed significantly. "Auto strada!" He shouted a lot more than that and it didn't sound particularly friendly. I was not allowed on this road and steered over to the pavement.

The day would end as miserably as it had started. I swapped the glorious sunshine for heavy clouds and similar rain. After a resupply at the Lidl in Tuttingen, I camped about 7pm among the damp trees of a logging plantation.

DAY 14. Sunday 29th March

I was on the road by 6.45am. It had rained heavily all night but I was dry in the tent. A light drizzle remained for the whole morning. There wasn't much traffic and most of the roads were downhill so I made good progress. The countryside was mainly fields and forest but it still came as a shock when a wild deer sprinted across the road in front of me. It disappeared before I could react with my camera.

By 9.30am I could see the snowy peaks of the Swiss Alps in the distance. I suddenly felt like Steve McQueen in *The Great Escape*, but of course he had headed for that frontier on a motorbike.

The huge lake at Bodensee looked very cold. I skirted round clockwise before picking up signs to Switzerland. I would need to cross the water via a large bridge. There was no disabled access, instead I had to negotiate seven separate flights of stairs to reach the footpath/cycle route. It was reminiscent of that scene in *The Untouchables* where the mother drags her pram slowly up, one step at a time.

225

I had reached the land of Toblerone by 1.30pm. There were border guards at the checkpoint but I was allowed through unhindered. The navigation was easy as the Swiss had created designated cycle lanes by simply widening the main road. By 5pm it was dark and I stopped to shelter in an open barn near Arbon. The distance and cold temperatures were taking their toll and my body was hurting. My stocks of ibuprofen were running out fast. There were no animals in the barn, instead it was being used as a garage for a long tractor trailer. It was dry and out of the strong wind but a bit too close to the farmhouse. The dog would bark occasionally and I was concerned every time the porch door opened. Would I be evicted from my illegal squat?

DAY 15. Monday 30th March

Farmers are habitually early risers so I would not be able to overstay in these cosy quarters. Once the early morning traffic noise had roused me, I was back on the road by 6.45am. It rained all day and I was very uncomfortable. My trousers and trainers were soaked and consequently my toes and feet were freezing. With no sunshine, my tablet soon died and navigation was difficult. A couple of times I had to ask for directions. Switzerland was beautiful though and I was impressed by all those intricately carved fascia boards on the wooden cottages. Still, I wasn't there for sightseeing. It was the wrong time of year and the weather was appalling.

Spurred on by the prospect of another scalp, I reached the open border with Liechtenstein at 1.39pm. A quick selfie on the bridge next to the welcome sign would be the only celebration. The place looked no different to Switzerland and the weather was identical, but Austria was only an hour away.

As I cycled towards the third virgin territory, I found myself recalling clips from the movie, A Knight's Tale, in which Heath Ledger assumed the character of 'Sir Ullrick Von Liechtenstein'.

By 2.25pm I was being interrogated by the Austrian border guards. They disappeared with my passport for a while as I stood outside shivering. Eventually they smiled and wished me good luck. I made my way into the nearest town and stocked up on supplies before heading further inland.

Inside this steep valley I was quite sheltered. There seemed to be less rain and the wind was certainly lighter but I was very tired now. I think I had pushed myself too hard and the weather had drained me but I was a day early and considered taking the next day off. By 6pm I had found a nice corner of a forest outside the town of Frastanz and built a luxurious camp. After filling my belly and downing a hot tea, I snuggled up in my sleeping bag and nodded off listening to music. I was in Austria and felt quite pleased with myself.

DAY 16. Tuesday 31st March

It was 8.40am before I stirred. There had been heavy rain that night but it wasn't a problem. The sun was out now. I was too restless to take a whole day off but I chose to relax for the morning. I did a kit inspection, some vehicle maintenance and some personal grooming. I also cooked a large meal. I was getting good at this standard diet of garlic, onions, peppers, eggs, rice, mixed spices and a tin of mackerel. It was hot, tasty and full of goodness. It was also much cheaper than the regular McDonald's meals of the last outing and chopping onions outdoors doesn't make the eyes water. My kit dried in the sun and my gadgets trickle-charged. I was in a good place and morale was high.

I felt incredibly privileged to be in Austria. It was already the most impressive country of the trip so far and made me feel happy to be alive. Every corner just made me say, "Wow!" and the constant clicking of my camera was slowing me down.

By 5.40pm I had found a beautiful spot for the night near Stallehr. It was in the woods just off the cycle route. I was on the bank of a small river and the main road was too far away to hear traffic over the ripples. I knew it would be cold but I braved up and took the plunge with my bar of soap. The icy water was so clean and refreshing. I felt great. I even did some laundry, hoping that it might dry in the wind.

DAY 17. Wednesday 1st April

Another lazy morning. I didn't want to leave this peaceful wilderness. At 8.30am when I poked my head out of the tent, it was snowing. Only a light sprinkling but a layer had fallen on my washing line, socks and boxer shorts. They were frozen like cardboard.

It had been a cold night and I didn't want to get out of my bag. I knew I had to get moving and away from this high ground. I didn't yet know it but this would be one of my longest days. I had been prepared for Arctic conditions. Wilson had been recruited to carry additional supplies such as winter clothing, fuel and food. I had enough equipment for five days comfortable living in the Alpine snow.

The clouds were preventing any solar charging. The mobile phone was full but I would lose access to the GPS on my tablet quite quickly.

The navigation was initially quite straightforward and well sign-posted. At

10.30am I had a breakfast of Alpen and morning tea at a large log cabin-style bus shelter. A local elderly gentleman advised me of impassable 'snay' higher up. My course would not change but I was grateful for the early warning.

The snow fell heavier the higher I went and would settle, making my route difficult. The roads were well-travelled, causing the white stuff to melt, but I was the only person using the cycle lanes and when the layer reached a depth of about 8 inches, the trailer had to be detached and used like a snowplough.

At one point I was being blinded by the flakes. Progress was very slow and tiring. I took shelter for a while under a road bridge. It was dry and mostly clear of snow but it was still cold and while there was daylight I wanted to keep moving.

When there was an opportunity, I left the cycle route and rejoined the busy road. I bought some more food from the Spar but quickly demolished those chocolate bars. This was hard work.

Still climbing, the road became white and riding was difficult. It was possible to pedal in a straight line on the compact snow but any slush would cause me to skid. Occasionally I would have a brief respite going through a long tunnel.

As I cleared the ski resort at Arlberg, I was warned of even more treacherous conditions ahead, but this was the only route available as the motorway was not an option. I had to either press on, wait for summer or abandon the trip. I was quite confident in my ability. I had survived three winters of Arctic training in Norway and this environment seemed familiar, so I carried on.

People started taking photographs of the crazy Englishman who was riding to the Black Sea. It started at the ski resort but continued along the climb. I trudged along the hairpin bends and moved to the roadside to escape the bow waves of snowploughs.

Various motorists stopped to quiz me in disbelief but I wasn't an ordinary cyclist. I had a trailer full of kit and this really wasn't a big deal as far as I was concerned. The hardest thing was pulling my stuff along the slippery road. All of the cars had snow chains. Having posed for the picture, I would ask how much further it was to the summit. 5 km shrank to half a mile. It was night-time but visibility was good because everything was white. It was very cold but at least the snowing had stopped. I reached the top and found the road signs at the fork junction. Which way?

I didn't recognise either route. The place names didn't feature on my map and my tablet was dead. Whilst I was weighing up my options, a large Mercedes van pulled up and the driver asked if I wanted a lift, Unlike the Greece trip, this was not a challenge. If he could accommodate my bike and trailer, I was more than happy to accept his kind invitation.

Martin opened the rear doors and lowered the ramp. We loaded up and minutes later I climbed in the front. Wow, it was warm. I was satisfied that I had made it to the summit but had been slightly apprehensive about the descent. Would I have sufficient grip? I had resigned myself to being stuck on the mountain all night and had been making plans to camp, come what may, by 4am. Martin would spare me that hardship.

He started the ignition and put the van in gear but we didn't move. We were wheel spinning. We weren't on a steep incline, it was just an adverse camber. I climbed on the front wing to give additional traction. That didn't work. Martin only had one snow chain. The other had broken earlier. We got out to put the chain on the opposite front wheel. That made no difference. Eventually we had only one option. We had to push the van backwards, turn it around and go back down the route I had just trudged. It had taken me three hours to get to the top. We made our descent in just fifteen minutes.

Martin was a musician and had been making his way home from an earlier gig. He had hoped to take the mountain route and avoid paying the toll charge for passing through the motorway tunnel. Unable to proceed without a full set of snow chains he cleared it with his boss and the lower route was authorised. I would have about forty-five minutes with Martin. That allowed me to dry my hat and gloves on the dashboard, put a tiny bit of charge into my tablet and make a full and safe descent from the harsh mountain environment.

Martin was fascinated by the trip details and offered advice on routes. He rang his girlfriend for confirmation of his suggestion before dropping me off by a fountain on the outskirts of Tams. His instructions were to follow the railway. There was a cycle lane running parallel and it would take me directly to Innsbruck. He pointed out the train line. Thank you, Martin.

I filled up my bottles and rode down to the track. I was heading east. North of the track was the main road. South of the track was a steep embankment. I was already on the cycle path. It wasn't very good. Not much of a track at all really. It was uneven gravel, almost impassable at points and very close to the track. The first train rushed by sending shivers down my spine. This couldn't be the cycle route. I abandoned my load, darted across the track and scaled the embankment. There was the designated lane. A wide tarmac path. Obstacles by instalment once more. This time I had to physically unpack the trailer and carry it empty before making numerous shuttle runs with the contents. It was exhausting.

I knew that I was 75 km from Innsbruck. I was ready for bed but needed somewhere to sleep. It was almost 11pm. In the middle of a field was a wooden shed. It was padlocked but some of the side panels were missing. I managed to squeeze through but my bike and trailer would have to stay outside. Walking to it had left tyre tracks and footprints in the snow but it was late and I'd be gone early morning. The shed contained wooden picket fence posts but it was dry. During the night there would be more snow and some flakes blew in through the missing panels. I tried to block these gaps with kit bags and my bivvy sheet. I wrapped up warm and went back to sleep.

DAY 18. Thursday 2nd April

The late finish meant I didn't rise early. It was still snowing when I surfaced about 9.15am so my tracks were covered. I couldn't stay there all day but I was too tired to move and my motivation was drained. I was ahead of schedule thanks to Martin. Perhaps it would stop snowing soon and brighten up? My camera and tablet were dead and there was not yet any sign of sun.

I really needed to get away from this high ground but opted for a few extra hours in my sleeping bag.

By 12.20pm I was recharged. The weather had not improved and I could certainly do better than this emergency accommodation. I decided to move on but today would be a real battle. The snow turned to sleet, and then freezing rain. It was a constant downpour which made the views less spectacular. The bike path was excellent but that was the only good thing about the whole day. I was pretty miserable. I stopped and cooked under a road bridge. I was out of the rain but my wet clothes made me shiver and it was very uncomfortable. It was so cold that the extra virgin olive oil I carried had frozen. I had to squeeze it out of its plastic bottle like toothpaste. I made notes in my diary but struggled to hold the pencil. Why was I doing this?

I passed an impressive stretch of river near Haiming. White-water rafting was just one of the outdoor pursuits offered at this site. With the opaque air it was not possible to determine whether I was still on high ground or lower down. I stopped quite early in a machinery store on the edge of some farmland. It was walled on just three sides and the roof leaked but it was better than the previous night.

DAY 19. Friday 3rd April

Good Friday — it was indeed. What a glorious day. The clouds had lifted and I watched the bright sunshine rise up from behind the snowy peaks before it drenched my lower valley with warm rays. For the first time in two days I had solar power. Such a morale boost. My tablet was fully charged inside thirty minutes and with my bike overturned to act as a clothes rack, my wet things soon dried.

I was in Telfs, about 20 miles from Innsbruck and only 110 miles from Zell am See. I set off about 9.20am.

With the increased visibility came some bad news. I had a severely buckled wheel on the trailer. A pothole during a high-speed descent was the most likely cause. I only needed Wilson for the Austrian phase. Once the snow theatre was complete I wouldn't require as much kit and could transfer the lighter load to my bike rack. Unfortunately there was no way the wheel would last that long and my pace would have to reduce to even reach Innsbruck.

Google told me there were five bike shops in that city. I spent two hours attempting to visit each one in turn. The first three were shut for lunch but the fourth one did the trick. He was a hoarder and although he didn't stock the needed replacement he had ad hoc spares in his cellar. To my relief he produced a compatible alternative to replace the wobbly wheel that had earlier suffered the puncture in Germany.

€25 later I was still rolling. After cooking in the sunshine I pressed on towards my first objective. I found a decent pair of gloves on the path. Mine were holed and worn at this stage so this was a bit of good fortune.

I camped that night in the treeline off the cycle track, southwest of Munster. I was next to a fast-flowing river. It was being fed by melted snow off the mountains and I was concerned that it might rise higher. I monitored it closely for the first few hours but it was OK.

DAY 20. Saturday 4th April

I was on the road by 9am and followed the cycle path through constant drizzle for most of the morning. In order to get warm I had a coffee and baguette in a Subway restaurant. That lifted my morale but I was also excited about reaching my target tomorrow.

Shortly after that, I developed seat wobble. I had packed a variety of tools for this trip but neglected to pack a number 6 Allen key. I tried in vain at several service stations and a ski resort. This was a desperate time. Without the seat I couldn't sit down, and I was unable to walk far because of my dodgy ankle. Completely by chance I came across a man doing some maintenance on his car and he was only too happy to lend me the relevant tool. My hero.

Today would turn into a finishing sprint. I was inching closer to Zell but instead of feeling tired I got more motivated. At 6pm I stopped for a McDonald's 'Big Tasty' meal. It was too cold for cooking and I was diverting my energy towards bigger prizes.

I cleared the final junction and found myself on the road that would lead me to my target. I still had a long way to go with several climbs and descents. It was night-time by now but there was very light traffic. One well-meaning motorist told me not to take the hazardous by-pass and directed me through a sleepy village to follow the cycle route. It sounded like good advice but the track was covered in thick snow and impassable so I had to abandon the idea. It cost me a lot of time as I had to ride back over old ground. I completed the steep climb out of the village. No one overtook me, so the by-pass wasn't that hazardous after all. I took a break at the summit and contemplated finding shelter but that meant riding until something appropriate presented itself.

Downhill stretches saw me clock up high mileage in just a few hours and it seemed silly to make camp when I was already so close. At 10.45pm I was stopped by a police patrol car. I had good lights, reflectors and a high visibility panel but the officer told me to get off the road and use the cycle lane provided. I hadn't seen it but took his advice. He was a good bloke but quite jealous that I was a retired police officer whereas he still had a few more years to do. He wished me luck.

By midnight I was there. At night-time the lake looked as big as the sea. It was too dark for photographs so I would complete the mission objective in the morning. I first had to find somewhere to sleep. There was nowhere discreet that I could see. Much of the shore was privately owned and fenced off. The high foliage was at the water's edge and everywhere else was exposed.

234

In desperation I camped by a pile of old logs on someone's private drive. I didn't get much sleep. I was unable to build a shelter that would conceal my presence and protect me from the weather so I hid the bike and trailer and slept in the open.

DAY 21. Sunday 5th April

It was an Easter Sunday that I'll never forget. It was cold at 5am when I woke up. I was covered in snow and even being motivated to move quickly, I was still shivering uncontrollably. I got rolling and started to look for somewhere to enter the water. The Strandbad boat-landing at Kurpark, Thumersbach provided the venue. I took refuge in the ferry terminal. It had two walls with benches alongside. It was open at both ends but had a roof. It would have been a good place to sleep if only I could have found it earlier.

First I needed to warm up, so I made a tea. That did the trick. I set up the tripod and camera. Which area would be best for my swim? Yes, swim.

In the final episode of *Band of Brothers*, the commanding officer took an early morning dip just here. Watching him on TV, I had decided that I'd like to do that one day. Major Dick Winters had his swim in July of 1945 just before the war ended. It would have been much warmer then but I couldn't wait until the seasons changed. I would be going in today.

I put some more water on the boil, stripped off and put on my trunks. I pressed the shutter and activated the self-timer before running into the water with my Union Jack.

A few seconds later I ran back to the camera and checked the shot on the digital display. It looked OK. Right, time for a swim. I did about ten breaststrokes before making a rapid exit back to the shelter. It was absolutely freezing. The tea did not thaw me out, so I made another and then another.

I threw away my first set of disposable clothes and donned a fresh outfit. It was at that point that I discovered the flag in my photograph was the wrong way up. I wasn't going back in. The upside-down Union Jack is a signal of distress and my early morning plunge certainly met that description.

I circumnavigated the lake, hoping to find a café for a celebratory breakfast. I had no such luck. I was used to the secular society in England but in Zell, everyone was dressed up smart and heading for church. There were no shops open anywhere.

I saw little point in sticking around and started to ride towards Salzburg. The sun came out mid-morning and reflected off the snowy peaks. There were blue skies, green fields and the occasional small but rapid stream. There were a few scattered Alpine cottages and farms too. It was very clean and quiet. At the time I considered it to be right up there among the most beautiful places in the world. I conversed briefly with some locals who were out walking their dog. I told them how lucky they were to live in such a place. Then I considered how lucky I was to be able to go there, effectively for free. The early weeks of miserable weather and cold nights were soon forgotten. This trip had been a success.

Today, for the first time, my route would be either flat or downhill. I stopped about 8.30am for tea and Alpen. About 1pm I dined at a large bus shelter. I occupied all three benches as my kitchen. I dried my other kit on an old abandoned flatbed trailer.

Despite the lower altitude and mostly sunny day, by late afternoon there were occasional snow flurries that stung my eyes as I rode through. Given the lack of sleep from the previous night I was very tired. When an open barn appeared I took full advantage. It housed some agricultural equipment and trailers but there was plenty of room for me to spread out on the straw-lined floor. This was luxury. I stood in the doorway sniggering at the weather and how I had cheated its inconvenience.

I was at Weißbach bei Lofer. Tonight I hoped for a straight twelve hours (7pm-7am). The news from home was that Leicester City had won. They had just twenty-two points and were four points from safety with only eight games remaining. Would this victory be too little too late?

DAY 22. Monday 6th April

After a great night's sleep I hit the road about 7.30am. It was a cold start and the snow had left a light layer on my cycle lane. Looking back, my tyre tracks left a trail leading to the barn doors. It was a cold, grey and miserable morning. I had to keep blowing into my gloves to stop my fingers from freezing. The navigation was easy though as Austria is very cyclist friendly. My route today would take me briefly back through the open border with Germany. With more blinding snow flurries, I considered taking refuge in a couple of barns but there were signs warning of hibernating adders. That caught me by surprise and I hadn't considered that the night before. It was difficult to tell where I made the actual crossing. It was somewhere near Bad Reichenhall.

Achtung Lebensgefahr !

bissige KREUZOTTERN

Salzburg was the target. I rode along the banks of a large and fast-flowing river. Looking back I could see the high snowy peaks that fed this channel. Looking forward I could see how the water raced over the rocks towards the lowlands. Not much further now, and the weather would surely improve.

It didn't improve. I was battered by wind, rain, sleet and snow for the whole day. I rode into the big city. It was a huge disappointment. A ghost town. Some of the big hotels were open and a couple of kebab shops but no supermarkets or tempting restaurants. I had been having mirages of a big fat juicy steak and chips and that was already twenty-four hours overdue, but of course this was Easter Monday, a Bank Holiday. To make matters worse it was still tipping it down and I was getting soaked.

There was a Turkish café that seemed an inappropriate venue for my banquet. I made a mental note of the Chinese takeaway to be regarded as a last resort but then stumbled across a local bar that made food. Steak was not on the menu, but a large rack of barbeque ribs, spicy roast potatoes, garlic bread and cobs of sweetcorn looked appetising. This celebratory meal was washed down with a local lager, my first beer for more than three weeks. It was warm in the bar. Outside, my bike and trailer were being drenched as the rain poured down. Then there were flashes of lightning which interrupted the TV screens. I would need to stay indoors for as long as I could. Hopefully the rain would stop.

I had a wash in the bathroom and checked my condition in the full mirror.

Hair was a bit longer and my beard was developing. I had agreed with Hannah that I would not shave until I got home but this facial hair irritated me. Weight-wise, I looked quite healthy. I did not have the same gaunt POW appearance which had transformed me by this stage on the Greece trip.

The food was superb. The beer was great, but I managed to resist the temptation for a refill. I was getting comfortable and sleepy so it was time to move. Fortunately, the rain had slowed and would soon stop.

Time to find a bed for the night. After buying some cookies and chocolate from a service station, I eventually reached the outskirts of Esch at 8.30pm. There was an old Roman bridge with several archways. I camped there. Mission A was accomplished.

Mission B. You WILL test the waters of the Black Sea and conduct a beach recce before demolishing a Bulgarian dish and eliminating all evidence by washing it down with a suitable Bulgarian beverage. Head north out of Austria and then transit Czech Republic, Slovakia, Hungary, Serbia and Kosovo.

DAY 23. Tuesday 7th April

The new mission didn't start well. There was a blizzard during the night and the temperature dropped to minus 7 degrees. With a shortage of anchorage points under the bridge, I had to erect my tent between the trailer and a sapling. It collapsed due to the strong winds and had to be rebuilt. Snow had been blown in through the arches and most of my kit was covered. The sun was quite powerful at 8am and I hung a lot of gear out to dry over a wire mesh fence. There was no real urgency. I had a very long way to go and intended to pace myself. I was quite content with my initial achievement and felt no pressure for additional success.

As I moved steadily further away from the high peaks and white fields, the snow started to melt. Patches of green appeared either side of my cycle track and eventually the only visible snow existed on the distant mountain tops. I liked it that way.

Snow was one of the things I would not miss. I rode along contemplating life and reflected on all those activities that I had experienced. With age and physical restrictions, there were some things I would never do again. I was too old to be a marine now, my marathon days were over and skiing was an unrealistic option. It didn't depress me though; I had done all of those things. I considered how much I had enjoyed the constant warmth of Malta and Thailand. Snow and the cold were things that I was happy to let fade from memory. I didn't want to experience either ever again.

That morning I made tea at a fountain in the village of Wankham. An amusing name. By 1pm the sun was high and I stopped at Strasswelchen for a resupply. I dried all my kit and recharged my gadgets. I was enjoying this more favourable climate and looking back, the Alps were steadily getting smaller.

My tripod was a little battered by this point. It had accompanied me to Brazil, through Europe to Greece, then Malta and Thailand. After three weeks on this trip, one of its legs would fall off down the hollow plastic inside of a fixed roadside bollard. I had positioned the device in order to take a photo of the distant mountain range but it'd collapsed. My salvage attempts were futile, but a pencil, fixed in position with masking tape, would make a suitable prosthetic.

On my travels I visited a Spar shop looking for Allen keys but was unsuccessful so I bought milk and replacement socks instead. I later found a hardware store but the woman didn't speak English. My sketch of an Allen key did the trick and I added a number 6 to my tool collection.

By 6.30pm I was at Vocklamart and made camp in a luxurious pine-tree forest.

DAY 24. Wednesday 8th April

It had been a comfortable night, cool and dry. The sun was up at 7.45am and I started pedalling. The ride was quite pleasant. I followed the 'Route 1' road for much of the day. I stopped mid-morning for tea and Alpen in a peaceful memorial garden for fallen Austrian and German Nazis. I was struck by the futility and stupidity of war. They had also fought believing 'God was on their side'.

My brakes were a problem now as the pads were severely worn. Excess snow had also dislodged the front set but I was able to adjust them. However, the rear set was down to bare metal and carving grooves into my wheel rim. They had to be removed and discarded altogether which meant I would have to ride slower. My tyres were in dire need of replacement too. I kept my eyes open for a bike shop but found a camping shop instead. I bought three replacement gas canisters. That would keep me comfortable for a few weeks.

I lost my gloves that day. They were in quite poor condition from the constant wet and dry routine. I had removed them and placed them on my cycle rack before taking a leak behind a tree. On my return I became distracted talking to a dog walker. When I set off again, I completely forgot about them. It was getting warmer but gloves were still needed. I would have to wear socks on my hands for the time being.

By 6.50pm I was camped in woods just off a cycle lane outside Traun. My compass was now missing as well. I was frustrated with myself. This was a fatigue-induced concentration issue. I had experienced similar on the road to Greece. I needed the compass, particularly when it was foggy, cloudy or when in built-up areas. This was quite unsatisfactory and unprofessional so I rebuked myself, but in truth I just needed some sleep.

DAY 25. Thursday 9th April

The woods had been difficult to enter because they were so dense. It had been an 'obstacle by instalment' routine again. Stepping out of the tent first thing, I came face to face with my compass. It had snagged on a branch as I'd concealed myself in the thicket. That was a relief. The night-time temperature had leapt from the minus 7 of Salzburg to a much more comfortable 11 degrees. For the first time on this trip, I'd had decent sleep and that made me feel better too. There had been a siren during the late evening. Sounded like an air-raid warning but I suspect it had something to do with the local waterworks.

I oiled up the mechanical moving parts and inspected the rest of my kit. I didn't want to lose anything today. The upper pannier pocket zip had broken and was beyond repair. I hacked away at the useless section with my scissors. That would save a tiny bit of weight.

By 8.45am I was riding again. Today I would join the Danube. That meant I was on the flats. Google Maps led me to a ferry crossing point. Unfortunately I was a month before season and had to take a long diversion to join the northern bank at Mauthausen. At 2.30pm I resupplied at Euro Spar and cooked a meal in their car park picnic area.

The river would be my companion for at least two days and that made navigation very simple. I was joined by a whole family of cyclists for a small stretch. They were following the Danube all the way to Vienna and stopping in hotels at 50-mile intervals. Peter was a German in his early sixties. He was the lead adventurer of his team but he was my first serious interviewer. Martin had asked questions before Innsbruck but I hadn't achieved much at that point. Now I was the crazy Englishman who had been cycling for nearly a month and had travelled through France, Belgium, Luxembourg, Germany, Switzerland and Liechtenstein before crossing the Austrian Alps. Peter yearned to be young again so as to replicate my journey. He got his wife to take our photograph. I was a celebrity.

I passed a bike shop in Grein but it was closed. The tyres and brakes were desperate now. As darkness fell, my sleeping arrangements would also become a concern. There was nowhere to camp. The river was flowing through a valley with steep banks. The main road ran parallel to the water. By 9.30pm I was just clear of Sarmingstein. Exhaustion took hold and I had to pitch my tent at the water's edge. The road was very close and frequent headlights disturbed me.

DAY 26. Friday 26th April

I opened my tent and looked out. I hadn't seen much when I'd arrived in the pitch darkness the night before. I was speechless. I had a room with a view.

This was the perfect spot for tea and breakfast at 7am.

A very pleasant ride through Granz and Kracking saw me arrive at Steindl's bike shop around 11.25am. Two brand-new puncture-resistant Continental tyres, a replacement inner tube, new brake pads and a tune up cost €150. That was quite expensive but it meant a new lease of life for my noble steed.

Wilson could make do without any treatment. He wouldn't be with us much longer. I expected to be in the Czech Republic tomorrow.

By mid-afternoon it was roasting and for the first time on this trip I was able to cycle topless. My milky skin needed a tan. I pressed on through vineyards and picturesque valley villages. Durnstein was worth a visit. A medieval town overlooking the river. It reminded me of 'Diagon Alley' in the Harry Potter films and was very popular with tourists.

Having cleared the city of Krems, I headed back into the countryside and encountered the very steep climb to a plateau supporting vineyards. On the ascent were a collection of one-storey houses built into the steep embankments. These were known as 'kellars'. Originally they had housed the vineyard workers but now most were converted into luxurious holiday homes. The kellars were linked by a seemingly endless cobbled road. It was impossible to ride because of the incline but the bike and trailer rattled and shook violently as I pushed them along.

I reached the top to see the sun go down and built a perfect shelter between some trees on the edge of one of the vineyards. I was startled once again by a wild deer that sprinted past and very low-flying owl swooped by my window.

DAY 27. Saturday 11th April

At my tent door, I lay watching the bright sun rise. I managed to get a photo of the big red ball as it appeared on the horizon near Langenlois. I had a fresh scalp planned for today so I was up early and on my way by 6.20am. As I filled up on Alpen, a hot-air balloon rose from a nearby field, the roar of its burners breaking the silence.

I was soon out of the plantations and back on the Radweg (cycle lane). I passed through the very old village of Zobing. Signs indicated that this settlement had existed since AD 1105. By mid-morning I came across some unusual graffiti. Painted in large characters on a roof were 1.7 Jordans 6.3. This was just outside the town of GraBreipersdorf. That sounded a bit like 'Grim Reaper' to me. My imagination spiralled. Was I the lone adventurer about to be sacrificed in the outback by some oddball religious sect? I didn't stop. I later googled the apparent verse but found no details.

I was quite relaxed and happy today. Weather-wise, I had finally turned that corner. The sun was out, the air was warm and I was in shorts for the first time. I would stay in shorts for the rest of my expedition.

I cycled along the road to see a young man descending a steep grass embankment on a unicycle. He was dressed up like an off-road mountain biker but only had the one wheel. I was impressed and shouted, "Bravo!" I would have been more impressed if he was towing a trailer uphill like myself.

During this day I discovered that my camera was damaged. Faint grey shadows appeared on the clear blue sky backgrounds of my photographs. This only happened on shots taken while zoomed in. I cleaned the lens thoroughly but couldn't get rid of the marks. I think perhaps dirt had managed to get inside. The only way to resolve this problem was to take pictures while holding the camera upside down. That way the shadows would be lost on the landscape detail but the skies would be clear. It meant that the disabled tripod would have to work even harder.

There was a Spar supermarket at the frontier town of Retz. I stocked up on supplies and used their outdoor tap for a water refill and a wash. I liked to make myself semi-presentable for border crossings.

By 2.10pm I had reached the Czech Republic. This was the fourth new

244

flag for my fridge. I took a selfie at the guard-free checkpoint and headed inland. The cycle route was signposted and the surface looked smooth and well-maintained. So far so good, but what was that up ahead in the distance?

Slightly concerned, I decelerated towards a tall lookout tower. I could see no guard but the sentry post was inside a barbed wire perimeter. Anti-tank obstacles formed an inner defensive barrier. I was now behind the 'Iron Curtain', in Warsaw Pact territory, but the Cold War was over, wasn't it?

I was riding towards a camouflaged bunker. A heavy artillery piece and a machine gun barrel occupied the firing positions. I was in the killing zone. Soldiers were walking around the site. Perhaps I should turn around and go back the other way?

To my relief, it was only a Cold War museum. This fortification was originally built to deter NATO. It was intended to stop me thirty years ago. I looked at the weapons and obstacles for a moment and considered how fortunate I was that we never did battle. I had time to make an internal bunker inspection but the beer tent opposite looked more inviting.

The regulars waved me over and seemed a friendly enough bunch. I bought a Svijany and toasted peace with my new Czech friends. I had no local currency but the staff accepted €1 and still gave me two 'Koruna Ceske' coins as change. The rowdy bar folk taught me to say a few words. 'Pivo' was beer. 'De kuji' (dickwee) was thank you.

It was 3pm on a sunny Saturday afternoon, the beer tasted good and I was tempted to stay for more. Another time perhaps.

I started pedalling again and could soon feel that alcohol in my veins. It had been wise to stop drinking. The cycle lane deteriorated to cobblestones, then broken tarmac and finally dirt and gravel tracks. This surface was biting chunks out of my expensive new tyres and was quite uncomfortable to ride on.

I became paranoid at one point. A saloon car had been following me for a while. I veered off down a narrow track and started an uphill stretch. Periodically I looked back. The car had parked up where I had turned off. Were they secret police? Were they advising other units? Would I be intercepted further up?

No; it was just my imagination. I passed through a number of villages, Satov, Jaroslavice and Dyjakovice, but the overall surface conditions were poor. I considered my options. I had originally intended to ride east to Slovakia. If I turned south, I could return to Austria, where I already knew the roads were good. I would also be able to see some of Vienna before crossing the Slovakian border outside Bratislava. This sounded a much better plan.

By 7pm I had reached the town of Hevlin and camped in the woods.

DAY 28. Sunday 12th April

It was another relaxing night. I really enjoyed the warmer temperatures and could look forward to those from now on. A busy woodpecker had forced me to rise at 7am. Did I really need my old Berghaus fleece? I hadn't worn it since Salzburg and it didn't provide much comfort as a pillow. I couldn't really justify keeping it as a passenger for the rest of the trip. I decided to cut out the zip-up pockets and throw the rest away. Initially I used one pocket to hold my cash and the other to protect my tablet.

Once packed up, I moved over across the open border. Austria was my favourite country so far and it was good to be back.

By 11.30am I was close to the town of Staatz. There was a scenic castle on top of a hill. It gave all-round observation of the low and flat countryside. The site resembled St Michael's Mount in Cornwall but without the sea. I was, however, flabbergasted to see that a row of wind turbines had been assembled alongside. I am a firm supporter of renewable energy but the installation at this ancient and photogenic scene was bizarre.

It was an otherwise uneventful day. I just kept riding south until I reached the lovely town of Korneuburg. I struggled to find a decent location for the night and eventually had to settle for some overgrown wasteland at the entrance to an industrial park. It was rather noisy there as I was close to the motorway and only about 10 miles from the capital city, Vienna. Fortunately I had brought some foam ear defenders with me.

DAY 29. Monday 13th April

It had been a pleasant 17 degrees when I went to bed and today promised to be a hot one. I was moving by 7.20am and my tablet was charging just fine. If I had ridden an hour longer last night I would have arrived at a perfect location, a nature reserve on the banks of the Danube. I was very tired when I stopped and it was the increasing traffic noise that persuaded me to go no further.

The route into the city centre was quite easy and cycle-friendly. There were good lanes and plenty of signs. I wasn't intending to be there for long but hoped to grab a selfie at some iconic spot. Weaving through the cars, trams and ornate horse-drawn carriages, I came to a grassed area in front of the cathedral. The building was covered in scaffolding, evoking memories of the Acropolis. I moved further into the centre and reached the town hall known at the 'Rathaus', but the Parliament building provided the best backdrop.

Vienna was quite stunning with so much to see and consequently there were lots of tourists. I couldn't hang around as I had an aeroplane to catch in just seventy-one days' time. I knew that in order to reach Slovakia, I had to cross the river again and started to make my way in that direction. Completely by chance I stumbled across even more palatial buildings including the Spanish Riding School.

Blue street taps would present periodically and provide drinking water or 'trink wasser'.

I stocked up at a supermarket and eventually found an arterial route out of the built-up areas. I crossed a large bridge over the Danube and weaved through an industrial estate until I came to a very long and straight cycle track. This vehicle-free route would serve me for most of my remaining time in Austria. It carved through a nature reserve which included plenty of wooded sections but also small lakes. It was almost silent. All I could hear were the birds and the sound of my tyres running over the gravel. The wild deer caught me off guard again. One sprinted away with its stumpy white tail waving at me. I was always too slow with the camera. This was a perfect spot for tonight.

DAY 30. Tuesday 14th April

There was a near-miss incident first thing. As I walked back to the track a sharp stick lanced itself through my training shoe. It could have impaled my foot but luckily it just tore the fabric, exposing my socks and toes to fresh air. I was rolling by 8am. I had my camera ready and within fifteen minutes I had snapped my first deer. Two of them crept out of the woods and stepped onto the track. They paused to look at me. I stood still. They were about 100 metres away. I slowly raised the camera and pressed the shutter on maximum zoom. "Gotcha!" I said, before they bounced away to the other side.

Navigation was easy this morning. It was a straight line for a couple of hours before crossing the Danube again. I found an abandoned gelled seat cover and added it to my saddle. Two seat covers were better than one; it was very comfortable. I picked up an appropriately named cycle route called 'Hollitzer Allee'. That led me to Hainberg and from there I could see Bratislava in the distance. I followed the main road. There was an old and derelict border crossing consisting of several lanes, leading to a number of vacant kiosks. Rather unceremoniously I had arrived in Slovakia.

The cycle lanes were fair but this was not Austria. As I rode back across the river and towards the capital, I came across another Cold War bunker, almost identical to the one in the Czech Republic. I was quite upbeat today. I had been in Austria for fourteen nights. That was almost half of my trip, but tonight I would be in a new country and tomorrow, I would be in Hungary. The virgin territories were now adding up.

I went to view the Presidential Palace and then decided to treat myself by dining out. I found a bar with an outside seating area and ordered a massive burger and chips. I washed it down with a local ale, 'Zlaty Bazant'.

I was then advised to make sure I got a photograph of the most famous icon, the 'Man at Work'.

I was enjoying this trip. The Chinese tourists didn't have the same enthusiasm as me. They weren't going to lie down next to the bronze sculpture but I think my photo will be better than theirs.

It was then time to leave. I wanted to be out of the city before nightfall and headed towards the next border. The Euro Velo 6 was the recommended cycle route but it was difficult to follow as the signs were too sporadic. By late afternoon I was firmly on course. The route was running parallel to the river. I inched towards Hungary but fatigue finally took hold and I camped in the treeline. The river looked so clean and clear so I also had a much-needed bath.

DAY 31. Wednesday 15th April

I was up at 6am to see the sun rise over the Danube. It was worth it. Then I discovered that my woolly hat was missing. That wasn't a major problem as things were generally warmer now but it provided a little comfort on chilly mornings. I think I probably left it at the fountain outside the Presidential Palace. I had replacement headgear, a floppy sun hat with a neck shade and full-face veil. It was time to get that out of storage. It was also time to put away my euros. They would not be national currency until reaching Latvia, if I got that far, and for the next three weeks I would be heading in the opposite direction.

The Danube at 6.24am, 15th April.

It was a casual ride towards the border. There was no welcome sign or new country acknowledgement but at the next town, the workmen confirmed that I was in Hungary. So far on this trip, the water had been free. That trend continued. Outside the church in Dunakilliti was an ornate public tap. I took full advantage by having a wash, filling my bottles, having a mug of tea and cleaning as much kit as was possible. I also took this opportunity to oil up the chain, axles and bearings.

Google-recommended cycle routes would not exist from here on. Many of the roads were off limits to cyclists, horse-drawn carriages or tractors. This meant I had to look at pedestrian routes. In any event, it made little difference. The roads were generally in a poor condition. The surfaces were like patchwork quilts made from different shades of tarmac. It was difficult to

251

tell which parts were original road and which were repairs. The alternative routes were just rough dirt and gravel tracks that stirred up intense clouds of dust whenever anything overtook me. The grit would go into my eyes and it was impossible to breathe.

It was around this time that I developed a problem with my knee. I felt a sharp pain when kneeling down one day. I couldn't see any injury and suspected an ingrowing hair might be responsible. I tried to pick it out with my tweezers but was unsuccessful. I treated it with iodine most days but the problem would persist and I needed to avoid kneeling on that side. I would suffer this sharp pain for the rest of the trip and for the first week after returning to England. When it was finally ready to be squeezed I discovered the culprit was a tiny sliver of glass.

I stocked up at a Tesco superstore in Mosonmagyarovar and then put in a full shift. Hungary was hard work and the least cycle-friendly country I had been to. There was a designated route, the Velo 6, but it led to unwanted destinations. It was intended for tourists following the banks of the Danube but I was heading for Gyor.

I dined mid-afternoon on a grass verge outside a graveyard. There was a tap there for watering the floral tributes. There was so many flowers.

There were several opportunities to make camp but it was a beautiful evening, the sun was still shining, people were fishing by the river banks and it seemed too early to stop.

I reached the main square in Gyor just as the sun was falling. People were dining outside listening to live music. It was very pleasant, but of course this was a built-up area and I now needed to find suitable quarters. I headed out on a compass bearing and got lost a couple of times. Finally I saw the railway track and used that as a guide. The trains were ancient diesels that I hadn't seen since I was very young.

I reached the countryside, where people lived in tiny and basic cottages.

Nothing more than wooden summer houses really. Darkness soon fell but I was struggling to find anywhere decent. Finally I occupied the treeline at the edge of a recently ploughed field. I could hear the motorway close by but I was exhausted and soon fell asleep. The traffic noise did not abate and probably affected my rest. I woke up at 3am. I had been having a nightmare. I was still a police officer and was involved in a serious disagreement with superiors who did not approve of my methods. I tried to break free of this dream by getting up and taking a leak but when I returned to my tent, the whole confrontation continued. I woke the next morning confused and disorientated. I was still very tired.

DAY 32. Thursday 16th April
    The sun was rising at 7am. I didn't need the woolly hat today. As I headed

down another dirt track I saw a car with a British registration plate. The would-be driver emerged from her house and I said, "Good morning," to the expat. We had a short chinwag about her move to this very different country. She was a bat enthusiast and various breeds were living in her garden sheds. The furry creatures, cost of living, massive but affordable house and more favourable climate had been powerful persuaders, but she advised me that the road conditions would not improve.

I took it very easy today and sauntered along. Most of the countryside was farmland. I cleared the village of Bony and saw a photo opportunity. I was shocked by my weight loss.

I took a slight diversion to reach the village of Dad. I had to get a photograph there. Most small settlements offered free water from fountains or communal taps and I questioned my logic at carrying four 2-litre bottles.

There were lots of Lada cars out here, old but still in excellent condition, relics of the communist era. I also made other observations this day. Each cemetery was overflowing with flowers. Literally every headstone had fresh tributes. The dead were being very well looked after here. I had mixed feelings about this and questioned the economics. Presumably it was staff rather than grieving relatives who tended these memorials. That suggested someone was paying a

maintenance fee. Notwithstanding, this was a very impressive display of colour, almost festive in appearance; the fact remains that everybody dies, so this was simply unsustainable. I decided that when my time came I'd settle for something less onerous.

Many of the apartment blocks were dull and grey with no character, almost like hastily constructed military barracks, and that implied oppression. Newly built apartments had more colour and were less uniform in appearance. That suggested freedom or liberation.

Finally, there were the women. I'm sure that there must have been some natural beauties lying around but disproportionately there was a large number that resembled the stereotypical Olympic weightlifter or shot-putter. As I rode past I would laugh to myself, trying to label each one.

I cooked in Tata Banya and made camp about 8.45pm just outside the town in a wooded area off the main road. Wild deer roamed freely and this was a great location. It was still 23 degrees.

DAY 33. Friday 17th April

Fatigue kicked in. Should I take the day off or do a half day and visit Budapest tomorrow? I needed a bit more rest before deciding and I didn't move until 11.30am. I stepped out from the woods onto Route 51 and casually cruised towards the capital. By late afternoon I was within striking distance. If I got there too late it would be dark and ruin any photo opportunities. If I camped now and rolled into the city tomorrow morning, the forecast was rain which would also ruin the photos. I took a gamble, picked up the pace and really went for it. After some initial climbs, I freewheeled down towards the River Danube. The west bank housed the Buda community. Pest was on the eastern side. Together they formed Budapest.

At 4.30pm I took the first available bridge and rolled into Pest. This place was every bit a modern western city. It easily rivalled London, Paris and Milan. It was busy and packed full of tourists. There was so much to see and do but I had only about an hour of daylight for my photos. I headed to the Parliament building. It looked similar to the Palace of Westminster but there was no Big Ben.

I explored a bit more and was careful not to get run over by the silent trams.

History will eventually credit former US President Ronald Reagan with ending the Cold War. He was already being celebrated here. In one of the squares there was a big bronze statue of the man. That had to be worth a photo too. I was very impressed so far and really enjoying the place.

I planned to dine out, so I moved back to the riverbank where the outdoor seating gave spectacular views. There I stumbled across a large crowd. I was at a modern monument called 'Shoes on the Danube'. It was a memorial to Jews killed towards the end of the Second World War. Women, children, men, young and old, were lined up, told to remove their shoes and then shot. Those dead or dying fell forward to be swept away by the river.

A selection of sculptured metal shoes had been affixed to the riverside. It was deeply disturbing. It represented the aftermath of a mass murder. I imagined it as a crime scene and in that frame of mind I was grief-stricken and ready to vomit. A lady's shoe, a small child's; it was very real. The monument had been opened in 2005 but the crowds were still there lighting candles and leaving messages of sympathy. It seriously dampened my mood. Then, almost without warning, it tipped down with rain.

I fought through the weather and traffic until I was called in by a waitress

to dine in her empty restaurant. The overhanging awning could shelter my bike but I had no Hungarian forint. That wasn't a problem as they accepted euros. I ordered a local Dreher beer and then went to freshen up in their bathroom. The mirror said I needed fattening up, so I ordered three courses. First the creamy garlic soup, which was served in a large hollowed-out bread bun. Next came my delicious and long overdue steak. That was helped down by another beer. I was full but it was still raining and showed no sign of stopping any time soon. I resigned myself to having to find shelter in the early hours and requested the dessert menu.

The Somloi Galuska was a national speciality and came highly recommended. A large bowl of trifle sponge, blancmange, ice cream and whipped cream, topped with chocolate sauce. I couldn't finish that. I couldn't even finish the third beer that I had ordered. I should have known better. After almost five weeks on the road, my stomach had shrunk. This was déjà vu and a flashback to that massive pizza in Montenegro.

I thanked my hosts and apologised for my failure to complete before heading out into the night. It was almost 9pm but it took another hour before I was sufficiently clear of the residential zones. I came across an abandoned gatehouse to a derelict industrial estate. It had four walls and a roof. There was some cardboard lying on the floor. I think someone may have slept there previously. I built barricades at the door and window to give me an early warning of intruders or even a displaced resident. It was good to lie down but my swollen stomach meant I had to sleep on my back. There was a noisy bird chirping from a nearby tree but I soon dozed off.

My slumber was disturbed in the early hours by a couple of barking dogs. They were snarling and growling too. They obviously knew I was in there but weren't quite brave enough to evict me. In the still of the night their racket seemed amplified and it went on for about fifty minutes. Eventually I got up and ran out to chase them away.

DAY 34. Saturday 18th April

Headed out at 6.20am and rejoined Route 51. It was a cold and grey start. A local Spar supermarket enabled me to stock up and a warm slice of pepperoni pizza made a pleasant breakfast. I rode through several housing estates that realistically needed knocking down and rebuilding. They looked such miserable and depressing places to live in. Permanently grey, it was like being in a black and white movie.

After following the main road for about an hour into the countryside a 'No cyclists' sign suddenly appeared. How ridiculous was that? Where was I supposed to go now? There was no cycle lane or turn-offs. I was not going to ride all the way back for an hour. I ignored the sign and prepared to justify my actions. I passed a field that seemed to be storing Soviet aircraft, including Hind helicopter gunships and MIG 21 fighter jets.

My next available alternate route took me past the Kiskunlachaza airport.

There were many more military aircraft there but I thought better of taking photographs. I didn't want to be accused of spying. Looking around at all this hardware, I wasn't entirely convinced that the Cold War was over.

I next arrived in the pretty town of Kunszentmiklos. The residential blocks still looked more appropriate for military garrisons but the main square had been landscaped with block paving, outside seating, fountains and gardens. I sat there for a while relaxing and browsing my maps.

By 5pm I was camped in the treeline overlooking open fields of the Kiskunsagi Nemzeti Park. It was very peaceful there, almost silent. That was perfect as I really needed to catch up on my sleep.

DAY 35. Sunday 19th April

The sun came up at 6.10am and the park ranger drove past me shortly afterwards. If he had scrutinised the treeline in his rear-view mirror, I would have been seen. I decided to depart before he returned. My presence wasn't doing any harm. I conscientiously never left any litter and chose to carry it until I could dispose of it responsibly. I hate litter, full stop. I rarely made fires and wasn't causing any damage; even so, it would be better to leave undetected.

My route for most of the day was through fields and along the dirt tracks of the national park. It was peaceful and quite relaxing in the warm sunshine. I saw a number of wild deer and hares. I got lots of insect bites today. Something had crept under the rim of my floppy hat and was biting a trail from my left temple across my forehead. Loads of tiny bloodsucking spiders had dined on my legs as I walked through the long grass.

What I saw of Hungary was just not ready for bicycle tourists and I hoped Serbia would be better. The bike and trailer would not tolerate this constant battering. Still, it could have been worse. The sun was shining and I had free water. I knew where I was and where I was going. Then came the epiphany. I had just discovered the formula for being content.

By 7pm I was camped in the roadside treeline.

DAY 36. Monday 20th April

On the road for 7.20am. Morning traffic had prompted me to rise; there were many noisy lorries today. My road led me to Baja (sadly this was not California).

I had a short rest on a bench and caught up with my messages. I had some roaming data allowance to use up before reaching the Serbian border. It was at this point that I got a message from Andy Shaw.

He was back in the Falklands on a reunion. He had spent an evening in one of the bars with another veteran. Major Mike Norman had commanded a small detachment of Royal Marines that had repelled the initial Argentine invasion in 1982. He had finally been ordered to surrender by Governor Rex Hunt. I had never met the commando officer myself but he was a legend in our Corps and his exploits had been captured in a film, *The Ungentlemanly Act*. Norman was played by Bob Peck, better known as the gamekeeper in the first *Jurassic Park* movie. Amongst their conversation topics was my bike ride across Europe.

The text from Andy was a few days old but read: 'Drinking with Mike Norman, I told him about your bike ride, he thinks you're a twat!'

Blokes are rarely complimentary to each other and usually trade insults even when they are being friendly or flattering. This made me chuckle and lifted my morale for the rest of the day.

At 1pm I made the crossing. The border guard told me off for taking photographs. I was only snapping the flag and he forgave me. My passport was finally stamped.

259

Within half an hour, my tablet was announcing incoming service messages. 'Welcome to Serbia'. Data roaming charges were £50 for 50 Mb. In Hungary it had been £20 for 100 Mb, but now I was outside the EU. My time in Serbia would work out expensive. I had at least 300 miles to do there and that meant six to seven days. My other problem was route planning. The Foreign Office advised me that owing to political tensions, I was unlikely to gain access to Kosovo through Serbia. They recommended that I divert to enter through Montenegro and exit via Macedonia. Extra miles and significant mountain ranges were likely to cause delays and therefore extend my stay.

I had other misgivings about this place. Atrocities and war crimes were committed by all sides during the Balkan Conflict of the 1990s but Serbian forces had been particularly brutal. Was I safe in this region? The roads were certainly better than Hungary but where was the free water? After three hours inside this seventh virgin territory I still hadn't seen a working public tap or fountain.

The day would end with a near disaster. I struggled to find a suitable campsite and sheltered at the base of a thick fir tree behind a roadside hedge.

As I prepared my meal, I discovered that toothpaste had leaked in my panniers and had clogged up the jets to my camping stove. I cleaned the device with my nail brush, rags, tooth picks and cotton buds. Finally it ignited and roared into flame. I expected the residue to burn off. I made dinner and the little appliance worked fine.

Later that same evening I decided to make a mug of tea. I usually did this inside the tent and today was no exception. Unfortunately the cooker would not ignite. I could hear the gas hissing but there was obviously still a blockage which resulted in a build-up of pressure. I clicked my lighter again and then there was a massive fireball. I jumped back as it singed my face. Whoa, that was close!

I looked at the tent ceiling. It was still there, but unfortunately there was now a grapefruit-sized hole in the mesh doorway. For security purposes, I slept with the zip door rolled back, leaving the mesh inner door as my only protection. This gaping hole meant that the eager and hungry mosquitoes would be all over me in seconds.

I zipped up the main door and cursed my incompetence. What now? Look for a new tent in this unfriendly country? I was supposed to be saving money. I couldn't simply stitch the hole together because that would create too much tension and prevent the zip from functioning. I needed a patch.

What could I use? I rummaged through my kit bag. Hey presto, the mesh lining to one of my Berghaus fleece pockets. It was the right size and just took a little bit of trimming with my scissors. I tacked it loosely in position and then did some more robust stitching. Feeling very pleased with my innovative repair, I sat back to admire the work.

DAY 37. Tuesday 21st April

A lazy morning saw me roll on at 9am. Found water at the next village. Hard to believe in this day and age that so many houses don't have what we consider to be the basics in England. There wasn't a queue at the public tap but as I made morning tea, there was a steady flow of local residents filling up their carriers and containers.

Fully hydrated, good roads, easy navigation and a pleasant sun meant my morning was relaxing. I hadn't realised the Serbs fought the Nazis during the Second World War. I came across a monument to one of their number, Mileta Protic, who had fled the country to join the RAF. Sadly he was killed in 1944, but if Serbia was celebrating him for joining the British, I was among friends after all.

I crossed the Danube again as I had to briefly enter Croatia for about an hour at Baca Palanka. Then I returned to Serbian territory. The border guard assured me that riding directly to Kosovo would not be a problem.

That was good news. It had been a constant concern since the planning stage; an issue I would have to tackle head-on when it came to it. This meant a shorter journey which enabled me to include a diversion through the capital, Belgrade. I was warming to this place.

I came to a steep decline. I knew that I needed to take the next left turn so I didn't want to go too fast and miss it. I picked up speed as I freewheeled. The heavy trailer was shunting me along. I could see the village at the bottom of the hill getting closer. The rapid descent created a refreshing breeze, so powerful in fact that it blew off my hat. My safe stopping distance was in excess of 100 metres. If I slammed the brakes on too hard, the trailer would try to overtake and cause me to jack-knife.

Somewhat annoyed, I ran back up the steep hill to collect my headgear. Then I jogged back down to carry on cycling. The road became a dirt track and headed towards a barn. The locals looked puzzled. What was I doing? Where was I going? I checked the GPS. I had missed the left turn. No!

I used the village fountain for a refill and then with the increased weight, I trudged almost all the way back up that which I had just freewheeled down. It was impossible to push the bike and tow the trailer directly uphill at the same time. I had to tack a course, zigzagging my way up. Finally and out of breath, I saw the concealed entrance of my missed turning. Into the woods I went. I was now in the Serbian National Park.

I found a picnic bench and utilised that as a field kitchen before dining al fresco. There were some forestry workers loading tractor trailers with the heavy logs that they had just carved up with chainsaws.

Soon afterwards, the noisy workers packed up for the day and the forest became silent but for a gentle breeze through the leaves. My mind was made up. This was the perfect place to spend the night. I rode a bit further along the track and then headed deeper into the trees.

I was able to construct a perfect shelter and suspend my solar panels from a tree in order to boost the battery on my tablet. It was only 4.30pm but I was about ready for an early night.

DAY 38. Wednesday 22nd April

I had taken two ibuprofen with each evening meal. That had been adequate so far but this morning my knees were very sore and I was concerned. Serbia had lots of mountains and the Black Sea in Bulgaria was a long way off. I contemplated using all my reserves of energy to achieve Mission B and gave myself the option of abandoning the return ride in favour of a flight. This was not meant to be a challenge and I had nothing to prove. This sounded like a sensible proposition and I pencilled it in as my new intention. I also had the Wilson issue. I was riding towards early summer and the need to carry extra kit and supplies was diminished. Did I really need this heavy trailer? It made packing up easy and reduced the wear on my back tyre. It also provided a buffer zone to protect me from cars that might overtake too closely. I decided to keep it for now.

I set off around 7.40am for a casual ride through this most scenic location. It was undulating terrain and the up-hills seemed to exceed the downhill sections. A working party of about six people had been dropped off by truck to scour the area looking for rubbish. I doubt they found much.

The tree branches supported new leaves and the spring flowers were in bloom. There was blue sky and warm sunshine. As the morning went on it seemed as though I was the only person in this wilderness. No traffic of any description. It was just me. I could hear my wheels turning, my footsteps and my heavy breathing, but when I stopped to listen, it was like being deaf. I could hear nothing. I concentrated, shut my eyes and held my breath. Nothing. Just an occasional breeze and a few song birds. I suddenly found myself singing Louis Armstrong's 'What A Wonderful World'.

I think being in a sound vacuum disorientated me. On the next downhill stretch and for no apparent reason, I was thrown off my bike and landed very heavily in a ditch. I sheared off part of the metal bracket holding my front brake calliper in place. I was able to bend it with tools so that it continued to function adequately. My front light had dismantled into several pieces, most of which vanished in the long grass. The parts I recovered were useless on their own. My backside and thigh had received a bad graze too. I felt so stupid. What had just happened?

Further along, my illusions of paradise were shattered by concrete pyramid roadblocks. They weren't deployed as a barrier, instead they were dumped together at the roadside. There were also rusted bullet casings lying about.

When I reached the high ground and broke out of the trees, I could see the surrounding countryside for miles. As I stopped to admire the view, I was joined by Pavel. He was a Polish cyclist, riding from his home in Lublin to Greece. It was very satisfying for me to be able to say, "Been there, done that."

We discussed our intended journeys and by way of co-operation we used each other's cameras instead of taking selfies.

Pavel's bike was loaded with front and rear panniers. His pace was much quicker than mine. It needed to be for his forty-day schedule. He told me to head for Nesebar in Bulgaria and invited me to call him if I reached his hometown on my way to Warsaw. I headed off alone while he had a picnic. Half an hour later he overtook me.

On this high ground I came across a TV broadcasting station. The tall concrete beacon had been shelled repeatedly. It was badly scarred and had whole chunks missing but remained standing.

It would have been sensible to spend a second night in the national park but I was spurred on by the freewheel descent towards the next town. On reaching Indija, I stocked up in the supermarket. I was just about to pedal away when in front of me walked the most stunningly beautiful woman. A young lad in the car park had seen her too. We both made comments. I don't think either of us understood the other's language but the sentiment was clear.

Getting out of Indija seemed to take an eternity. I kept riding but was unable to clear the built-up area and there seemed to be no end in sight. Eventually I moved into a small orchard between two industrial units. There were plenty of dense bushes but a guard dog had detected my presence and started yapping.

I was too tired to care and laughed him off. "Bark all you want, I'm not moving," I muttered under my breath. He quietened down an hour later and I slept well.

DAY 39. Thursday 23rd April

My desperate position meant I needed to be out early before the workers arrived. It was a chilly start at 5.30am but the dog stayed quiet and I was soon on the road to Belgrade.

By 10.15am I had crossed the Danube again and was in the capital. I had ridden past the Hotel Yugoslavia and reached McDonald's for a wash, a 'Big Tasty' and to make use of their free Wi-Fi.

After a selfie at the Temple of St Sava and a refill with some 'holy water' I headed out of the city. I stumbled across the football stadium of Red Star Belgrade. The gates were open and I was allowed in to survey the pitch. Then it was time to trudge along.

Already requiring another £50 data top-up prompted me to ask Noi to stop sending pictures of enticing beers and sunsets.

I returned to the hills and high ground. Looking back I could see the skyscrapers and high-rise accommodation blocks of Belgrade. In front of me was the Avala Tower. At the time it was the tallest telecommunications tower in the Balkans. Its predecessor had been bombed by NATO during the conflict.

I camped that night in the forest between Ripanj and Mala Ivanca. The midges and flies attacked me as I made my shelter so I put on my trousers over my shorts and tucked the bottoms into my socks.

DAY 40. Friday 24th April

Back on Route 149 for 8am. As I was packing up I saw a small leech crawling along one of the guide ropes, looking for a way in. I flicked off the unwanted passenger. One of the neighbours had his garden sprinkler activated. The hosepipe was leaking at the roadside and I got an opportunistic refill.

It was quite a tough day with lots of riding ascents. I cleared the town of Mladenovac. I was unsure of the pronunciation but reading it made me think someone should sack the cleaner: 'my lady no vac'.

Met up with Luica Radivojevic, a local Serb. He was fascinated by my journey and was himself in training for a bike ride to Greece which he would go on to successfully complete later that year. He gave me some useful advice regarding routes that avoided the mountains. Later that afternoon I could see those mountains behind me on the skyline. I was so glad to have taken that recommended diversion at Topola. Thank you, Luica.

I camped about 6.45pm, off a dirt track in the trees on the edge of a ploughed field.

DAY 41. Saturday 25th April

Up at 5.30am. I was keen to get out of Serbia. I enjoyed the place but data roaming charges were piling up. My tablet was showing 80% used since the last top-up just thirty-six hours before. The sooner I was in EU Bulgaria, the better.

Had a decent wash with some holy water outside the church at Bagrdan but today would be another punishing ride. I was able to stock up at a supermarket and the good news from home was that Leicester City had won four games in a row. Their Premiership survival was almost assured.

After a long climb with many hairpin bends I camped in the trees of a high roadside embankment near Zlatan Reservoir. My legs were hurting again and the mosquitoes were out in force.

DAY 42. Sunday 26th April

A bright start and on the road at 7am. I had already done a lot of climbing and for much of the morning, it plateaued. I was cycling through glorious scenery. I was flanked by mountains but there were several lakes up here and early morning anglers lined the shores.

It was another tough day with a determined ride. I wanted to be in Kosovo tonight. Head down, I just went for it. I rode through the town of Kastrat. Sounded painful. Then I started the steep ascent towards the border.

I noticed that the higher I went or indeed the closer I got to Kosovo, the more litter there was. It was quite disgusting how much. Over to my left was the river. The trees along the banks were decorated in plastic and paper waste from when the water levels had been higher. I tried to work out why this was. My mind spiralled over conspiracy theories and diverted to the issue of water ownership.

If a river flows through two bordering countries, which owns the water? Surely it is the country in control of the source. Take the example of Egypt and Sudan. Egypt's economy relies on the River Nile. Sudan is an emerging nation with mouths to feed and industries needing energy. The Sudanese are closer to the river's source. They have now learnt to harness the power through hydro-electricity and have started to build dams. They are draining the associated reservoirs to irrigate their crops but that means the water flow to Egypt could vanish. As Sudan's demand for water grows, Egypt will inevitably suffer a drought. It would be nice if the river could serve both nations but I expect this will eventually result in conflict. Water is taken for granted and is so undervalued. Today we fight over oil. Tomorrow it will be water.

I arrived at the barrier checkpoint. Legally the Kosovo region still belonged to Serbia but they had declared themselves autonomous. Consequently I did not get my passport stamped for leaving Serbia. I did have to present it in Kosovo but there they considered themselves part of the EU. They weren't actual members but were proudly flying the flag and had adopted the euro as their currency.

I was made very welcome. The first guard called his supervisor over and he shook my hand and smiled as he quizzed me. He seemed very excited that an Englishman was visiting his country. He told me that Pristine was 36 km (22.5 miles) away. I wanted to be in and out tonight and put my foot down. I rode like a madman until I reached the capital at 5.30pm.

It struck me as odd that the place was called Pristine. The English literal meaning is 'immaculate'. This place was far from that. It was generally dirty. There seemed to be a language dispute too. Many of the road signs gave detail in two versions but often one would be spray painted over or scribbled out with marker pen. Other than some ornate mosques there were few obvious landmarks for a decent selfie. There were some statues and the main square looked a good place to be but I needed food. The Islamic version of McDonald's beckoned.

I placed an order and got their Wi-Fi password. I had been so desperate to communicate with the outside world again that I forgot to collect my cash card. It was promptly brought over to me at my seat. I demolished the meal and set off again to clear the built-up area while there was still some daylight.

People were sat in outside restaurants having a nice evening. There was a whole squad of American soldiers dining at one, all wearing their uniforms.

What struck me as odd was that my tablet was not working. I had not been offered roaming data by my service provider and the Serbian subscription for which I had already paid was not giving me any access. I suspected Big Brother was jamming me and the people of Kosovo.

I had to rely on my maps to get me out. That wasn't a problem though as there were few roads. I was soon on the main carriageway back towards the mountains. As the darkness fell, I struggled to find anywhere decent to sleep. I was flanked by high mountain peaks and with no street lighting it was very dark. Occasionally I would be blinded by headlights and had started to close at least one eye to protect my night vision.

The Sunday-night silence was broken by two short bursts of automatic gunfire. They were followed by a single shot. I had seen signs for a bear sanctuary a few miles earlier and considered it might be poachers. It could have been an execution. All I know is that the bullets were flying in the hills and it didn't make me feel particularly safe about sleeping rough.

Exhaustion got the better of me and I had to settle for a poorly constructed shelter in a roadside lay-by.

DAY 43. Monday 27th April

I was up at 6.15am and started my climb through the mountains towards my favourite country so far, Serbia. Austria had been beautiful but that was Western Europe so it didn't count.

I had only been riding for about 500 metres before I came to a public fountain with the constant flow pipe filling a trough-like basin. There was also some picnic area seating. This was perfect. The sun was rising but the traffic hadn't started. I made up my mind. I was going to have a shower. I filled all my bottles and went for the ship's routine. I emptied the first bottle over me to get wet and then lathered up all over. Then I rinsed off with my other three bottles. I was soon dry in the sun and decided that a fresh set of clothes would be appropriate. I felt amazing.

I made a big mug of tea and started to do my laundry. I hung out each item on tree branches; in this sun they wouldn't take long to dry. My T-shirt had been worn since Easter Sunday. That was ready for the bin so I used it as an oil rag for my chain and axle bearings. I put my gadgets on charge, had some breakfast, wrote up my diary and studied my maps. I now had eight new flags for my fridge and tried to imagine what that would look like.

After my full-service pit stop I followed the only road choice, Route 9. It went higher and meandered through the mountains. I was quite chilled and relaxed.

There was potential for trouble at the next checkpoint but I felt as fresh as day one and was ready for anything.

Mid-morning I met two Germans coming downhill on their bikes. The road was hardly used so it was inevitable that we would converse. They were only doing a short route between the two countries but I was reassured about my pending border crossing. They told me that the guards knew I was coming. Was that a wind-up? How could they possibly know?

About midday I stopped to admire the view of the surrounding countryside. From my high vantage point it was quite spectacular. I was stood there eating an apple when the border police patrol pulled up. They were friendly chaps and had indeed been expecting me. One of their shift had driven past me during my early ascent. They knew I would reach them eventually and had intended to make me a tea but I had taken too long and they were to complete their duties elsewhere. I thanked them for their kind consideration and complimented their splendid country and its magnificent views.

I rolled up at the official Serbian post about thirty minutes later. This shift wasn't as welcoming. They had the sniffer dogs around me and I had to open a couple of bags. The 'grail diary map' helped to reveal my intention.

I suppose I should explain that term. The 'grail diary' was used by Indiana Jones's father to record everything he needed to remember about his quest for the holy relic. Having been in that movie and now possessing a similar-sized notebook, it was an obvious title.

Then it was a steep freewheel back into Serbia. I was so relieved and Bulgaria was not far away. Everything was fine. Everything apart from my brakes. I was descending too fast and the pads were squealing from friction heat.

When I reached the valley below, I came to a pretty little stream and made my dinner. Wilson was proving quite versatile. He served as a windbreak, a cooker splashback, as a dining table and also as a chair. He justified his continued participation.

After my meal break I rode on for a couple of hours but then the fatigue hit me. A combination of overexertion to get in and out of Kosovo plus the mental stress and anxiety of potential border crossing problems had taken their toll. Despite being clean, well fed and having sky-high morale, I was absolutely exhausted. I was in my sleeping bag by 3.30pm and fast asleep before 6pm.

DAY 44. Tuesday 28th April

I had a great night and lazy relaxing lie-in. There is something therapeutic about raindrops falling on the tent roof when you're tucked up warm and dry inside.

When the weather eased off about 8am I pressed on. I had to take a picture of a rickety old bridge. It was still in use linking communities together. Having lost one camera on the Thames and another in the Mediterranean, I was extra cautious this time.

It was a slow lazy ride today. I knew that Bulgaria was too far to achieve, so I was resigned to at least one more night here. I rode through several picture postcard villages before arriving at the city of Lescovac. The place was bustling and chaotic. One of the market traders wanted my trailer. I hadn't a clue what she was saying but I gave her the instruction manual and wrote 'eBay' on it. Wilson was not for sale and I intended him to accompany me to the Black Sea.

The main road out was a cobbled highway. Almost

The bridge at Medveda.

impossible to ride on. The shaking and vibration was too intense and I had to walk often. This really slowed my progress. The mountains and weather conspired against me too. It was as if the local gods wanted to keep me there.

There had been bright sunshine around midday. At 2pm I stopped for lunch by a pretty river and laid out all of my kit to dry. That was a waste of time because by 3pm I was riding uphill into an electrical storm. I was instantly soaked and at times it was difficult to see where I was going. The lightning was a concern but shelter opportunities were scarce. The trees gave little cover and the cliff overhangs weren't much better.

Eventually I found a derelict building. It was an old 'one up, one down' but was crumbling and part of the upper floor had collapsed. It was dry downstairs but as I took temporary refuge it occurred to me that the added weight from rainfall could cause the entire structure to collapse and entomb me. I was already wet and there was little chance of getting dry today. I would have to brave up and face the elements again. I headed back out into the freezing rain and sleet.

Almost as suddenly as it had started, the inclement weather returned to bright sunshine. I had been tested and survived. I continued towards the border, hoping the warm sun would dry me out a little.

About 6.30pm, I made camp beside the river. My location was stunning.

DAY 45. Wednesday 29th April

Everything was wet. I hadn't managed to get dry after the previous day's deluge and there had been further rain during the night. Typical valley weather. At 6am when I headed out there was still a light misty rain. The kind that soaks you silently.

I rode through an amazing mountain pass, far better than Cheddar Gorge, and by some photogenic waterfalls. I hadn't realised when I set out but most of the morning would be downhill. A rapid freewheel descent to the lowlands. This must have taken over an hour and I was frozen stiff when I finally reached the flats.

I went into a service station at Pirot and bought a hot coffee to thaw me out. Then it was along the main road towards Bulgaria. I had that 'new country' motivation again and made rapid progress along the straight arterial route.

A large Bulgarian flag announced my imminent reaching of the border. It was only 2.15pm; I had arrived quicker than anticipated and this was quite a shock. I had made it – my final country and my target destination for Mission B. It was another flag for my fridge and cheaper internet (£12 for 200 Mb). I was ecstatic.

I was also exhausted. I continued inland to clear the busy crossing and camped very early in a blissful pine tree forest outside Dragoman. The pressure was off and I could relax. I was very content. I made a special note in my diary. It said:

'Chillin! I amaze myself. I made this happen. FUCKING AWESOME!'

DAY 46. Thursday 30ᵗʰ April

It was twenty-five years to the day since I had joined Leicestershire Constabulary as a fresh and invincible bobby. A quarter of a century later I felt old. I had done a lot though, and hopefully there was a lot more to come.

Nesebar was 280 miles away and at my snail's pace, that was six to seven days' ride. Navigation was easy though. Route 6 all the way. I didn't get started until 10am. I had earnt that lie-in and I was in no danger of being disturbed where I camped. After an easy couple of hours pedalling I arrived on the outskirts of Sofia. I hoped that there would be no more snow, but just outside the capital was a massive mountain. Stood prominent and in isolation, it reminded me of Ayers Rock in Australia, only this had white peaks.

McDonald's enticed me in for a banquet. I had no food left and a supermarket resupply was urgently needed, but for now a 'Big Tasty', McFlurry and a McMuffin would have to do. 13.36 leva was the equivalent of £4.50. That was a bargain.

From there I found a bike shop. Wilson's tyres needed attention. The replacement from Innsbruck had some tread left but the other was an original that had existed since England. It was worn out and the internal cords were now exposed.

The first shop couldn't supply me but gave directions to his cousin's shop a few streets away. I had been ready to pay £20 for one replacement but ended up paying just £8 for two brand-new sports tyres. The cost of living in Bulgaria was so cheap.

There were many beautiful buildings in Sofia and I very soon fell in love with the place. It was and remains to this day the best capital city I have ever been in. I will hopefully return one day for a longer stay. Google recommended that I see the Alexander Nevsky Cathedral and I headed in that direction.

I was joined by a pretty student at the traffic lights. She could see how awestruck I was at her home town. Bulgaria was in a festive mood. It was celebrating 1,300 years of culture. The girl invited me to stick around until tomorrow when there would be a carnival in the main square. I had to resist that temptation and stay focussed on the objective. One day of partying would have almost certainly ended my journey.

The smartly dressed, white-gloved policeman marshalled the traffic and it was then my turn to roll.

It occurred to me that if I wasn't careful my trip album would be a collection of church photographs. They were often the most ornate and impressive buildings and that annoyed me a little. Surely religious donations would be better spent assisting the poor and disabled rather than building so many

luxurious places of worship? Parliament buildings, statues and theatres houses would make suitable alternative snaps.

After a Lidl stop, it was back on the road. Unfortunately they didn't sell PG Tips or milk powder here. The next thing I noticed about this place was the manhole and drain covers. Many had sunk causing the same effect as potholes. They had the potential to destroy my wheels and the first couple had caught me off guard. Some holes were missing their covers completely. That meant riding at night was out of the question. It looked as though the tarmac itself was melting. The effect of heavy lorry tyres was like that of a rolling pin on pastry. They would push the road surface sideways and cause it to raise and buckle kerbside.

Leaving the industrial outskirts of the ring road I became aware of the ladies loitering in lay-bys. I hadn't seen many on this trip but that would change. By the end of the evening I had seen dozens. This caused me problems with camping. I had to clear the red light areas but they seemed to be endless. Eventually, I gave up and built a hasty shelter in the treeline next to the main road. It was noisy but there would be no one stopping or parking by this busy section.

DAY 47. Friday 1st May

Happy birthday to my big brother. I was on the road by 8am and had a pleasurable ride on generally good but undulating roads. I had a problem finding water though. There were fewer village fountains or public taps.

Sometimes there would be a road sign suggesting the existence of a water tap at the next lay-by, but on arrival it wouldn't work any longer and the site would instead be a fly-tipping location.

As I went up into the hills, I came across a mountain stream. It was clear and there were freshwater shrimp swimming in it. That was reassuring and I spent ages collecting the precious liquid in my metal mug before transferring it to bottles. It would be fine if I boiled it.

About an hour later I came across a picnic area with a fountain. How ironic. I emptied, rinsed and refilled my bottles.

Early evening, I stopped at a service station to buy some supplies. That Magnum ice cream looked good and tasted even better. Over here it was called a 'Boss' but I soon stamped my authority over it. I had ran out of milk powder so I also bought two small cartons from the fridge. At 7pm I set up camp in a comfortable pine tree forest just west of Anton village and opened one of my milks. That would quench my thirst. I had made about three full gulps before realising I had actually purchased yoghurt… again.

DAY 48. Saturday 2nd May

After moving on at 7.30am, I found a lay-by with a fast-flowing fountain. Water is supposed to be colourless and tasteless but that is not so. Here I found the most delicious and fresh-tasting water I had ever drank. It was

278

obviously mineral water, filtered through the mountains, but I was impressed. I took this opportunity to bathe and do a bit of laundry. A local man pulled up in his car and filled a bottle. We got talking.

The Bulgarian told me that he was heading to a nearby village for a festival marking the 1,300 years. He invited me along and offered to give me a lift. I pointed out my bike also had a trailer and that it would not fit in his vehicle. The village was a considerable diversion too but I thanked him for the invitation. He told me that the fresh water on this side of the valley was better than the other side. Different mountains with different rock filters. I had definitely filled up at the right place.

Today would present some of the most spectacular scenery from the whole trip. The Central Balkan National Park was simply breathtaking. Each corner or bend in the road would usurp the last amazing landscape.

The news from home was that Princess Charlotte had just been born. Unable to 'splice the mainbrace', I had to settle for a mug of Earl Grey without milk.

On reaching Kanare, I was ravenous and it had started to rain. I put up my bivvy sheet between some roadside trees and cooked a meal. By the time I had finished eating, the shower was over. As I packed up ready to continue I was approached by a young man with his two children of about five to seven years old. We shared no common language but I understood he was begging. He first gestured for money, rubbing his thumb against his forefinger. I had no money, only plastic. He then indicated that he and his children were hungry. He was quite genuine and I felt bad that I had very little food left. My stomach was full and I wouldn't need to eat again today. All I had left was my emergency ration apple. I hope they enjoyed it.

I camped about 5pm in another perfect pine tree forest. Leicester beat Newcastle 3-0. Come on!

DAY 49. Sunday 3rd May

I was up at 6.55am. Fourteen hours' rest was quite sufficient and that constant "Cuckoo!" was annoying. Only 100 miles remained. If I unhitched the trailer and sprinted, I could be in Nesebar tonight but we had started together and we were going to finish together.

The roadkill was interesting this far south. I came across the usual snakes and geckos but also a wasp that was the size of a king prawn. There were freshwater turtles too. I kept an eye out for a complete shell for use as a souvenir bowl but they were all crushed.

I was a bit mardy today. The shops were shut in most villages and I couldn't find anywhere that sold milk. None of the petrol stations had any. Having tea without or muesli with water is so dull. The roadside litter annoyed me too and I started to curse the missing drain covers that presented a dangerous obstacle. The kerbs were twice as high as those in England but none were dropped and this meant frequent dismounts for me so as to not buckle my wheels. Instead people had to build either wooden ramps or lay a slope of concrete. There was a good reason for this and I would later find out why but at that time it added to my frustration.

I stopped for a water refill at a roadside lay-by. There was a picnic area but this place was serving as a fly-tipping location. It was disgusting. As I filled up, I was propositioned by a hideous-looking lady. She was my age and invited me to join her on the bench. I believe sex was on offer but this woman made me shiver. I told her I was in a hurry and rode off. There was no milk at the next service station but I enjoyed the ice cream.

I rode by one particular village and it was clearly poverty stricken. People had very squalid conditions with basic houses, some nothing more than sheds with blanket doors, but it struck me as odd that most still had a satellite dish outside. I sympathised with poor people but why did they need to throw their litter all over the place? They were living in beautiful open countryside and ruining it.

I camped in a roadside field. There were some trees but I was quite exposed. I was, however, in the middle of nowhere, so I was unlikely to be disturbed. It had been dark when I stopped and I intended to be up early. Nearly there now.

DAY 50. Monday 4th May

"Whooah, we're halfway there, whooah, living on a prayer!" I sang to myself. A good solid ride today would ensure an easy cruise to the final objective tomorrow.

I started out at 6.30am and just pressed on. By mid-afternoon I was in the Karnobat wine region. Scores of manual workers were tending to vines. As I trudged uphill, one group started to wave and cheer me. That lifted my spirits and I waved back with a beaming smile. I intended to buy some of their label on return to England but to this day I haven't seen any.

I reached the main town and bought some fresh supplies. UHT milk was better than no milk. I was amazed at how fast I could gulp it down. I continued riding until about 7pm when I passed a newly deceased dog. Its legs were pointing skywards through rigor mortis. Why was it still in the road causing an obstruction?

I was within striking distance of my objective. An early start tomorrow and I could be in the sea for midday. An almond orchard beckoned me over for the night.

DAY 51. Tuesday 5th May

The swimming trunks went on first and at 6.20am I was out of the door. I passed the statue at Ajtos and headed to Burgas. I desperately needed camping gas and had been looking everywhere for a resupply. The big port city would be more likely to have it than the tiny seaside resort. I rode around Burgas in vain but I had finally seen the coveted water.

The road out took me to a more impressive and very blue section of the Black Sea. That was 11.30am and my target was only a few miles further along. Unfortunately, the route was now against me. I was not allowed on the main road and the cycle lane running parallel wasn't fit for purpose. I spent most of the time walking. Signs kept repeating my destination but the finish line remained elusive.

I passed two young lads trying to replace the flat tyre on their car without a wheel brace. My adjustable spanner proved inadequate and I had to leave them to their own salvation. They overtook me half an hour later tooting their horn and waving.

At 2.30pm I turned a corner. THE BLACK SEA. I stripped and ran into the water like some desert-stranded survivor who had reached an oasis.

I was fortunate to not get stung by all of the jellyfish.

283

The entrance road to Nesebar Resort.

Putting our feet up after the reconnaissance on Sunny Beach.

Dish demolition commences

Eliminating the evidence. Job done.

Nesebar and Sunny Beach would be worth another visit sometime. They were already popular with the discerning Brits and very good value for money. After posing for a photo with some of my fellow countrymen who were very excited about being able to tell 'my' story when they got home, it was time to complete the final stage of my mission.

The main course, dessert and two beers went down very well and no trace remained. I made an entry in my diary. Simply said, 'Done it!' That was an understatement.

I had reached the target on Day 51 but in terms of time, it had taken me exactly fifty days. My next problem was getting home. I had provisionally booked a flight for Day 100 from Sweden. It only cost £48 and I could cancel that if need be. Wilson was OK with two new tyres and José was still up for the adventure. It was entirely up to me. I looked at the map. I recalled the last fifty days. It was a long way but the summer was fast approaching and there would be no more snowy peaks or Alps. It was time to 'mount up and move out'.

I headed northwest towards the border. After about two hours of steady uphill riding, I came to a small wooded area. I looked back towards the coast. The sun was falling rapidly behind me. Day 51 was over. Mission B was accomplished.

DAY 52. Wednesday 6th May

I got up at 6am and ran back to the road to watch the sun rise over the Black Sea. I should have stayed in bed. It was an overcast and grey sky. The sun could not penetrate the clouds, let alone appear over the horizon.

The day did not improve. I packed up and hit the road quite promptly but soon after felt a minor irritation to my right calf. I looked down to see a greedy mosquito sucking away like a fat kid on a thick milkshake. I splatted the little vampire. I soon came across a communal fountain and did a refill. It was quite early with hardly anyone around so I also had a bird bath and did my laundry. I then pressed on through the villages. The houses were pretty crude DIY jobs but it was pleasant enough and quite tranquil. One washing line caught my attention as there was a Union Jack towel.

I entered a corner shop and stocked up on food. I had walked in at the right time. The shopkeeper was sharing out a box of chocolates and I was offered one which I gratefully accepted. The apples were as big as pomegranates.

From then on it was uphill for most of the day. At one particular point the steep gradient was so severe that I had to lean that far forward my hands were touching the road. When that stretch plateaued I had a rest and took in the view. Scattered around the local high ground were many wind turbines.

Google Maps led me down a track and this would become one of those satnav horror stories. The road condition was poor. I couldn't ride as it was crude rock chippings. Something suitable for a Land Rover but not a bike or trailer. I was flanked by thick forest and could only see a short distance in front or behind. I knew there was a river ahead and I was descending, so things looked promising, but then I heard an engine. Slowly a Land Rover was driving towards me. I pushed my bike and load to the side in order to allow them to pass.

They braked alongside and quick as a flash, the three men jumped out and surrounded me. I'm not sure that they quite knew what to make of me. I had a vagrant or castaway appearance and was pulling a trailer with solar panels attached. Apparently I was trespassing and worst still I was in the middle of a live firing and hunting range. Thanks Google. I showed the lead chap where I was going and he laughed. The river was too big an obstacle and there was no bridge. In any event I could not proceed further without being in harm's way. The alternative route was a massive diversion that contoured up and down around that mountain. They escorted back to the main road.

I had lost a great deal of time and was tired from too much walking. I sat down for a rest and a drink, only to notice that one of Wilson's tyres was flat. I now had to do a puncture repair before continuing.

I cooked on my final gas cylinder but it started to cough and splutter. It was running out and I still hadn't found a replacement. I had candles and a lighter but campfires were prohibited in this area and on the high ground my smoke would be a clear giveaway.

Then my large plastic water bottle sprang a leak. It soaked into my kit bag. I could still use it if I tightened the lid and carried the bottle upside-down.

At some point during my ill-fated day, one of my pedals slipped and took chunks of flesh off my shin. My leg was sore.

A local farmer approached to converse and he invited me to help myself to the leftovers from the village banquet. There was plenty of roast lamb remaining. It was a kind invitation but the village was 3 miles in the other direction. That meant another 6-mile diversion just to get back to where I was already standing. I declined the offer.

I trudged along. Mostly on foot now. It was too steep to ride. I reached the summit. Looking southeast, I could still see Nesebar in the distance. I was high up and it was quite chilly.

Looking northwest I collapsed with sorrow and depression. Before me lay row after row after row of mountains. I didn't want to do this anymore. I'd had enough. When I set out that morning, the next big town, Shumen, was 96 km away. It was still 82 km. I had travelled all day but achieved less than 10 miles.

I camped on the windswept peak. Tomorrow would be better, wouldn't it?

DAY 53. Thursday 7th May

Yesterday had taken its toll. Had an early night and a lie-in but I was still tired. It was peaceful up here and there was a refreshing breeze but in order to get home I needed to attack the hurdles.

Fortunately my route was less strenuous than I had anticipated. I rolled from 8am, initially all downhill. I meandered through various villages, each with a single minaret, before joining the main road which ran parallel to the river. The Land Rover men had done me a great favour. I could have swam the river but there was no way of getting my bike and trailer across.

It tipped it down that afternoon so I took shelter at a bus stop and watched the impressive downpour. I had never seen it rain that hard before and it made such a racket as it bounced off surfaces. The thunder and lightning joined in. Very quickly the road was covered in water and the levels continued to rise. Within minutes the carriageway was a canal of fast-flowing brown water. This explained the need for those high kerbs.

The rain continued but eased up a little and the waters subsided. I continued along the wet road, drawing small comfort from the prospect that this lubrication might preserve the tread on my tyres.

I rode further and harder than I had intended in order to recoup some lost time from yesterday. To my surprise I actually reached Shumen by late afternoon. I found a camping shop and thought my luck was in. I showed my camping stove and got a positive response from the shop assistant. I was taken to the relevant shelves but there were no Bluet stoves or compatible replacement canisters. I would have to continue my search.

I reached a traffic light junction and was joined by another cyclist. He gave me the casual greeting nod and I responded in kind. Did he speak English? I asked, and fortunately he replied in my language. I then asked about potential outlets for replacement canisters. He knew a place but instead of giving me directions, told me to follow him. We rode about 400 metres and he led me into a promising hardware shop. All sorts of canisters and gas appliances were on sale, but nothing compatible with my stove. My guide pondered a while and had a brief discussion with the shopkeeper in their own tongue.

"I know another place," he said and then led me on a forty-five minute bike ride around the city. He was fast too. Conscious of the fact that this chap was my best hope and appreciating the assistance, I needed to ensure I didn't delay him any longer than necessary. I was riding so hard to keep up but at the same time trying to hide my fatigue. We made several stops, all of which were in vain. The last place was a large hardware store. They didn't have my item either. I was desperate now. Forty-eight hours without a mug of tea was too long. The shop had similar cookers and I decided to splash out and buy one. I should point out that my cooker cost £10 in England and the canisters were £5 each. The equivalent cooker in this shop and three canisters totalled £8.70. I just couldn't believe how cheap it was.

I made the purchase as the whole shop quizzed me over my adventure. Only my guide spoke English and he was very busy translating all the questions and replies. My grail diary map impressed them and I was offered use of their toilet while they refilled my water bottles.

I wanted to reward my guide with my remaining currency but he wouldn't accept any payment. He was just happy to have assisted a fellow cyclist. He told me his name but I couldn't repeat or pronounce it. I got him to write it in my diary.

'Sevdalin' or 'Seb' for short.

Seb and the shop staff browsed my map and pointed out my best route before waving me off. Such nice people. I had only ever heard bad things about Bulgaria, usually from people who had never been. Well, I can emphatically say it was the most welcoming and friendly place that I had visited so far.

I stocked up at Lidl, where I immediately downed a full litre of real milk. Then I made camp in the roadside treeline of the main arterial route north.

After washing down my meal with a big mug of tea (with milk) I suddenly felt so much better. The combination of yesterday's niggles and mishaps had continued to stress me today, but now I was mellow. It occurred to me just how typically 'English' I was. A mug of tea had made everything OK again.

It was 8.30pm by the time I finally laid down to rest. It had been a very long day.

DAY 54. Friday 8th May

The intense traffic noise stirred me and by 7am I had joined it. The Conservatives had won the general election. The best of a bad bunch, I suppose, as I found Milliband and Balls quite odious.

It was a sunny day and the roads were good. By 1pm I had reached a lorry park with a natural fountain. I took full advantage. I bathed, did my laundry and hung everything out to dry on a wire mesh fence. I started to prepare a meal.

The occasional lorry would arrive and park up. Some drivers would fill buckets of water and start cleaning the dirt and dust accumulations from their windscreens.

I was interviewed by one driver. His name was Rumen. He was delighted to see an Englishman in his country and was desperate to shake my hand. He saw that I was preparing to eat and gave me his remaining half loaf of sliced bread to compliment my meal. What a nice chap.

I had earlier been overtaken by a campervan. It had a British registration plate and a GB sticker on the rear end. I had waved at it but I hadn't noticed any response and the vehicle hadn't stopped. That same campervan pulled up at the fountain and I spoke to the driver. He was an elderly gent who had been travelling for nine months with his wife. They had been through Russia, Kazakhstan, Iran, Turkey, Cyprus and were now cruising slowly back to England via Bulgaria and Romania. They'd certainly be home before me but what an amazing adventure. They had needed to be accompanied by an approved guide all the way through Iran but otherwise it had been problem free.

I had a small amount of local currency to get rid of, and a local beer in the town of Tsar Kaloyan seemed to be money well spent. I was certainly going to miss this place and my imminent departure was tinged with sadness. In addition to all those random acts of kindness, so many passing motorists tooted their horns in support and in most villages the people smiled and waved.

I ended the day camped in woods outside the village of Pisanets. It was 7pm and I had done close to 50 miles. Tomorrow should be easier though. It would be downhill towards the Danube and a bridge crossing to my next country.

Just before falling asleep I heard a single shot being fired in the distance.

DAY 55. Saturday 9th May

Up at 6.40am after a very comfortable night. There was quite a bit of dew on my tent and that would need to be dried out later. I still had 9 lev (£3.60) to spend. I bought some rice and chocolate at a corner shop but still had change. I kept one coin as a souvenir and the rest went in their charity box.

By 11.20am I had been waved through the checkpoint and rolled onto the bridge. The border was mid-river and I took my final photographs of the Danube.

It was an open EU border so I just rode in unchecked. I picked up the signs for Route 5 to Bucharest and started pedalling. I was slightly apprehensive about this place. Once again, I had heard bad things from those who had never been but I was ready to make my own mind up.

It was immediately apparent that this place was poorer than Bulgaria. Many more horse-drawn carts and most of the local cars were Dacia Berlinas.

I found a roadside communal fountain sponsored by the Rotary Club. Fresh water was gushing out of two pipes. There was also picnic area seating so I dried my kit there, had a welcome wash and cooked a meal. My Bulgarian cooker was slightly heavier than the Bluet but worked equally as well.

It was a lovely sunny day and I made great progress along the main road. This was a surprise. I had expected a rough and potholed carriageway but the long, straight, Roman roads were the best I had been on. The surface was so good the groups in sponsored Lycra outfits were practising time trials. My speed would have to be steady though. My rear wheel was buckled and one of the spokes was broken. I held it in position by binding it with masking tape to its neighbour.

The next thing I noticed about Romania was that most roofs were made from metal rather than tiles. The climate was no different to Bulgaria so I could rule out that explanation, but I never managed to find out why they preferred this material.

I camped about 7.20pm in some overgrown wasteland on the outskirts of I Decembrie; it wasn't perfect but the riverbanks were lined with Saturday night parties and barbeques.

DAY 56. Sunday 10th May

I was due a lie-in and it was 8.30am before I set off for Bucharest. It was a grey start with a little light drizzle. Within two hours I entered the capital and some festivities were taking place in the recreational park. There was a fountain but it was too small for my large plastic bottle. I had to keep filling my mug and transferring the contents. It took a while but I was eventually fully loaded.

Bucharesti was a normal thriving capital and certainly looked worthy of a longer stay. I took a selfie at the Parliament building and then tried to fight my way out. The grey sky started to produce rain and the constant checking of my tablet for directions was a problem. McDonald's would provide me with a chance to get warm and dry so I took advantage. I was quizzed by a student before I could enter. The trailer was such a magnet to intrigue. Where are you from? Where are you going? Why? These were the typical questions. My answers would prompt more questions. My travels were certainly capturing people's imaginations and for some it would fuel their spirit of adventure. I'm sure my enthusiastic interviewer would have chatted all day but I was cold and hungry so I told him I needed the toilet and said goodbye.

I left the warmth for more rain. I had tried waiting it out but the skies showed no sign of abatement. The map said I had a long way to go. Moldova was many miles away and so was Ukraine. I hadn't properly decided on a course. I needed to see enough of those countries to say that I had been there and be able to 'bag a flag' for the fridge, but I had already completed my missions. All I wanted was to get home by the easiest and shortest possible route via the remaining accessible virgin territories.

My new heading was Buzau along Route 2. The sun came out mid-afternoon and I was by then in open countryside on a nice straight road. Romania was so easy compared to previous countries. I could see a parked car up ahead and a well-dressed man was waving an empty plastic bottle at passing vehicles. No one was stopping to help him. Believing I would be of no use without jump leads, I carried on riding. The man shouted over to me but I couldn't understand. "I'm English; I don't know what you're saying!" I shouted across to the opposite side of the road to where he stood.

"Please tell me you have some water in that trailer?" he replied. I understood that much and stopped to help. I was carrying 6 litres. He had suffered a radiator leak. He had managed to trim the pipe and stem the flow of coolant but the system was now completely dry. He was in an urgent hurry to get to a wedding and had four bridesmaids with him. His car guzzled 2.5 litres, almost half of my supply, and he insisted on paying me for the water. I insisted on rejecting any payment. He and the ladies were all trying to stuff bank notes into my hands but I dismissed them. It was Romanian water. I had received it for free and they needed it more than me. We compromised. They could keep their money in exchange for a photo. Everyone was happy.

I was glad to have finally been of some assistance. So many people had already helped me on this trip and it felt good to have given something back. I could just imagine the stories being told at the wedding. They had broken down and were rescued by a crazy Englishman who had ridden to Bulgaria from France and was on his way to Sweden. Who would believe that?

A little further along there was a crossroads. Police and an ambulance were in attendance. There had been a two-car collision and the recovery wagon was removing one of the damaged vehicles. There was a traffic jam for miles in both directions. I was able to ride clear of the obstruction but for the next couple of miles the frustrated motorists were asking me for situation updates. With no local language skill I had to resort to charades. It took a while.

It was strange entering new villages. I was on one of the main arterial routes but people's front gardens came close to the roadside. Residents would be sat out on benches and stop talking to stare as the stranger rode into town. I would just smile and wave. Looking confused, they would smile and wave back.

Many of the houses were basic wooden cottages and instead of public taps, there were usually communal drinking wells. I couldn't believe that such things still existed in Europe. These were garden features in England. An old man went to get a drink from one. He turned the handle to lower the rusty old bucket and then wound it back up again to fill his cup. He assured me it was quite safe to drink. There were freshwater shrimp inside but I spooned those out and was soon back up to 6 litres.

I camped about 7.20pm in the roadside forest approximately 5 miles from Urziceni.

DAY 57. Monday 11th May

The traffic got me up at 6.50am and I had a good day. The road was mostly straight and flat but there were some strong crosswinds. Some of the little girls went to school wearing traditional pretty white dresses with flamboyant floral designs. It was very cultural and I would have liked a photograph but regrettably I felt awkward about using my camera.

I stopped for lunch about midday. I was riding into a headwind and it was quite difficult. Using an old filled-in well and Wilson as a windbreak, I set about preparing my meal in a roadside lay-by. As I sat there with my small vegetable knife, peeling garlic and chopping onions, two rather attractive females walked past me. We startled each other before smiling and saying hello. They went to sit on the picnic bench and started eating sandwiches and crisps. I dismissed their presence as simply being two local factory workers on a lunch break, but I hadn't noticed any nearby premises. They soon finished their meal and took up position in the lay-by. The lorries and vans drove by, tooting their horns at the women. Then I realised that they were prostitutes and I was encroaching on their territory. I finished my food and bid them farewell.

The Carpathian Mountains stood menacingly to my left. I really needed to avoid those. Not because of the ascent, but coming down was very hard on my brake pads and I hoped to reach the ferry in Estonia without any more pit stops.

I ended the day about 10 miles north of Buzau. The flat open countryside was exposed and with no decent cover so I camped in a roadside hedgerow. The occasional horse-drawn cart rode past but at the edge of a ploughed field I was unlikely to be discovered or disturbed.

DAY 58. Tuesday 12th May

The sun was up at 6am and I watched it rise over the fields. It was a warm day but very windy again. I noticed that there were an unusually large number of dead dogs in this country. So many strays decaying on the road. Sometimes the smell would announce their presence and get stronger as I rode closer. The stench was so powerful that occasionally I had to turn away for a final gulp of fresh air and then cycle as far and fast as I could while holding my breath. I saw all sorts. The recently hit or those with rigor mortis limbs sticking out. There were the bloated or maggot-swollen and even the completely sundried rugs with the tell-tale bones and teeth. This sight was so frequent that I decided to count as many corpses as I could in an hour. ELEVEN!

I cleared Focasani before Google sent me on a shortcut. The distance was much less but the route was dirt or gravel tracks that forced me to dismount. The walk took me over a large and impressive hydro-electric dam. At the next village, Movileni, there was a beautiful community well. A middle-aged man in a Manchester United football shirt was filling his own containers but let me push in. I didn't want to go first but he insisted. He went further than that. He took my bottles and filled them for me. Such hospitality was heart-warming. If similar wells existed in England, some idiot or attention-seeker would pollute them. Out here the people were more sensible and my confidence in this water was growing.

I camped early in a perfect wooded area on the outskirts of Furcenii Noi. It was only about 5pm but I needed to catch up on some quality rest.

DAY 59. Wednesday 13th May

Another fine morning. I started out at 7am. By midday I was at the village of Tutova. Horse and carts were common in Romania but in this village they even had registration plates. I made a note of one: BX06TNE. That was a British registration and I'm pretty confident that DVLA has no record of it being allocated to this horse-drawn wagon.

I stopped in a lay-by at 12.30pm. There was a picnic area and a tap with a trough-style basin. I seized the opportunity and headed into the trees with my bottles and soap for a refreshing shower. Next I did my laundry and while I waited for it to dry, prepared a meal. I moved on at 2pm and did a Lidl resupply. My trainers had finally given up so I bought a cheap pair which were sold in a handy zip-up mesh bag. That could have some useful purpose, particularly if my Bulgarian stove set fire to the tent.

I stopped for the night at 6pm. All of the best sleeping places were occupied. Every time I saw an appealing collection of trees, there would be a little cottage or small community inside. Even the sheltered areas of the mountains had goat herder huts or wigwam-style constructions. The goat herders themselves would be sat round tiny campfires. How simple life was out here. I eventually had to make do behind another hedgerow at the edge of a ploughed field. I could see the farmhouse but hoped I was far enough away to go unnoticed.

DAY 60. Thursday 14th May

Route 24 was serving me well but I had concerns about Ukraine. I was likely to be there for five or six days and didn't want to have to pay expensive data roaming charges. The only alternative routes involved going over the Carpathians. Perhaps I could just buy a more detailed map on arrival and run silent for a week. Moldova was next in line but I hoped that by skirting northwards just inside the border, I would still receive the Romanian network.

I headed out at 8am. Romania had so much space, open fields and farmland. It had a better climate than England and free water coming off the mountains. Back home, we are struggling for space, we cannot grow the crops to feed ourselves and the weather is less favourable. It occurred to me that instead of moaning about EU migrants coming to Britain, the British should all move out here.

Some of the houses were spectacular. They had verandas for all seasons and times of day. Our builders could make a fortune. Subsidence seemed to be a common issue but that was presumably down to poor foundation work.

I reached the impressive statue of King Stefan Cel Mare before riding on into Vaslui. I knew I had been spotted and that my next two interviewers were preparing. I responded to the usual questions with the usual answers. At this stage the grail diary map looked quite impressive. I was no longer setting out on an adventure, I was going home after completing one. To be able to say that I had swum in the lake at Zell am See on Easter Sunday and had been sunbathing by the Black Sea just a few days ago, really enthused my audience.

They welcomed me to their village and encouraged me to sample some of the local wines and Palinca (rum). My first host wished me good luck and left me to answer Andrei Focsa's additional questions. He was only a young lad, an agricultural student, but my story fascinated him and he was keen to do a similar adventure himself. He guided me through the town to my exit route which was about 100 metres from his house. I was invited back for a break and to sample some of that local wine. Why not? We sat in his garden. There were grapevines around the perimeter and chickens roaming freely. He ran inside to fetch two glasses and I tried the wine. It was good, very local indeed. It was homemade.

I gave my host the journey details supported by the first 450 photographs and the future intentions. It was good to sit down and talk for twenty minutes but that wine was kicking in very fast. I could feel it tingling in my face. My athletic and well-drilled body didn't accept alcohol as readily as before. The shot of Palinca had to be the last drink. We raised our glasses and said "Noroc!" (Cheers).

My new friend had lessons to attend and I still had a plane to catch so I thanked him for the reception and stood up to leave. Andrei hadn't finished yet. He wanted to send me off with some extra supplies. Against my protestations he ran back in, grabbed some freshly laid eggs, oranges and a jar of stewed plums. Thanks, Andrei.

I rode away thinking how wonderful life was. I was a foreigner and a complete stranger. In England, someone like me would have been greeted with mistrust and caution but out here I witnessed Romanian hospitality. It was friendly, kind and generous just as it was in Bulgaria but that Palinca was dynamite and I needed to take extra care on my bike.

I stopped at 6.55pm and made camp in the roadside forest just outside Schitu Duca. I was hidden from the road and had gone a good distance into the trees. The steep gradient made it an obstacle by instalment incursion. Darkness was falling and there was light drizzle. I couldn't believe it when I looked out of my tent window to see an old lady hobbling around picking natural herbs. She had seen my camp but said nothing and carried on regardless.

DAY 61. Friday 15th May

It was a bad start. At 7am it was still dark under the tree canopy. I filled my mug to make tea and started to heat it but knocked the whole thing over. My sleeping bag absorbed most of the spillage but I had to use my sock as a sponge for the remainder. Fortunately the water wasn't hot. I was packed up and ready to continue but a motorist pulled up to take a roadside call of nature. I froze and remained unseen. Had my judgement of suitable campsites really become so poor?

On I rode, up through the winding Route 24. When I neared the summit two hours later, there was a picnic area and a well. I knew it would be downhill to Iasi and from there I could expect to reach Moldova later that day. It was time to dry my kit and have a decent wash to make myself look presentable before reaching the border. I met a local old lady at the well. She chatted away at me. I hadn't a clue what she was saying. Probably senile but we had a great conversation. She did all the talking and I just nodded.

I was unable to weigh myself but ribcage

photographs advised me that I was losing too much weight. On reaching the fantastic city of Iasi, I ordered a KFC bucket meal for two. Iasi had everything you'd expect to find in a modern Western city. The taps in the main shopping centre had motion sensors. Such a contrast to the wind-up bucket wells that I had got used to.

The local Parliamentary Palace.

I enjoyed this place and it would be worth a longer stay but time was ticking and Moldova beckoned. A couple of hours later I joined the long queues at the Sculeni border post. As a cyclist I was eventually ushered forward and managed to jump a few places. I was expecting to breeze through but my facial appearance would cause a hold-up. I no longer matched my passport photograph. The guard did not accept that I was the same person. I produced the grail diary map and my digital camera. With my fuller face in March and by scrolling through to my present gaunt features I was able to satisfy the diligent officer. My little red book was stamped and I was waved in.

I didn't enter the country far enough to give it a full assessment. I bought a local Chisinau beer at the first service station and then looked for my route north.

The main A-class road was pretty poor. This was the route taken by the import and export trucks. Their big wheels could cope with the rough surface, but mine could not. The B-class road that I needed was just a dirt track. Fortunately I made the turning before losing network coverage.

I slept in an orchard at the top of a valley. It was quite comfortable. If I held my tablet on one side of the tent I would receive service messages welcoming me to Moldova. When I moved it to the other side I would be welcomed back to Romania.

Just as in Bulgaria, I had heard a single shot being fired in the distance. Perhaps it was a farmer warning off the predators.

DAY 62. Saturday 16th May. A BIG DAY in the PREMIER LEAGUE!

I was on the move for 7am. It was downhill initially and then on the flats for the rest of the day. Moldova was primitive in many ways. The preferred method of travel was a horse and cart. I didn't see many cars that day. An ancient ambulance was doing community visits. Ducks, geese, chickens and baby chicks roamed freely and the wells were more intricately decorated.

I was challenged by the frontier police. One of them chased after me in his combat uniform, carrying his gun and wearing body armour. He was friendly enough after I explained my movements. He was there to stop illegal immigrants from Romania. From what I had seen I couldn't understand why he would be needed. There was nothing here. That said, I quite liked what I saw.

No cars meant fewer roads, no traffic lights and less noise. The horses ate the grass, their manure fertilised the soil. The population drank water from the wells, burnt wood from the forest, ate fish, chicken, eggs and crops from natural and sustainable sources. There was absolutely no litter. It was a basic and simple way of life that had probably existed for hundreds of years. In some ways I envied these people. The West is obsessed with purchasing things they don't need, eating junk food and generating mountains of waste, but of course we're more civilised. Apparently.

In one village there were dozens of little yellow ducklings, feeding from a plate at the roadside. A little girl was petting them. As I approached, she ran away to a nearby garden and the gate was slammed shut. I stopped to take a photograph of the cute, fluffy bundles. As I snapped away I was aware that the little girl and possibly her mother were spying on me through a gap in the fence. These people weren't used to strangers.

Two boys disturbed me as I made lunch overlooking a large lake. They were only about nine or ten but already skilled horsemen. Terribly rotten teeth though. I tried to explain that I was English. They'd never heard of that place. I elaborated, "The land of football and David Beckham." They looked on bewildered. They were happy for me to take their picture though.

I completed my 39-mile route through the peaceful countryside. After travelling through Tomestii Noi and Balatina, I reached the Costesti border post. It was 3.30pm and I was the only person making the crossing. The guard took my passport and made loads of phone calls. Forty-five minutes later, I was allowed to proceed across the frontier which was another hydro-electric dam. By 4.30pm I was back in Romania. I bought some comfort food and an ice lolly from a service station. It was good to be back. By 7pm I had found a perfect roadside forest for the night.

Leicester City had won again and consequently they made history by pulling off one of the greatest escapes from almost certain relegation. They would finish in fourteenth place but no one could have predicted the season that followed. Favourites once again for the drop, they went on to defy odds of 5000/1 by becoming Premier League champions (with two games to spare). Incredible. Some 70% of Leicester's population attended the victory parade to celebrate Claudio Ranieri's team and the occasion united all colours and creeds in a unique party atmosphere; such is the awesome power of football.

Photo by Hannah Hollis.

DAY 63. Sunday 17th May
I was quite relaxed this morning and didn't start pedalling until 8.40am. I stocked up at a supermarket in Botosani before making a determined effort to reach the woods at Pomarla, just 3 miles from the border with Ukraine.

It would be 9.40pm before I got there but it was one of the most peaceful nights and I likened it to camping at Center Parcs, for free.

DAY 64. Monday 18ᵗʰ May

An absolutely magical start. After breakfast I made my way back to the road and hitched up my trailer. It was exactly 8am. As I did so, I saw a wild boar emerge from the forest that we'd shared the night before. He was followed by another adult, then two more and then five babies and some more adults. I was scurrying around, frantic to get my camera quickly and silently. Then a car came in the opposite direction and blasted its horn, sending them all scurrying back from whence they came.

I stood still with my camera ready for about five minutes but the moment was lost. I walked along quietly and about 50 metres further up, the lead scout reappeared. He went across by himself and then the others followed as a single stampede. I managed to snap a few blurred images but felt truly fortunate to have witnessed this display. Yesterday I had seen my first ever pine marten as it ran up a tree and next I would see a massive eagle fly overhead. Could today be any better?

No. I had an easy freewheel descent to the border post at Racovat but it was closed. The sheriff approached the barrier but told me I would have to try and cross at Siret over 30 miles away. This was a devastating blow. It meant going all the way back up the hill that I had just descended. It meant retracing my route for about 15 wasteful miles that I had completed yesterday. That meant more climbing and mountainous roads. There was no guarantee that I would be allowed through at Siret as it was a vehicle crossing and I would be classed as a pedestrian.

If Siret could not accommodate me I would have to give up on Ukraine and divert through 200 miles of Carpathian Mountains. There was no time to lose, so I cracked on. Within minutes I was stop-checked by border police. They were dressed up like soldiers. It took me about an hour to reach where I had started at 8am. In that period I was stopped three times by separate border patrols. They started in a dynamic and almost aggressive mode but quickly shifted through the gears to passive questioning when they realised I was not a threat. They didn't like the Ukrainians very much. They all radioed my details through for the relevant checks but I wasn't thoroughly searched. The grail diary and map spoke volumes. The final set of officers told me I had got a long and difficult ride ahead of me and they weren't going my way.

One small consolation of retracing my route was that it presented me with an opportunity to photograph a crane bird that had built its nest on top of a telegraph pole. I had tried the day before but the sky had been a bit too dark and the flash wouldn't illuminate at that distance. When I reached it today, there was a perfect blue sky. I just needed to wait patiently for the head to appear over the parapet.

There was a shortcut through the mountains but the track looked ominous so I chose to stick to the road and take the long way round. I reached the border at 2.15pm but would they let me through?

Ukraine was a country at war. The

border guards were armed with Kalashnikov assault rifles, and the border checks were thorough. This caused a massive queue. Having said, "Drum bun" (farewell) to the Romanian guard I was handed a movement receipt by a Ukrainian soldier. I then joined the slow-moving queue. The main inspection zone was like a petrol station forecourt. I looked forward to reaching the shade because it was quite intense sunshine out in the open. Some of the soldiers were young females. Quite athletic looking with blond hair. Very attractive, I'd say. One of them came along gathering up about a dozen passports at a time. Periodically she'd return from her office and hand them back to the owners. She knew who to return them to by checking the photographs. She didn't return mine.

Eventually I reached the forecourt. Customs came and inspected my cargo. They were friendly enough. The diary map helped to explain my quest. Other travellers shared the interest and I was becoming the regular entertainment. The thing was, I was receiving fresh audiences each time new vehicles arrived at the forecourt, but I wasn't going anywhere. Eventually one of the soldiers came back and asked if I had other papers. I didn't need a visa. I had checked the website that morning and was permitted entry as a tourist for sixty days. The only other documentation I had was my travel insurance certificate and flight confirmation from Sweden. I showed those items but they dismissed them.

One car was turned around and would not be allowed to enter. They extended the return queue for Romania. I really did not want to join them. I was asked the purpose of my visit. "Tourism and a shortcut to Poland," I said and pointed out my intended route. They were unhappy that I had visited Moldova and couldn't understand why I would have done so. They seemed to regard Moldova as an ally of their enemy, Russia. They could see that my visit had been just one day which I innocently explained as being due to poor roads. I was made to wait a while longer.

Eventually my passport was handed back to me. It had been stamped and the guard just pointed the direction for me to go. Customs had checked me over an hour ago and they waved me through. I got clear of the final machine gun and kept pedalling in case they changed their minds. I had been at the crossing for exactly two hours but I was now in Ukraine. Virgin territory number twelve. All that anxiety and extra mileage had left me shattered.

In a bid to avoid data roaming charges, I headed to a service station looking for a map. The cashier was a helpful chap and spoke a little English. He helped choose the best map for me. Then I decided that I wanted to celebrate my arrival with a local ale. The fridge was well stocked with Russian lagers but I wanted a Ukrainian. He pointed out my options and I selected one before settling in the dining area with the map and beverage. The cashier came over with a bottle opener. He was looking after me well. I then fumbled with the tripod to take a selfie in my raised beer bottle pose. The cashier did the honours. Unbeknown to me, the fuel attendant had crept in behind to photobomb.

The two of them studied my map and helped plot the best route. They then translated all of the relevant place names from Russian into English. Then they tried to fix me up with the rather beautiful blond from the currency exchange. She ran back to her booth embarrassed and giggling over their suggestions. I'm not sure exactly what they were saying. Then they taught me to say 'farewell' which is something like 'Shas lee voy door rogga'. And finally they gave me a Ukrainian flag to mount on the back of my trailer. I had never had so much fun and laughter in a shop.

I mounted up, thanked my new friends and waved goodbye. "Shaslevoydoorrogga!" I said. They replied with the same word and I sounded almost fluent.

By 8.30pm I had camped in the roadside forest at Bibat. It was quite comfortable. I had moved too far from Romanian network coverage but to my delight, the charges for Ukraine were equally as cheap. It had been a very long day but it was probably the best of the trip so far. Despite the diversion, I had seen that family of wild boar and an eagle in flight. I had been concerned about coming to Ukraine but had been made very welcome.

DAY 65. Tuesday 19th May

After another free and relaxing night in 'Center Parcs', I was on the move by 6.45am. The roads weren't perfect. They had the rolling-pin effect in places caused by heavy truck tyres on melting tarmac. The signs were good though and navigation was not difficult. I really wanted to see one of the iconic onion domes, typical of that region. It wasn't long before I found one. They looked impressive from afar but close up the sectional joints were more pronounced.

It was a very patriotic place. Some of the bridges had railings painted in the style of the national flag. Each village, town or city had a welcome monument, usually featuring the national colours.

At this early stage, there were few signs to suggest the country was fighting mighty Russia but every war memorial was covered in floral tributes.

At the first big town, Chernivtsi, troops in uniform were actively recruiting passers-by. I stopped in the main square to take in the views. Electric buses were a sight I was unused to and there was a serious number of Ladas.

By 1.30pm I had joined the locals cooling off in the River Prut. This area was effectively used like the seaside. People were sunbathing on the banks and having barbeques. I took the opportunity to get clean, do my laundry and prepare a meal.

Finding clean drinking water was a problem. There were fewer fountains and public taps. I still had about 4 litres but needed to keep my eyes open. The bike tyres were wearing very thin, especially the rear. It occurred to me that neither the bike nor the trailer were in good condition any longer. I didn't think either was capable of going the full distance. I didn't want to pay for expensive repairs at this late stage and decided I would push the team until it collapsed and if need be continue alone by alternative means, namely, boots, bus, truck, train or taxi.

By late afternoon I had reach Orshivtsi. It looked like there was a tap in the main village square. I headed over but had to give way to a man walking along the pavement in the opposite direction. He spoke to me. I shrugged, not knowing what he had just said. "I'm English; sorry, I don't understand."

The man was Vasyl Todoryuk and he could speak perfect English. That was a relief. He quizzed what I was doing in his village. He was the local councillor.

The grail diary map helped explain and I was suddenly given ambassador status.

He wanted to talk to me, and invited me for coffee at the village hall. I was ready for a break and here was an opportunity to fill up my water bottles. We entered the hall and the coffee and biscuits were soon laid on by one of his staff. I was shown around the old building. One of the corridors had a photo gallery of all the villagers who had put on uniforms to fight for their country. They started as black and white portraits but reaching the other end were the more recent colour photos of those currently deployed to the modern Eastern Front.

We sat in his office. It was very dated. It looked a bit 1970s. I told Vasyl how much I had enjoyed his country so far and that Ukraine had some of the most impressive houses I had ever seen. He told me that the houses might look impressive but Ukraine was very poor. It quickly became apparent that I was not there to tell him about my adventure. He wanted me to hear about the suffering of his countrymen. Why was the world ignoring Putin's aggression? Did we not know or care that people were being killed? Ukraine felt abandoned by the West.

The army needed volunteers to defend the eastern border. Ten had gone from this village in recent months but the military had limited funds. Each time someone went, the community would have to make a donation in order to pay for a uniform and boots. The winter had been tough for those deployed on operations.

My host was quite depressed about the situation. He loved his country and couldn't bear to see such injustice dispensed by his Russian neighbours. I felt completely impotent. I was not a diplomat and had no power or avenues for influence. I could only sympathise. Having vented his frustration, he invited me to use the village hall as accommodation for the night. I declined the kind offer as there was still plenty of daylight for riding. He tried to hand me his desktop flag as a gift. I respectfully rejected this and told him that I was already flying those colours from my trailer. It was then clear that he desperately wanted me to receive a memento of his village.

He insisted on taking me to the village shop. I could have anything that I wanted. I told him the water, coffee and biscuits had been quite generous enough. Then he revealed his true anxiety. He had volunteered for the army and would be joining tomorrow. My heart sank. I felt as though I knew this man and I was already concerned for his safety. He told me he had three weeks of training to complete and then would be deployed to the Eastern Front. He was fifty-two years old. I had joined the military with boyish enthusiasm at sixteen. I was forty-six now and did not relish the associated hardships of his predicament. Six years my senior, Vasyl was far too old for battle, but he felt compelled to go owing to his position on the village council. I proposed a toast to his success. A beer in his honour. We entered the shop and he chose the best beer available and asked what else I would like. He wasn't having a beer. He didn't want to impair his fitness before starting his basic training, so I told him to forget about the beer and that I'd have a choc ice instead. I left the shop with both. I got Vasyl to teach me how to say 'thank you' and 'good luck'.

"D'ja koo yu, Harrnoh and Shaslevoydoorrogga!" I said to the brave man.

I was quite sad cycling away. War is just so tragic. The Europe I had seen on this trip was covered with graveyards from the various conflicts. As a father of four, I so wished there was another way.

At the next village there was a pretty fountain. I sat down to drink my Robert Doms beer. At the other end of the town was a well-tended memorial. There were fresh flowers and candles in abundance and national flags at half mast. Beside it was a poster featuring the names and faces of those killed in the conflict over the last twelve months. There were 117 victims. This was so depressing and I felt as though we were letting the side down. Despite these tragic losses, there was no shortage of recruitment posters. Some of the large roadside advertising boards had images of troops sat on a tank. I thought back to what Vasyl had said about the uniforms. Sure enough, all of the soldiers wore different-style boots.

Putin had so much power and could easily open up Russia as a friend and partner of the West. Had he done so, he would have most likely been celebrated and remembered forever through paintings and statues. Instead, the self-honouring egotist commissioned his own monuments which will probably be removed or desecrated after his demise.

I pressed on through some horrific stretches of road. The surface of one section was like skiing over moguls. The oncoming traffic had to zigzag across both lanes at a snail's pace in order to proceed. When darkness fell about 9pm I camped in the roadside treeline.

DAY 66. Wednesday 20th May

Yesterday had taken its toll and so I had a proper lie-in until about 9.15am before continuing. I came across a well by a tiny chapel with a picket-fence garden. Holy water was a blessing, right?

Wrong. A little further on there was a crashing sound. My trailer had dumped itself in the middle of the road. It had never become detached before. Closer inspection revealed that the main towing arm had sheared off. The 6-inch section holding the two linchpins no longer existed. I was stranded in the middle of nowhere. Was it time to abandon Wilson and transfer the stores to my bike rack and panniers? The extra load would certainly accelerate the bike's decline. The rear wheel was already badly buckled and the tyre was completely worn out.

I knew that the trailer arm was a hollow metal tube and discovered that I could splay the relevant end with my adjustable spanner to maintain the connection. This would be sufficient for a few more miles at least. The old bootlaces, retained since Schramberg, and some masking tape contributed to this bodge repair.

I was initially quite pleased with my handiwork but it nearly ended in disaster. I had done sufficient to enable the bike to pull the trailer but I had not taken into account the effects of braking or descents. As I freewheeled down a steep hill, the trailer accelerated and shunted forward. The towing arm slid straight through the female housing which was welded to the chassis and the splayed section connected with the rear wheel of the trailer. This acted like a handbrake turn and almost threw me off my bike. This destabilising effect lasted for about 100 metres before I was safely able to stop. I could easily have been thrown into the path of an overtaking vehicle and had been lucky to survive unscathed. With the second bootlace and a lot more masking tape I was able to prevent that forward motion from recurring.

Slightly shaken, I considered my options. My new plan was to just try and reach the Polish capital and fly home from there. I reached the next big town of Kolomyya. I was delighted to have made it that far and bought some supplies from the supermarket. I didn't know what I was buying or how much things cost. Onions and peppers had to be bagged and weighed on a machine. I was expected to punch in the various commodity codes in order to print the pricing label. The alphabet was completely alien to me but another shopper kindly helped out.

As I neared the centre of town, I saw a bike shop and headed in for an emergency pit stop. There was nothing they could do for the trailer but they were able to 'true' my rear wheel, replace some spokes and fit a brand-new tyre. It was cash only so I was directed to the nearby ATM.

I was expecting a bill close to £100 so I worked out the exchange rate and started to push the buttons. I had no idea what I was reading and the glare on the screen made the numbers difficult to see. I pressed the wrong buttons and my card was swallowed up but out of the machine came a huge wad of banknotes (2,000 hryvnia). It worked out at approximately £58. Not enough for my bike repair, they didn't accept credit cards and I had no other method of payment. I didn't want to risk losing my Mastercard in the ATM as well so I went back to tell the pair of bike-shop workers to cease what they were doing for me. Too late. They had been fast and efficient. I waited for my bill.

They charged me about £6.60; I couldn't believe it. They had been on it about an hour and even adjusted my gears and brakes. I queried the charge and they broke it down between parts and labour. I rounded it up to the equivalent of a tenner. They were baffled as to why I was paying so much. I told them I was giving a tip for such good service. Ringing my bank to cancel my card would be another tenner but José was reinvigorated.

I toured the town and had a few conversations with locals. It was a very hospitable place. There was a big recreational park with a boating lake in its centre. On this hot day it was like being at the beach.

I rode out of town towards the dark clouds and by 5.10pm I was camped in the roadside treeline as the rain started to fall.

DAY 67. Thursday 21st May

On the road for 7am and made steady progress, passing a beautiful domed church which was broadcasting high-pitched choir music. I couldn't tell if it was a service or a recording.

I stopped for lunch in the car park of an abandoned old restaurant and then made my way to the city of Ivano Frankivsk. There were armed police at roadblocks along the arterial routes in and out. Probably more for reassurance than a formal cordon or defensive perimeter.

The inner city was very cultural with live music being played and people drinking or dining outside in the sunshine. I was taken by surprise to see black and Indian people. I had only seen white or tanned faces since leaving Austria. This sudden change of demographic was refreshing. It suggested an inclusive and forward-thinking society. Many of the people wore traditional clothing which was best described as white shirts or dresses with colourful embroidered patterns down the front. I hadn't bought any gifts or souvenirs on my trip but I felt an affinity to this place, a solidarity with the underdogs standing up to the bully. For my daughters I bought hand-painted trinket boxes and I got myself a traditional shirt.

It was a long trek out of town and I missed my intended road. There was an alternative so I didn't turn back. I had by now developed a pain in my hip. That was a bad sign. Typically my pain management signals had four phases. The ankle, knee, hip and back. The ankle always hurts. Overdoing things would extend pain to my knee and prompt me to take ibuprofen. When the hip became painful I was in trouble and if that pain reached the final stage of my lower back, I would be a total write-off. By some strange coincidence the pain had started yesterday, which meant that José, Wilson and I had all worn out on day 66.

I camped in trees off the main road near Pavlivka. My massive stock of ibuprofen had run out. All I had now were some antibiotics and two Lemsip sachet powders. They contained paracetamol and would have to be saved as a last resort.

That night I had problems. I couldn't sleep. My hip was excruciating and it didn't matter what position I was in. It hurt when I was on the road, but since stopping it had become much more pronounced.

DAY 68. Friday 22nd May

The day didn't start well. Distracted through pain, I missed my alternative turn and had to backtrack, repeating agonising miles. The suggested route took me down country lanes and through fields. There had been heavy rain the night before and it wasn't long before my feet were soaked and squelching through the wet grass and my four wheels were clogged with sticky mud and clay.

I was using my bike as a crutch for much of the time and I was making some quite pathetic whimpering noises. I needed to find a pharmacy quick and it looked very much as though this little expedition would end today. Eventually, my so-called shortcut reunited me with the correct road, H09, and I could carry on. Where was the sun? The cold, grey and damp sky was doing nothing to alleviate my symptoms or mood. I trudged along, hoping someone would take pity on me and offer me a lift.

I reached a small village and there was a single shop that sold everything. Socks, umbrellas, canned food, bottled drinks and all manner of supplies. I hobbled in and scanned the shelves looking for medicine. The old lady behind the counter spoke no English but through a game of charades and after viewing my grail diary map, she understood that I was in great pain. I understood that she did not sell medicine and there was nowhere that did in this village.

From all the items loaded on her shelves, there was nothing I could buy that would fix my problem but she bent down behind the counter and opened her handbag. She took out a blister pack containing 2 green tablets and then fetched a cup of water. She instructed me to swallow her medication and drink. I had no idea what I was taking. Could have been hormone tablets for

317

all I knew. She insisted I swallow both tablets. I felt better immediately. Maybe it was psychological. Maybe it was getting warm in the shop or perhaps even the warmth of her generosity. To show my appreciation, I bought an armful of supplies which included a microwave cheeseburger. The lady heated it up for me. I gestured my sincere thanks and returned to my bike.

As I finished my burger, the bread-delivery lady arrived to drop off the daily order. As she returned to her van, she took out a loaf and offered it to me. I smiled and waved my hand to say, "No no no," but she insisted. She mimed that I had ridden far, and gave me the Ukrainian equivalent of 'bravo' and applauded. The corner-shop lady must have told her of my crippling ride and now she was rewarding me for my effort. These two ladies had made such kind and sincere gestures. I was truly humbled and the pain dissolved very quickly.

At the next village there were many shops but the signs held no clues as to the items being sold. Which was the pharmacy? I window-shopped until I found the most obvious. I had indeed found the right place but they had no ibuprofen. The green tablets were doing well but I now had the anxiety of reaching the next village before they wore off.

There was another armed police roadblock at the village exit. This caused a traffic jam but I was waved on along the pavement.

I finally managed to buy the medicine in Burshytn. I spent the equivalent of £10 on a few days' dose of tablets but they were worth every penny.

I camped in the roadside treeline just outside Natashyne.

DAY 69. Saturday 23rd May

My hip still hurt but was much better than the day before. It was another miserable start but I pressed on about 8am. I could hear a siren further ahead. I was riding towards it so it would obviously approach me very soon. The siren continued to blare out but nothing appeared over the horizon. On and on it went, getting louder as I got closer.

Then there it was in the distance. Some sort of parade. A police car led the procession and was followed by a taxi which was flying a huge Ukrainian flag. A large convoy of vehicles was in tow. Crowds lined the road either side. It was a protest demonstration, I thought.

As I got closer I realised that the crowd were holding candles and throwing flowers at one of the cars. Many of the ladies were clearly crying and some of the men were on their haunches rubbing their eyes.

This was a sight we had seen too often in England. It was a Royal Wootton Bassett-style homecoming for one of Ukraine's fallen soldiers. I had realised a little too late but got off my bike to stand as the cortege passed through.

At the village well, an elderly man confirmed that they had lost one of their own and he cursed the man responsible. "Down with Putin!" he said.

The weather didn't really improve all day and I camped quite early in trees at the edge of a roadside field.

DAY 70. Sunday 24th May

There was a heavy downpour during the night but the trees gave some protection. I was rolling towards Lviv from 7.30am and reached there about 10am. It was an obvious tourist attraction and worth a longer stay but I didn't want to stop because I was cold and wet.

Seeing three Ladas parked alongside each other suggested an episode of *Top Gear* was being filmed but in reality this was just normal life.

It took four hours to get back on the road towards Poland. I looked back at Lviv. On the skyline there appeared to be snowy peaks. I put my camera on maximum zoom and took a photograph. I then examined the picture. It was an overflowing landfill site.

The weather brightened up briefly by late afternoon but only provided a partial charge to my tablet. I relaxed in the peaceful setting of a roadside forest just short of the border.

DAY 71. Monday 25th May

For the third day in a row I was greeted by miserable weather. A grey and misty fog with a light drizzle. I reached the border village of Rava Ruska about 9.20am and found an old-style water pump. It was clearly used by the local residents and was a welcome top-up. Then I had a cooked breakfast under the canopy of an outdoor restaurant. I still had too much Ukrainian currency and swapped it for Polish Zloty before making the crossing.

As I cycled up to the frontier, the soldiers stopped me. I was not allowed to pass through as this crossing was for vehicles only. I assured the guards that I could ride quite quickly without causing a traffic jam but they wouldn't permit me to try. I had no idea where to go now. This was a real hammer blow.

The supervisor tried to explain but also offered a potential solution. If I was in agreement they would try to secure me a lift across the border in the back of another vehicle. I was absolutely fine with that idea.

She gave some instructions to the soldiers and they sought co-operation of the next empty truck. Wilson and José were quickly loaded up into the back of a lorry and I joined my new travel partners in the cab. They were two Ukrainian men on their way to Krakow for some 'dark business'.

The driver's passport had so many stamps in it. I gathered he made weekly cross-border runs. I didn't want to ask too many questions. We were soon in the EU. The Polish guard was quite impressed by my trip and said he intended to ride to Gdansk that summer (the equivalent of John O'Groats to Land's End).

By 11.40am the 'bootleggers' had dropped me off on the main road. They offered to take me to Krakow but I was heading for Lublin. I tried to hand over some Zloty for their help but they flatly rejected this. I had been helped once more. Ukraine had been the most hospitable place of my trip and the small flag that accompanied me through that country continues to fly in my kitchen window. D'ya koo yu, Ukraine.

My first impression of Poland was good. I was surrounded by forest, fields and farms. The roads were excellent and even had solar panels to power certain traffic lights or illuminated road signs. By the time I had reached the first big town I suddenly felt underdressed and out of place. I was quite clean and had combed my hair but was still conscious that I was making this immaculate place look untidy.

The supermarket had everything I would buy back home. Fresh milk was such a treat. I had been used to buying and carrying food to last for three days. I didn't need to do that here as I could shop at will and therefore travel lighter. Were it not for the unpronounceable language and acres of space between houses, Poland was almost the same as England.

By 8.20pm I was camped in the woods outside Majdan Krynicki.

DAY 72. Tuesday 26th May

Up at 6.25am. There had been heavy rain, thunder and lightning overnight and it was a chilly grey start.

The black T-shirt that I had worn since Kosovo was finally rejected. Despite washing it, the sun had bleached the fabric and it looked dirty. I felt the need to dress a little smarter here, so I put on a fresh top. The old rag would be used for oiling my chain and bearings.

I arrived at the beautiful town of Zamosc mid-morning and later prepared lunch on some old benches near Izbica station. The sun was out and I used the opportunity to air and dry all of my kit. The trend of free water continued as I found a public tap. I worked out that the ferry in Estonia was only 735 miles away. In order to be on my pre-arranged flight I would have to ride just 29 miles a day from now on. A slower pace was welcome news. The rear wheel was buckled again and had lost another spoke. Being so far ahead of schedule enabled me to finish early and make a more luxurious shelter in the roadside forest.

DAY 73. Wednesday 27th May

There was heavy rain, thunder and lightning during the night, but I remained warm and dry. The sun had not risen by 7am and through the trees I could see that the cars still had their headlights on. It was still raining.

I casually packed up as it was quite sheltered under the trees, but as soon as I reached the open road I got drenched. I was in shorts and a T-shirt with a Gore-Tex jacket but the wind and rain made me uncomfortably cold. Poland was indeed similar to England. It seemed that my arrival in northern Europe had been premature. I had expected to be greeted by early summer sunshine but this recent spell of bad weather was a worrying trend.

Wilson had suffered a slow puncture. I needed to reinflate every three days but had forgotten to do so this morning and it now looked quite urgent. The Statoil service station outside Praski had an appealing forecourt which enticed me over. It would give me brief respite from the constant downpour. When I dismounted I realised that I was soaked through to the skin. This was very unpleasant and I started shivering. I tried to use the bike pump but my fingers were frozen and didn't work. I was a pathetic case and quite useless now.

The intrigue magnet pulled in the station manager. The grail diary map impressed once again but my shaking body and jittering speech prompted Slawek to invite me inside to get warm.

I went to the shop and selected a chicken baguette which the cashier zapped in the microwave as I removed my wet things. I grabbed that hot baguette in both hands to warm my fingers and then gorged on my first mouthful. Slawek then asked if I would like some Polish soup. "Is it warm?" I asked.

It was, but my host was just getting started. In addition to managing the service station, he also ran the restaurant next door. It was normally closed during the daytime but he went in and opened it up just for me. He put the radiators on full blast and set up a table directly alongside for me to thaw out.

He brought me a hot latte from the shop and a basket of bread. The soup arrived shortly after. He called it 'Zurek' or 'Easter soup'. It contained portions of boiled egg and slices of German sausage. The delicious, warm and creamy appetizer soon made me feel better. Steam was starting to rise off my shorts and T-shirt.

Then I was offered Pierogi, which were like giant pieces of ravioli, stuffed with cheese, onion and minced bacon. I didn't deserve this treatment. I wasn't anyone special. I was just a nomadic vagrant on a three-month tour of Europe, but to Slawek and his wife I was an honoured guest. That meant that they would not accept any payment. I was truly astonished and humbled by this generous Polish hospitality. Thank you so much.

Fully recharged I headed back to the road. It had stopped raining too. I soon reached Lublin but I was there well in advance of Pavel's return so there would be no reunion. The city looked interesting with its castles and museums, but the cold, grey skies encouraged me to keep moving. After warming up with a McDonald's 'Big Tasty' meal, I pressed on to find somewhere to sleep.

I ended up in the roadside treeline behind someone's garden fence.

Another leg fell off my camera tripod so I had to carve a second prosthetic from a stick.

DAY 74. Thursday 28th May

There was nothing particularly significant about this day. I spent most of it riding through the Polish countryside which was similar to the first day's description of 'forest, fields and farms'. I was entertained for about five minutes by a very confident woodpecker. I ended the day in woods about 80 miles from Warsaw.

DAY 75. Friday 29th May

Today had pleasant sunshine and I pressed hard. By 7.15pm I was only 15 miles from the capital and spent a comfortable night camped in Chojnowski Park.

DAY 76. Saturday 30th May

It was dry for most of the day. I set out at 6.30am and within two hours I had reached the outskirts of the big city. I rode past several impressive buildings, including palaces and international embassies. I visited the Chopin Memorial Garden and many of the city landmarks. Old Town was probably the best place to be with its bars, restaurants, and horse and carriage rides, but I wasn't in a tourist frame of mind. To me, Warsaw was just a checkpoint.

It was time to reconsider the options. Should we continue as a trio, a pair or solo? The ferry was still 600 miles away but time was on our side. I hoped we could all make it as far as the boat and decided we should stick together. I refilled at a fountain and crossed the river.

Old Town Warsaw.

Just clear of the ring road was a large retail park which included a huge camping store. Finally I could get replacement tent poles but I couldn't see the point. I had managed this far and it was probably cheaper to buy a new tent. What I did need was replacement gas canisters. The Bulgarian stove still had some life in it but these shelves stocked the previously elusive Bluet gas. I bought three. That should be adequate for the remaining timetable, I thought.

By 8pm I was camped in the woods outside Marki.

DAY 77. Sunday 31st May

A sunny morning at last. I was on the road by 6.30am. I had to step over a sleeping local. He had presumably drunk too much the night before and had just slept where he fell. He looked quite comfortable so I left him to his slumber. I tanked along the E67 and enjoyed a McDonald's breakfast about 8.30am. I did a Lidl stop at Ostrow Mazowiecka. I also found a public tap which enabled me to refill, have a wash and do some laundry.

I camped in the roadside forest about 5pm. It was very peaceful until 7.30pm when two cars drove along the dirt track. One had loud music blaring and I expected this was to be the site for an evening barbeque. If more people arrived I would almost certainly be discovered. The cars parked up and the respective drivers got out. There was a blond lady in her forties and a man in his late twenties. They kissed and embraced before getting into the back seat of his car. A short while later the car started to bounce up and down.

I had a limited view so this was hardly a 'dogging diary entry' but I was very close and could hear their passion. I hoped that I could muffle the sound of my tablet. Any incoming message alert would surely give me away. I laid still and silent about 10 metres from the fun. The door opened and out flew a condom. Why did he have to litter the place? A short while later they were at it again and I wished the darkness could fall quicker to conceal my presence. Activities seemed longer than they actually were and the secret lovers kissed openly once more before driving their separate ways.

DAY 78. Monday 1st June

It was light at 4am and I hit the road before 6.30am. It was another sunny day and, carrying less weight, I made good progress. I ended the day at 8pm. I was only 50 miles from Lithuania but I really needed a street-tap refill, a supermarket for food and a decent lake or river for a bath.

DAY 79. Tuesday 2nd June

Some of my needs were addressed. Another beautifully sunny morning offered a tranquil early swim in the lake at Rajgrod. I dived straight in. It felt amazing to be clean again. I dried on the jetty as I made tea and breakfast.

I passed through several pretty villages and the border was getting closer. I soon realised that I could make the crossing that night and I felt like celebrating. I had about £7 of zloty remaining and I intended to spend it all. At the first shop in Giby I bought some milk, a bottle of Warka beer, some chocolate and crisps but I seemed to leave the shop with more money than when I started. I relaxed in the sunshine drinking my refreshing ale. I continued towards the border and stopped at a service station for a Lomza beer. It was the equivalent of just 51p. The final opportunity was at a corner shop just before the border; I got free water from their outdoor tap, but purchased more chocolate, biscuits and a Tyskie. I still had the equivalent of £3.50 left but was feeling the effects of the alcohol so I gave up trying to spend my money.

I decided that from now on I would have three beers in each new country just prior to leaving. There would be one beer for each team member, although I would obviously have to help my colleagues with this task. I named this new ritual 'departure beers'.

I was straight through the open border at 6.20pm. Lithuania was virgin territory number fourteen.

DAY 80. Wednesday 3rd June

I hadn't gone quite as far as Phileas Fogg or Michael Palin but twenty countries on a pushbike was impressive. I considered straying into Belarus for a bonus flag. It wasn't far away but I required a visa. Perhaps I could just run across a field and briefly enter as an illegal immigrant before dashing back out again unnoticed? If I was caught by border guards, I could plead ignorance and claim to be lost. I was tempted but then dismissed the silly idea. Belarus was a close friend of Russia's and may have reacted unkindly to my incursion. If they took away my camera, diary or tablet, the trip details would be lost, so I planned my route through Kaunas instead.

I wasn't in a hurry today and had a lie-in till 8am. I had been badly bitten during the night and had been kept awake by a constant urge to scratch the itchy bumps around my throat, torso, feet, arms, back and buttocks. It wasn't a mosquito. There were swarms of them outside my tent, trying unsuccessfully to creep in through the mesh windows and door. I suspected it was a delayed reaction to something in the lake the day before. That morning swim had been a bad idea.

I had been impressed by Poland. The infrastructure was equal if not better than the UK's. The weather was certainly on par. The cost of living was a lot cheaper and there was so much open space. Instead of people back home moaning about the Poles invading England, perhaps the English should move to Poland. If we remain in the EU that will probably happen. As a shrinking island with a housing crisis and an increasing population, a mass resettlement to the Continent will be the only realistic solution.

By comparison, Lithuania was no match. It may have broken free of its Soviet shackles but it was underdeveloped and looked like a ghost town. The road surface was poor and there were abandoned farms, factories and houses. Many of these were built from chipboard panels and had corrugated asbestos roofs. They all had modern wheelie bins though, probably an EU rule, but the contrast of old and new looked odd.

It was a hot day and fatigue soon hit me. I had pushed hard to exit Poland

and needed to slow down. The rear wheel was buckled so badly by now that it clipped the rear frame with each revolution. I bent it back to workable by kicking and jumping on it.

I stocked up at a supermarket and was then approached by a beggar outside. I had no cash other than my remaining zloty. The currency was litas or euros here and I was using my credit card. The low value of my Polish coins did not justify their weight, so I handed them over. The man was delighted and patted my shoulder before running straight into the store for some alcohol.

I stopped about 4.30pm; I decided to have an early night in the Selena Woods.

DAY 81. Thursday 4th June

I slept straight through. It was nearly 9am before I surfaced. A tractor had fired up to start pulling a trailer full of felled logs. It was time to get moving. I was only 25 miles from Kaunas and reached it by lunchtime. This place was the second biggest city in Lithuania. It was very busy, packed with cars and trams, but I found the complete absence of dropped kerbs intolerable. There were lots of uniformed soldiers walking about but they weren't carrying weapons.

I visited the Hesburger fast food restaurant for the equivalent of a McDonald's meal. I hereby declare that it was much better quality than my usual junk food.

I was quizzed by a local as I headed out towards the ring road. He was a young lad on his bike but my trailer prompted the usual questions. I asked about the availability of free water and he told me there was none. Lithuania was almost completely flat with low-lying marshlands. He offered to supply me from his house and after giving me directions, agreed to meet me by the road further up. Unfortunately, I didn't find him again.

I joined the arterial highway but stopped early and camped in the roadside treeline.

DAY 82. Friday 5th June

I had another lazy lie-in. Just 335 miles remained. Late starts and early finishes should be the method from here on.

I bought my first bottle of water at the supermarket in Kedainiai. Almost three months of free water had been an unexpected bonus. I stopped to eat in a public park by the pretty lake and took a selfie on the bridge over a weir. As I rode away, the hot sun reminded me to put my floppy hat back on my head. Where was it? It was needed to shade me from the harmful rays. I retraced my route but there was no sign of it. I checked my camera. The hat featured in my recent selfie. It was resting on top of my trailer. Had it blown into the lake or drifted down the weir? No.

Then I remembered there had been a woman and two young children who crossed the bridge when I did. I considered that perhaps one of the children had found my headdress and I went in search of them. Eventually I found them in the play area. I asked the mother but she had no English. I showed her a photograph of my hat and made various hand gestures. Her response indicated that my hat had blown into the river. I went back for another look.

She was right. I had missed it initially in my haste but there it was balanced on top of the weir directly underneath the footbridge. I could have climbed down to retrieve it easily enough but wouldn't be able to get back up again. I could swim for it but the water was less inviting than the crystal clear Polish lake and I didn't want to be eaten alive as before.

The 'reach, throw, wade, row', song started playing in my head. Could I dislodge the hat with a rock or stick and recover it further downstream? No. Then it came to me. I linked two bungees together and 'crab-lined' the hat. This small victory was the highlight of my day.

I camped in the National Forest just north of Krekenova. Only 296 miles to go.

DAY 83. Saturday 6th June

It was another easy day. Glorious sunshine. By midday I had stopped to admire a beautiful village lake. Sand had been brought in to make a beach area and two children were diving off the pier. It was hot and I fancied another swim but those earlier bites dissuaded me again.

I found a public tap in one of the villages but, disappointingly, it had been padlocked out of operation. The traffic was quite light by the afternoon and I was soon within striking distance of the border. As I rode through the countryside I found a €10 note. Was that karma? Whatever it was, it was time for 'departure beers'. At 4.20pm I bought a Svyturys from a service station. At 5.40pm it was a Taurus from a roadside convenience store. Finally, at 7.30pm, I bought a Kalnapilis from a service station. I carried that in my pannier and drank it in my tent. I had camped in the roadside forest at Raubonys, close to the border, just north of Pasvalys.

DAY 84. Sunday 7th June

The beer and outdoor exercise meant I had an excellent night's sleep. There had been lots of animal noises which included barking deer and peacocks. I was back on the E67 for 9am. I hadn't done much cooking lately and was having fewer hot drinks. I decided to lighten the load by dumping my Bulgarian cooker. It still had half a canister but I left it in the car park of a roadside diner.

By 11.30am I had ridden through the unmanned border into Latvia. Not far to go now. I rode casually along the quiet main road. I was daydreaming when the siren blasted out behind me. The loud noise and shock caused me to wobble and almost fall off my bike. I looked behind to see a police escort signalling me to pull over. Behind the flashing blue lights was a military convoy. The lead vehicle was an armoured Hummer. There was a mounted machine gun in the turret and a soldier stood aloft. They wore American uniforms but were Latvian forces. The convoy seemed endless. I got off my bike to stand and watch as about thirty vehicles paraded past. The troops were all smiling, waving or giving thumbs up. It was an impressive sight but somewhat depressing at the same time. My map indicated that this country was flanked to the east by Russia. These troop movements represented a ratcheting up of military tension. Putin wasn't going to push through here as well, was he? The 'tail end Charlie' was another Hummer with a machine gunner lookout.

As the noisy convoy disappeared, I was left alone in the peaceful countryside. I continued a little further through the tiny villages of Gaujas and Arce. I thought it would be better if those two were united like Budapest. Gorgeous Arse has a nice ring to it. I then stopped to cook at a bus shelter. The silence was soon shattered by the thunder of four Apache helicopters flying north in formation. That was a sight. Had a conflict started or was this just more flexing of military muscle? I checked my tablet for news and sighed a relief.

I restocked at Bauska and then pressed further inland. The bus stop sign at Rudzi was riddled with bullet holes which I suspected was the result of regular target practice. I headed down what started as a freshly laid tarmac road. I could make rapid progress on that. Unfortunately it stopped after about a ½ mile and turned into a dirt and gravel track. Each time a vehicle drove past it would generate a cloud of dust. I would have to stop and cover my eyes, nose and mouth while holding my breath until the air cleared. This was a serious problem especially when fast cars or large lorries approached. It was imperative that I clear this section before the anticipated traffic increase of Monday morning.

The track just went on and on. Eventually I gave in to exhaustion. It was 9pm and the light was fading. I built a shelter in the woods near a level crossing 2 miles south of Vecumnieki.

DAY 85. Monday 8th June

I was up at 8am. The trains had started and there were many. I remained on the dusty highway for most of the morning. I travelled through open swampland on the road to Ogre. Was this the home of Shrek? I saw several adders basking on the road. I gave them a wide berth but they were now a concern, particularly when it came to camping in the woods.

I took a few selfies at the welcome sign but the town of Ogre was otherwise disappointing. I did a supermarket visit and carried on towards the capital. A decent road would take me to within 20 miles and I spent the night in the thicket by some roadside waste ground.

DAY 86. Tuesday 9th June

I had a slow and relaxing morning. The early sunshine provided a chance to air my kit on some old concrete tubes. As I stood there brushing my teeth, a wild deer came out of the woods. I slowly went for my camera but startled the graceful animal and it bounced back to the trees with me clicking away.

I rode into Riga about midday. People were taking off from the river on motorised hang-gliders but I used the water to clean up before entering the centre. It was a beautiful place and reminded me of Bruges but without the canals. It was full of tourists, little cafes, bars, museums, spectacular buildings and gift shops. It would certainly be worth a longer stay one day.

It was a quite a trek getting out of the big city but I eventually camped in some peaceful trees off the main road.

DAY 87. Wednesday 10th June

After a good night's sleep I was rolling by 8.30am. The sun was shining, which was a relief as I hoped to swim in the Baltic Sea later. After a steady ride through a landscape of forests, swamps and lakes, I reached the beach resort of Saulkrasti. This was popular with Dutch caravaners. I had discovered their secret escape. I soon headed down to the almost deserted beach and waded in for some hydrotherapy. It wasn't as cold as the name suggested. Quite warm, in fact. After half an hour's sunbathing I moved back to the clifftop to cook dinner.

The place was beautiful. Not over-commercialised. It was effectively 'Center Parcs by the sea'. After my lunch I continued towards Estonia. Somewhere over the next few miles, I lost my floppy hat. I was distraught. I had worn it since Hungary, every day for fifty days. I went back looking for it, clocking up extra miles in vain.

I saw another eagle later that day. It swooped down into the long grass and presumably caught its prey because I didn't see it return to the skies.

333

I set Tuja as my target for the day. I didn't arrive until 9pm but found a shop and bought some supplies which included the first of my 'departure beers', a bottle of Lacplesis. I then made camp in a pine forest. There was great pressure to erect my tent quickly and exaggerate all of my movements to keep the mosquitoes away. I had repellent but didn't like wearing it as it would make my sleeping bag smelly and oily. I was bitten a few times.

DAY 88. Thursday 11th June

I had the best night so far. Pine forests are so comfortable. My tent was suspended between two trees and the ground was a combination of soft peat, pine needles and heather. Luxurious. It was completely silent during the night and by morning most of the mosquitoes had given up trying to enter my tent. I saw another eagle. It flew low between the trees and came to rest on a nearby branch. I took a picture but sadly all I got was a view of its tail feathers.

By 2.20pm I was at the port town of Salacgriva. I visited the supermarket and bought the second bottle of beer, a Tervete. I reached the final Latvian town of Ainazi about 3.30pm. I dined at the Hesburger restaurant and bought my last 'departure beer', a Gaisais. An hour later I crossed my only remaining land border. Two low-flying A10 Tank Buster jets escorted me in Estonia.

I moved down to the beach and camped in the sand dunes outside Ikla. It was so relaxing there. I watched the tide come in and waited until 10.20pm to catch the sunset. I was stood there for ages trying to get that golden globe touching the sea horizon. The results were disappointing as there was too much cloud. Consoled by my beer I considered that the sunrise might be better.

DAY 89. Friday 12th June

I was up at 4am but the early morning event was equally unspectacular and I went back to bed. I considered taking today off as I was well ahead of schedule and in a great location. By 11am I was bored and restless. It was time to move on.

With the exception of a few elderly folk in ancient wooden shacks, the place was deserted. I came to one village where the bus shelter had been designed as a Viking ship. I took a photo of this and then my camera died. It had taken 720 photos but had suffered a few knocks and was now quite lifeless. I sat at the shelter pressing its buttons hoping for some magical resurrection.

I was joined by a local chap. It was midday and he had already drank a bit. I could smell it on his breath. Most of his front teeth were missing and he looked like he'd been hit a few times but he was quite chatty. I wasn't in a rush and we spoke for about half an hour. He claimed to be the architect of this fine building. His son had burnt down the old wooden shelter playing with matches. This replacement was atonement for his village. He explained that no one liked the Russian occupation but after their withdrawal the economy had slumped. Most people had moved to the capital or Riga.

He was right. I didn't see anyone for the rest of the day. There were good roads but I was the only one using them. It was a very lonely planet. Was I was the only survivor after Armageddon? No, two more A10 jets flew overhead.

By 7.30pm I was camped in the roadside trees at Reiu. I had prepared for the mosquitoes. The mesh bag that had accompanied the purchase of those cheap Lidl trainers in Romania made a perfect head net. I laughed at my potential attackers. "Do your worst; come on!"

DAY 90. Saturday 13th June

I rode into Parnu mid-morning. People at last! I visited a couple of large shopping centres looking for a new camera battery but didn't find one. I checked out the lively beach and some of the old town. There were fireworks going off and live bands playing. It was quite an exciting place. I bought some supermarket supplies and dined once again at Hesburger. I was going to miss those. I spent the rest of the day slowly cruising towards the capital. At a service station I bought the first of my 'departure beers', an Alexander.

I camped on a dead-end track by the side of a field. The nearby forest was fenced off and looked marshy. There were only 50 miles to the big boat.

DAY 91. Sunday 14th June

I was on the road for 7.30am. Today could be the last of my riding. I had options. The ferry would take me to Helsinki and from there a different ferry could take me to Stockholm. I didn't necessarily have to ride any more after today. Was it really over?

The skies were grey and there were darker clouds to the north. I was riding towards rain. I passed a large group of charity bike riders in a lay-by. They soon caught up and overtook me. I challenged myself to keep up with them but I couldn't sustain that pace. When the heavens opened I took refuge at a large bus shelter. It was like a log cabin. Being a Sunday, the buses were infrequent, so I moved in and made myself at home. I cooked most of my remaining food and then got comfy in my sleeping bag. Some motorcyclists also stopped by. They were drenched and seeking a brief respite from the deluge. They were from Finland and were hoping to board the ferry home tonight. I made them a hot tea and we swapped a few stories.

It rained so hard that I was able to fill my metal mug just by leaving it outside on the pavement. I was at this shelter for about two and a half hours until the rain slowed to a light drizzle and then I pressed on for the remaining 25 miles.

I reached the outskirts of the big city at 7.02pm. A large illuminated electronic clock was positioned at the roadside. Finding a place to sleep was a priority now. The further I rode into the capital, the harder it would be to find a secluded spot. There were no ideal locations but it was getting dark and I settled for the dog walking area. There were plenty of trees and I doubted I would be disturbed.

DAY 92. Monday 15th June

I was packed up and back on the road for 5am. Most of my kit was wet and I was cold. It was another miserable day. I walked around a deserted early morning capital. It was an impressive place and one which I would recommend for a short break. I made a mug of hot tea in one of the plazas and then headed to the ferry terminal. My ticket to Finland cost €44; not bad for a bike and trailer. My crossing was not until 10.30am. The boarding gates opened at 9am but it was still only 7am. Fortunately I was able to wait inside the warm building and browsed the tourist information to pass the time. Outside, the rain had started again so I parked José and Wilson in the foyer. Puddles formed underneath but they were still operational and it looked as though the three of us were going all the way.

When the time came, cyclists were directed to the front of the queue so that they could be first to embark. I was joined by Rainer Klein. He was a young Estonian, studying in Finland. He wanted to hear about my adventure so we boarded and headed for the bar. The bad weather had drained my tablet and I was relying on this device for photos. Rainer had a USB connector and we were able to sit by a charging point.

My new pal for the two-hour crossing was a former soldier but was now an engineering student working on designs for more energy efficient engines. He now became my teacher. The Estonian words for cheers are 'terviseks' and 'nastravee'! We practised those sayings over a couple of beers.

The Fins say 'moi' for hello and 'moi moi' for goodbye.

I needed no persuasion to accept the offer of a hot shower and an indoor camp bed for the night. Rainer had lectures to attend first and that would give me time to explore Helsinki. He gave me his address and lent me his second mobile phone.

We disembarked and went our separate ways. It was brightening up in the capital but it was still very cloudy. I had very little power in my tablet so picture-taking was limited. I eventually found a camera shop and a replacement battery but it didn't fix the problem.

My first observations of Finland were that burgers and bottled water were very expensive. Consequently, the place was almost litter-free but full of beggars.

I rode towards my host's and stopped at the students' supermarket for a few items. When I came back outside I saw a red squirrel. I ran around like an excited child, trying to snap it on my tablet. With no flash or zoom, my picture was nothing more than a silhouette. A bemused elderly gent had been watching me as I chased the fluffy rodent under his parked car. He told me that there were loads of red squirrels in Finland. They even had an island sanctuary where you could feed them nuts and they came up to sit on your head or shoulders. I must have looked rather silly chasing what I thought to be a rare sight.

Rainer made contact and rode out to join me before leading us back to his student lodgings. I hung my kit out to dry in the late evening sunshine and went for that hot shower. I was in there for ages but he assured me that there was endless hot water. That was good. I spent more time cleaning the mess that I had made than showering. I was conscious that my kit reeked and so I left most of it outside his front door. He made up the camp bed and lent me his charger and then left me alone while he went to play squash.

I was used to going to sleep early and was out like a light. I heard him come home later but we didn't properly speak until morning.

DAY 93. Tuesday 16th June

No lie-in. I was back on the road by 8am. I had made the morning tea while Rainer sorted out my next ferry. He advised me that if I wanted to see some of Finland I could ride another 100 miles to the west port of Turku. That sounded a good idea and he checked the timetables. He offered some supplies from his fridge. Cured ham and smoked salmon were a bit too rich for my insides but the rye bread was fine. By way of exchange I left my unopened pack of coffee creamer. I didn't need it now and I threw away the old tripod too. I was gradually lightening the load. Then it was time to say farewell or moi moi.

Once again I had been astonished by random acts of kindness and generosity. I had done nothing to betray the trust I was given but I don't think we treat people this way in England. Maybe as islanders we are cautious of outsiders. Our innate default setting is clearly a flaw in our culture. Thank you so much, Rainer Klein.

Finland was quite beautiful. Lots of forest, excellent cycle lanes, some of which were even open to mopeds. Many of the houses looked like something out of an Ikea catalogue and yes, stereotypically all of the people are blond. The brush with civilisation had made me soft though. Instead of being rejuvenated I was sluggish and slow. There was no real explanation. I think the adrenaline had worn off as the body prepared itself for an easier lifestyle.

I stopped about 5.40pm and made camp by a lakeside wood near Paksaloa. I had only done 30 miles. There were 70 more to the next boat. That would obviously take two more days. Hopefully I would return to full power tomorrow.

DAY 94. Wednesday 17th June

Up at 7.10am after a good night. I was ready and fired up. It was sunny

338

today but there was rain forecast for the next week. Could I do 70 miles as a 'finishing' sprint? No pun intended. That was a tall order and was a daily mileage well in excess of any completed so far. There would be a relaxing ferry crossing for the following day and I was travelling lighter now with just 2 litres of water.

I went for it. I just pedalled like a madman. The road signs told me I was getting closer by indicating the remaining mileage countdown. When my water ran out, I rode without any until I was thirsty. I eventually replaced it with a new 1.5 litre bottle but my next drink was a 'departure beer'. I bought a can of Lapin Kulta from a corner shop. It was very expensive. The beer was a welcome boost and acted like an energy drink.

By 8.30pm I was in Turku. I found the ferry terminal and bought a ticket for the next morning. It was only €23, which was half the price of the Tallinn ferry but I was going twice as far. Breaking my own rules, I was now in a built-up area with nowhere to go. I moved to the castle gardens and bedded down inside a large bush.

DAY 95. Thursday 18th June

I was awake at 5am, excited as a child on Christmas morning. Sweden was the final virgin territory and I would be there tonight. I opened my water bottle for a mug of tea. There was froth and spray everywhere. I had bought carbonated water again. Everything was soaked but it didn't matter. I packed up and organised myself on and around a park bench as the early morning joggers beat the path.

About 9.30am I made my way to the boarding gate and it seemed that I had won celebrity status. The ticket lady from last night had mentioned me in the staff room and the gate officer knew exactly who I was. "You're the crazy Englishman who has ridden all around Europe with that trailer," she said.

I boarded and made myself comfortable. Appropriately, I was on a Viking ferry. The crossing would last all day. No riding, for a change. Periodically the sun would shine through the clouds and I'd go out on deck to admire the view. It occurred to me that I could possibly swim or canoe from

Finland to Sweden. On the map it is a vast stretch of blue but actually on the water there were small islands acting like giant stepping stones all the way across.

We docked midday at Mariehamn, Aland. I had never heard of that country but it would be a bonus flag for my fridge, taking the total to nineteen. That also meant another 'departure beer', so I headed to the HMS *Victory* bar for a Stalhagen.

It was about 6pm when we disembarked at a dark and wet Stockholm. I was making it up as I went along now. My return flight was not until Wednesday 24th but I had no intention of staying. I had no money, no food, no clothes and no camera. I was in one of the most expensive countries in Europe and it was tipping it down with rain. I intended to ride to the airport and try to get an earlier flight home.

Stockholm would have been nice in the sunshine but it was unpleasant at that time. I thought about abandoning José and Wilson, I could get a taxi from here, but noticed signs for the train station. Just a short ride and I was there. I packed up the kit I needed and then tried to find a suitable home for my colleagues. A taxi driver snapped up the offer. They would be ideal for his seventeen-year-old student son. A new back wheel and a service was all José needed. Wilson had reasonable tyres and plenty of life left in him too.

I raced on foot into the station, boarded a train and headed for Arlanda. There was a stop for the airport and I entered the departure terminal. My original flight reservation had cost £48.80. For an extra £100, I could fly home tomorrow evening at 5pm via a two-hour stop in Copenhagen. It was only 8pm. I had no intention of sleeping on the airport floor.

The Clarion Hotel was close by. I entered the upmarket establishment and immediately felt out of place. I apologised and explained my dishevelled appearance. £120 for one night was a bit extravagant but I had saved more than £2,500 during this trip so I could afford it and the grail diary map earnt me a free room upgrade. I headed off to find the door of 1 1 1 1 and filled the bath.

I did not recognise the naked man I saw in the mirror. A very thin and bony shipwreck survivor. Why was my beard ginger? I was just 11st 4lb. I sank into the bubbles and exhaled slowly. Was I dreaming? Was I really going home tomorrow? I had nowhere left to ride to. I had no bike or trailer. This was weird and confusing. Then I noticed a filthy tidemark on the side of the bath. The dirt was coming off me but I didn't want to soak in that grimy water. I pulled the plug, had a thorough shower and then filled the tub all over again.

It was getting late but I was not ready for sleeping. There was some expensive wine in the room but I really fancied a beer. Unfortunately I had no clean clothes and my trainers were malodorous. I remembered my Ukrainian shirt. That would have to do. I unpacked it and put on my Ron Hill tracksters and a pair of socks before heading down to the bar for three Swedish Eriksberg.

DAY 96. Friday 19th June

I didn't sleep well and was wide awake by 5.30am. The bed was comfortable and the sheets luxurious but all those pillows were superfluous after fourteen weeks without. Outside, the weather was foggy and grey so I was glad to be leaving. I just hoped the poor visibility wouldn't cause flight delays or cancellations.

I spent much of the morning freshening up my trainers. I didn't want to offend anyone on the plane so I scrubbed them in the bath and subjected them to some intense hair dryer sessions. I didn't check out until lunchtime and then sat around in the lounge. I occasionally went out to use the shops and the time soon flew by. I asked the reception staff to dump my old kit bag containing the poleless tent, sleeping bag, roll mat and anything else I no longer needed. It was mid-summer weekend and that was a cause for celebration in Sweden. It was effectively a Bank Holiday. The female staff were wearing flowers in their hair and there were complimentary strawberries being handed out.

I was only carrying a small bag now. Airport security seized my gas canisters, scissors, adjustable spanner and blades. In the departure lounge there was a group of musicians known as the 'Ye Banished Privateers'. They were dressed as pirates and entertaining the travellers, free for all to see. They were brilliant and continued their performance on my flight to Copenhagen.

As I waited in Denmark for my connection to Heathrow, I toasted my absent friends by downing a Carlsberg. Probably the best 'departure beer' in the world.

I touched down in Blighty and with hand luggage only, I raced to immigration. "Where have you been?" they asked. I burst out laughing. "Well..." I started.

My journey had taken me from England to France, Belgium, Luxembourg, Germany, Switzerland, Liechtenstein, Austria, Czech Republic, Slovakia, Hungary, Serbia, Croatia, Kosovo, Bulgaria, Romania, Moldova, Ukraine, Poland, Lithuania, Latvia, Estonia, Finland, Aland, Sweden and Denmark. A tube to St Pancras and the last train to Leicester meant I would arrive home in the early hours of Day 97.

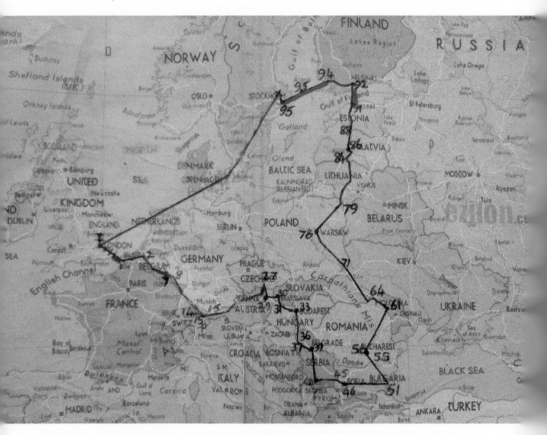

Original map by Ezilon.com sourced through Vidiani.com

Chapter 20.

Adios

Some people asked me why the big adventure had not been a charity fundraising challenge. There were many reasons. Not least, I was making it up as I went along. I had no firm plans or route. My intention was to do some travelling and save money at the same time. The freedom to roam or stray as I pleased meant quality 'me time' and a chance to unwind in the sun… and wind, rain, snow and sleet. In any case, 40 miles per day wasn't that difficult.

A sponsored event would need fixed qualifying criteria, a timetable and some corroboration of my achievements. Feeling obliged to succeed and not let anyone down, I would have inevitably pushed myself harder and probably fallen ill. I didn't want that stress burden. I had dealt with more than enough pressure in my life and this was about chilling out. There was a chosen charitable cause: me! It was self-help therapy.

Sponsorship could have raised potential adverse perceptions. The first was from clearing £2,500 of debt at the end of a charity ride. That already sounds suspicious. Another was the question of how could a disabled ex-cop manage a 4,000-mile cycle trip? Strange that people don't ask how blind or limbless wounded soldiers can ski to the North Pole or climb Mount Everest but of course, policemen are far less endearing.

It was easier to just do it for fun. That gave me total freedom and breathing space. An opportunity to completely empty my mind and put things back together.

So what good did it do?

It was inevitable that my ankle condition would get worse over time. I think all that riding has accelerated the deterioration and consequently, more than one year on, I still haven't replaced the bike, but I'd say it was definitely a worthwhile experience. It was a life-changing journey and the biggest thing I have ever done. I had achieved this, not as a marine or a policeman but as a slightly disabled pensioner. It satisfied my lifelong desire to push and prove myself. It ended my search for something bigger or better. It was enough. There will be no more silly stunts. It'll be taxis and hotels from now on… Honestly.

The simplicity of my adventure was very liberating. Each morning I would ask myself the same four questions:

Have I got water?

What's the weather like today?

Do I know where I am?

Do I know where I'm going?

Metaphorically, these are the same questions we all need to ask.

Water is your basic need or urgent priority.

Weather is your external pressure. You have no power over weather. Just try and be prepared for it.

Location is your status, where you are now.

Destination is where or what you aspire to be.

Life doesn't have to be complicated. My advice: turn off the TV, turn off the PlayStation and ditch your smartphone. There is a whole world full of adventure waiting for you out there.

The last trip also provided a suitable grand finale to my story. For a long time, Hannah had been pressing me to write a book about my life but I'd procrastinated, needing a fitting climax. That said, I hope there is a lot more to come but this will have to suffice for now. There were many episodes that I did not want to revisit. Having to relive those early days filled me with dread but it's done now. Recording the details in a book means my experiences can be shared without me having to remember or recite them. I hope that someone finds them useful or inspiring.

I have no bitterness towards anyone and harbour no hatred. I am pretty much at ease with myself and my life. Having travelled the globe and seen how other people live and the hardships they endure, by comparison, I have had an amazing time and consider myself extremely fortunate.

Next stop… ARGENTINA.